SYMBOL, MYTH, AND RITUAL SERIES
General Editor: Victor Turner

SYMBOL AND
Public Rit
in Santa F

Sh

M
F
R
R

SYMBOL AND CONQUEST

Public Ritual and Drama in Santa Fe, New Mexico

RONALD L. GRIMES

Cornell University Press

ITHACA AND LONDON

First published 1976 by Cornell University Press.
Published in the United Kingdom by Cornell University Press Ltd., 2–4 Brook Street, London W1Y 1AA.

International Standard Book Number 0–8014–1037–1
Library of Congress Catalog Card Number 76-13657
Printed in the United States of America by Vail-Ballou Press, Inc.
Librarians: Library of Congress cataloging information appears on the last page of the book.

For Milton, Nadine,
Darrell, Sherry, and Terry,
who weather the windiness
of living on the Texas side of Santa Fe

Foreword

Recently both the research and theoretical concerns of many anthropologists have once again been directed toward the role of symbols—religious, mythic, aesthetic, political, and even economic—in social and cultural processes. Whether this revival is a belated response to developments in other disciplines (psychology, ethology, philosophy, linguistics, to name only a few), or whether it reflects a return to a central concern after a period of neglect, is difficult to say. In recent field studies, anthropologists have been collecting myths and rituals in the context of social action, and improvements in anthropological field technique have produced data that are richer and more refined than heretofore; these new data have probably challenged theoreticians to provide more adequate explanatory frames. Whatever may have been the causes, there is no denying a renewed curiosity about the nature of the connections between culture, cognition, and perception, as these connections are revealed in symbolic forms.

Although excellent individual monographs and articles in symbolic anthropology or comparative symbology have recently appeared, a common focus or forum that can be provided by a topically organized series of books has not been available. The present series is intended to fill this lacuna. It is designed to include not only field monographs and theoretical and comparative studies by anthropologists, but also work by scholars in other disciplines, both scientific and humanistic. The appearance of studies in such a forum encourages emulation, and emulation can produce fruitful new theories. It is therefore our hope that the series will serve as a house of many mansions, providing hospitality for the practitioners of any discipline that has a serious and creative concern with comparative symbology. Too often, disciplines are sealed off, in sterile pedantry, from significant intellectual influences. Nevertheless, our primary aim is to bring to public attention works on ritual and myth written by anthropologists, and our readers will find a variety of strictly anthropological approaches ranging from formal analyses of systems of symbols to empathetic accounts of divinatory and initiatory rituals.

Symbol and Conquest makes a number of innovative analytical distinctions which Professor Grimes interweaves skillfully with his descriptions of the rituals and symbols of the two dominant public celebrations in modern Santa Fe. This New Mexican city is an especially appropriate subject for the study of symbolic action in a contemporary setting. Santa Fe not only has inherited a rich store of icons, emblems, and insignia from its dramatic past and an arena of conflict and alliance between "Hispano," "Anglo," and "Indo" peoples and cultures, but also has generated new "signifiers." In addition to the processions and pageants that are the main focus of his book, Grimes considers such important modern sources of symbolism as tourism, the Chamber of Commerce, the civic "establishment," and other by-products of commercialism. He is also sensitive to the ways in which public symbolism is influenced by the resident artistic community and by immigrant, mostly "Anglo," religious groups who are seeking to construct liturgical forms more in keeping with contemporary experience than those of their matrical churches and sects.

Grimes resolves apparent contradictions of form and interpretation found at the surface level of celebrations by distinguishing three modes of organizing and enacting deep cultural concerns in Santa Fe: *civitas* ("city-mindedness"), *ecclesia* (institutionalized religious procedures), and *ethnos* (organizational styles typical of each of the three Santa Fean cultures). These modes overlap and interpenetrate in the organization of ritual performance, and account for "the division of labor" Grimes finds among the symbols. "By appealing to any one of these symbols on a given occasion, Hispano Santa Feans can emphasize alternately the ecclesiastical, ethnic, or civic aspects of the city. And because they do not inquire into the consistency of the symbols as a system but treat them as a varied collection, the contradictions of public ritual seldom become an issue" (p. 264).

Grimes's examination of public ritual as an evolving system throws light on performances as "metalanguage": no mere reflection or expression of reality, but the very means by which a city reflects upon its own growth and development and reminds itself of its flaws and shortcomings. In confronting these issues Grimes has valuable things to say about the perennial question whether symbols are "best understood systemically in terms of their contemporary relations to one another or chronologically in terms of their historical development" (p. 45).

Not the least of Grimes's contributions to comparative symbology is the typological precision of his distinctions between pilgrimages, processions, and parades. Each of these institutionalized forms of symbolic action is a metasocial commentary made from a particular cultural perspective. One of the most fruitful lines of future anthropological investigation must surely be the detailed study of public genres of metacommunication: from seasonal rituals, through carnivals, charivaris, and miracle plays, through pilgrimages, pageants, religious processions, and parades, to sports spectacles, demonstrations, revolutionary scenarios, and mass entertainment. Sociocultural reflexivity continually finds expression in the symbolic processes of these and similar performative genres.

VICTOR TURNER

University of Chicago

Contents

Illustrations

Preface

This work interprets a system of public symbols in the ritualistic and dramatic contexts provided by the city of Santa Fe in north central New Mexico. Specifically, it focuses on the processions and novenas of a Marian image, La Conquistadora, and the events of the Santa Fe Fiesta in order to show how religious and dramatic actions are systematically linked to ethnic and civil symbols in a modern, urban, interethnic setting. We have a tendency to treat symbols solely as the private creations of poetic genius. Consequently, we are far too ignorant and suspicious of public symbols. We are also too preoccupied with verbal and literary symbolism. The present study is grounded on the belief that public, nonliterary symbols should be taken seriously in order to understand how religion is as much a matter of symbolic action and gesture as it is of verbal symbol and theological idea.

In the first chapter I have tried to illustrate the complexity of the symbolic ethos of Santa Fe, heavily loaded as it is with archetypal, stereotypical, and commercial uses of symbols. Also I have provided a very brief sketch of the social contexts and methodological presuppositions underlying my approach to the performances that were the object of my field study. Chapters 2 through 5 concentrate specifically on fiesta and processional symbolism. In the second chapter I investigate the symbolic use of space in the early summer novena-processions. Chapter 3 considers the struggles over symbols of power, particularly those clustering around the fiesta's De

Vargas figure. My Chapter 4 looks at a variety of performances, including pageants and melodramas, which condense Santa Fe's history into symbolic actions. Finally, I inquire into the meaning of two feminine symbols, Our Lady of the Conquest and the fiesta queen, and conclude with a consolidation of the symbol system in terms of which they have their meaning and power.

For enthusiastic encouragement and kind criticism I owe a tremendous debt to Victor Turner, as well as to his wife, Edith. I am also indebted to the Committee on Social Thought of the University of Chicago for extending to me the privileges of a guest scholar while I was finishing this work in consultation with Professor Turner.

I am grateful to the National Endowment for the Humanities for bearing the financial burden of my investigation, and to Lawrence University of Wisconsin and Wilfrid Laurier University of Ontario for assisting me with incidental expenses.

I appreciate the careful editorial help of the Cornell University Press staff, as well as the secretarial and proofreading assistance of Linda Glenn and Ken Ludlow of the School of Religion and Culture, Wilfrid Laurier University.

Thanks are due also to the New Mexico State Library, and to Brother Brendan Wilkinson, F.S.C., and Anna Ortiz of the College of Santa Fe library staff for allowing me access to their Southwest collections and providing me with space in which to work.

Part of the work of taping, translating, and data gathering was done by a team of student research assistants: Mary Forde, Deborah Halberstadt, Paco Ramirez, Laura Tietjen, and Tom Wolfe. Because of the complexity and simultaneity of events, some of the rituals would have been difficult to observe and interpret without their help.

Pedro Ribera-Ortega, *mayordomo* (president) of the Confraternity of La Conquistadora, served as primary consultant and informant. Without his endless hours of patient briefing, his critical candor, and his willingness to grant me full access to his clippings and files, this book would not have been written. His influence on it is strong, even on points where we disagree. The tenor of my study is interpretive, analytical, and critical, and Peter encouraged such an approach, regarding it as "a gift of Our Lady," even when my interpretations ran counter to his. I hope other Santa Feans will receive my views in the same spirit of friendly, critical dialogue.

For receptivity during their busiest time of year I thank Bennie Duran, president of the 1973 Fiesta Council; Father Austin Ernstes, O.F.M., rector of St. Francis Cathedral; Faustin Chavez, the 1973 De Vargas figure; Reies Lopez Tijerina of the Institute for the Research and Study of Justice; Father Blase Schauer, O.P., and Father Clifford Stevens, director and assistant director of Liturgy in Santa Fe; and Sister Giotto Moots of Sagrada Studios. The map of fiesta activities is reproduced with the kind permission of Edward L. Gonzales ("Gonzo"). The official seal of Santa Fe is reproduced by permission of Mayor Joseph E. Valdes.

Quotations and interpretations from many unidentified Santa Feans appear here. I have intentionally muted the names of private and public sources, not for lack of appreciation, but to protect confidentiality, to minimize possible controversies about individuals, and to maximize the emphasis upon structures rather than personalities. Historians and journalists are properly the ones to provide names, dates, and personalities. I mention names in the text only when they are unavoidable. So I would like to offer my profound thanks to the many Santa Feans who talked freely and frankly with me and my apologies to any who felt their names deserved to appear but received only protective quotation marks.

RONALD L. GRIMES

Waterloo, Ontario, Canada

SYMBOL AND CONQUEST
Public Ritual and Drama
in Santa Fe, New Mexico

CHAPTER 1

Interpreting Ritual Symbols in Santa Fe

Do not find it strange if there has been no manifestation of joy and enthusiasm in seeing this city occupied by your military forces. To us the power of the Mexican Republic is dead. No matter what her condition, she was our mother. What child will not shed abundant tears at the tomb of its parents?

Today we belong to a great and powerful nation. Its flag, with its stars and stripes, covers the horizon of New Mexico, and its brilliant light shall grow like a good seed well cultivated.

In the name, then, of the entire Department, I swear obedience to the Northern Republic and I tender my respect to its laws and authority.

Governor Juan Bautista Vigil y Alarid,
Santa Fe, August 19, 1846 (Twitchell 1967:34)

Even though the story of man in the southwestern United States began around 10,000 B.C. and a discernible Pueblo (or Anasazi) culture developed along the Rio Grande River between 1100 and 1300 A.D., the story of Santa Fe did not begin until 1598, when Don Juan de Oñate began colonization of what is now New Mexico and set up the first capital at San Juan de los Caballeros. In 1610 the capital was moved by Pedro de Peralta to what is now Santa Fe.

In 1680 a revolt of the Pueblo Indians drove the Spaniards out of Santa Fe and down the Rio Grande valley to a place near present-day El Paso, Texas, where they remained until 1692. In this year Don Diego de Vargas led the "bloodless reconquest" of Santa Fe. He obtained the resubmission of the revolutionaries to both state and church and credited the inspiration of his victory to La Conquistadora (The Conqueress, or more devotionally, Our Lady of the Conquest), whose image he returned after it had been rescued from a fire set by the revolting Indians.

Popular tradition maintains that De Vargas vowed to commemorate this re-establishment of peace between Spaniard and Indian with a religious celebration and a chapel. In 1712 Don Juan Paez Hurtado, who had been De Vargas' lieutenant governor and then governor upon De Vargas' death, led the citizens of Santa Fe in drafting a resolution of the City Council which would ensure that the reconquest would be commemorated with an annual fiesta; in 1717 La Conquistadora Chapel was built to honor and house the twenty-eight-inch Marian statue.

Today the existence of two chapels, Rosario Chapel and the La Conquistadora Chapel (the north transept of the cathedral), and two celebrations, a religious procession and novena (series of nine Masses) in the early summer and a more secular fiesta on the Labor Day weekend, create an interesting but complex historical problem best handled by Fray Angélico Chávez in *Our Lady of the Conquest* (1948), where he pursues the continuities and differences between popular tradition and historical research.

The main focus of this book is not on the history but on the rituals and symbols of the two celebrations in present-day Santa Fe. The primary symbols are the Marian image of La Conquistadora, the fiesta queen, and the role of Don Diego de Vargas played by a local Santa Fean in the Entrada pageant, a re-enactment of the bloodless reconquest. Yet these symbols can best be understood if one has some knowledge of Santa Fe as a uniquely symbol-conscious city. Artists, politicians, Indians, and non-Hispano groups also have considerable interest in the natural, religious, civic, and ethnic symbols of these two celebrations, even though Indian and Anglo participation in them is not as central as Hispano involvement. Hispano-Catholics, largely responsible for defining the symbols of the novena-procession and the fiesta, must do so in terms of the stereotypes, archetypes, images, iconoclasm, and iconophilia of other Santa Feans and tourists. Conflicting interpretations and valuations of these symbols in modern Santa Fe reflect the cultural and religious upheavals generated by the Spanish conquest of the late seventeenth century, the imposition of Mexican rule in 1821, and the subsequent take-over by the United States in 1848.

The Santa Fe Image

The city of Santa Fe is located in north central New Mexico between the Sangre de Cristo Mountains on the east and the Jemez Mountains on the west. The city is closer to the base of the Sangre de Cristos and sits at the opening of a great plain extending southward, where the mountains eventually taper out into prairie and desert. The Santa Fe River, really only a creek, runs through the city and meets the Rio Grande River just a few miles away to the west. The Rio Grande runs from north to south and bisects the state; it passes through Albuquerque sixty miles to the south. According to the 1970 census Santa Fe has a population of 41,167 people; 22,405 claim Spanish as their mother tongue, and 14,606 claim English. The total Spanish-speaking and Spanish-surnamed population is listed in the 1970 census as 26,641. Three major cultures meet in Santa Fe and the immediately surrounding area: Hispano, Anglo, and Indian (largely Pueblo).

According to the director of the Santa Fe Chamber of Commerce, the city ranks eighty-first in the nation in per capita income, yet one fourth of its population is receiving food stamps. Popular opinion has it that there are well over a hundred millionaires in the area, but the Chamber of Commerce estimates that a more realistic guess is thirty. In any case, New Mexico is a very poor state, and the income of Santa Feans is clustered about the extremes.

Economically considered the most important industries are government and tourism, along with its allied services (such as motels, restaurants, gas stations). Approximately 60 percent of the city's population is employed by some agency of the city, county, state, or federal governments. From this statistic alone it is obvious that symbols of civil piety have the possibility of attaining a status in Santa Fe not typical of other American cities.

According to the Chamber of Commerce, the city has about 1,600 artists, compared to approximately 500 in Taos, New Mexico's other major art colony. Of course, defining who is and who is not an artist is difficult in Santa Fe, since so many pursue art as a hobby or part-time vocation. Santa Fe (not necessarily the rest of New Mexico) has affinities with some sections of Florida. It vies with St. Augustine over certain "oldest" claims, and its attraction is strongly based on three related factors—tourism, climate, and leisure.

No systematic census data exists on the religious constituency of Santa Fe, but the director of the New Mexico Interchurch Agency offered this approximate ranking of the denominations based on size of membership: Roman Catholic, Methodist, and Baptist, and then Presbyterian, Episcopalian, and Lutheran.

Santa Fe has created many slogans to support its self-image and its claims of age and uniqueness. Some of them appear only in tourist literature, but most are also heard from the lips of residents. Some of the most popular are: (1) "site of the Nation's oldest capitol" [the Governor's Palace], (2) "city of tricultural harmony," (3) "most exciting region in North America," (4) "the city different," (5) "home of the nation's oldest community celebration" [the fiesta], (6) "site of the oldest chapel in the U.S." [San Miguel], (7) "home of the most ancient image of the Blessed Virgin Mary in the U.S." [La Conquistadora], (8) "Santa Fe Opera—internationally recognized as America's finest summer opera," (9) "capital of the Land of Enchantment," (10) "site of the oldest house in the U.S.," (11) "the major arts and crafts center of the Southwest," (12) "ever changing yet ever the same," (13) "a tourist Mecca," (14) "the royal city of St. Francis."

Santa Fe is convinced of its uniqueness and holds a certain disdain for mainstream mid-America. In a recent article, whose exact date I could not determine,[1] Oliver LaFarge criticizes those who wear poke bonnets during the fiesta. This, he remarks, is "copying what would be standard procedure for Square Corners, Indiana, or West Bend, Kansas." After deploring the 1890s in Santa Fe because of that period's interest in replacing "shapeless adobe" with modern architecture, LaFarge concludes, "Not until after 1910, with the beginning of the art colony and coming of the anthropologists, did Santa Fe turn away from a drive to turn itself into an imitation of a minor Indiana town. With three and a half centuries to choose from, these are the last decades to emphasize." One informant re-echoes this value judgment: "There are three 'different' cities in America—San Francisco, New Orleans, and Santa Fe—and Santa Fe is the *most* different." The latest Department of Development tourist brochure remarks, "New Mexico is so different from the rest of the United States that some people still think it must be another country. It's not. It's another world."

Preservation, more than modernization, is important to Santa Fe. Architecture, art, folklore, traditional foods, landscape, archeological remains, and general ethnic flavor are resources to be protected. Preservation in these areas is regarded as identical with maintenance of the city's uniqueness, which must be protected from bland, middle-class fads. Creativity in Santa Fe is expected to preserve the social and physical environment.

In addition to the many museums, galleries, archives, and collections which preserve the cultures of Santa Fe, at least three organizations, the Old Santa Fe Association, La Sociedad Folklorica, and the Historic Santa Fe Foundation, are

---

[1] Sources such as this one and a few others for which I am unable to provide complete bibliographic data are from a collection of clippings owned by Pedro Ribera-Ortega.

constantly at work preserving. "History helps progress," one of them notes. The Old Santa Fe Association "works for an urban renewal program that renews through preservation." Many of my informants subscribe to the ideology of renewing by preserving. The "magnetic charm" of the city is directly dependent upon its uniqueness, which, in turn, is dependent upon preserving its multiple ethnic heritages, according to several informants. So strong is the sentiment about preserving Santa Fe's architectural image, for example, that one informant wryly commented that "a big white glass building would probably be burned or bombed before it could be finished in Santa Fe." "The adobe ethic," as one person tagged it, constitutes a powerful force.

As its name implies, Santa Fe is the city of "holy faith," and faith is closely linked to civility and ethnicity. The official insignia of Santa Fe draws on symbols of three nations and fuses them into something belonging to the city as a legal entity, thus fostering civil piety while drawing on ethnic identity. The mayor's card bears this seal and an interpretation (see Figure 1). The interpretation associates the castle with Oñate, the early Spanish colonizer of New Mexico (1606), the lion with De Vargas, and the eagle with Mexican

CITY OF SANTA FE   NEW MEXICO

Figure 1. The official seal of La Villa Real de Santa Fé de San Francisco de Asís

Independence (1822). The stars and stripes are motifs symbolizing the United States presence in Santa Fe, which began in 1846. The description refers to Santa Fe as "a successful blend of three cultures."

The problem with this interpretation of the insignia is that it confuses ethnic with civil symbols. These symbols represent a succession of governments rather than a confluence of cultures. Its motifs are from flags, and its dates commemorate the initial presence of those flags in Santa Fe; the city seal does not represent all three cultures. Spain, Mexico, and the United States are not coextensive with Hispanos, Anglos, and Indians. A logo which one often sees in Santa Fe, and which does symbolize the three cultures rather than the succession of governments, is composed of three stylized heads—an Indian, a conquistador, and a cowboy.

The New Mexico Image

The state, as well as the city and region, has an interest in projecting an image. The New Mexico resident not only searches for, discovers, and propagates images, he also experiences images as they are heaped upon him by the media. Particularly revealing are the *New Mexico Blue Books*, the annual civil compendia. For example, the 1971–1972 *Blue Book* begins with pictures of three people—the secretary of state, the governor, and John Wayne—all of whom are on horseback. Except for those of a few government officials, every other picture in the book relates to the movie-making industry in New Mexico. Even the pictures of the officers of the New Mexico Motion Picture Industries Commission are present. New Mexico ranks second to California as a locus for feature-film production (Fiorina 1971:61).

The movie industry and the advertising industry are two of America's powerful makers of popular mythology. Even though they do not manufacture symbols from nothing, but draw on the resources available to them, they nevertheless transform what they appropriate. Hence, New Mexico serves as a mine for regional symbolic resources, but it also consumes those very symbols when they return in print, on television, or on the screen. During the period of my field study, several movies filmed in the area were shown. To understand the power of images generated in New Mexico and inflated to mythic proportions in Hollywood one only has to observe the tumultuous cheering which greets the credits at the end of the movie, not to mention the "there's-so-and-so's" throughout the showing of the movie. Growing, manufacturing, inflating, marketing, and consuming symbols is a cycle of immense strength in New Mexico.

A cycle also exists between the multiple New Mexican cultures and those industries which market symbols, primarily tourism, the arts, literature, government, motion pictures, and advertising. New Mexico is a producer of raw symbolic ore which is refined elsewhere, often according to a very different set of values, and then shipped back in for popular consumption. The very fact that the adjective "dramatic" occurs so frequently in the rhetoric of Santa Feans when they speak of their histories and cultures is in part due to the movie industry, which is the modern counterpart of the very old New Mexican tradition of folk drama and pageantry (see Chapter 4). Symbol consumerism should not be mistaken as the purview of tourists. It is an activity pursued by a symbol-conscious citizenry—the indigenous complaining about cultural exploitation and tourism notwithstanding.

New Mexicans tend to regard their own traditions and images as authentic in contrast to what they regard as the concrete world of the East and the plastic world of the West, particularly California. A popular bumper sticker reads, "Do Not Californicate New Mexico." Santa Fe is even more convinced of the authenticity of its symbolic heritage because of its nearness to the Pueblos, its being an early Spanish settlement and also the present capital, and the presence of so many artists and writers. Hence, it is not unusual to hear comments like, "Albuquerque [or California] has no soul; Santa Fe does."

When a symbol's primary function is its economic value, it has become that species of a symbol we refer to as a "trademark," a quality prominent in Santa Fe symbolism. The romanticism of New Mexico feeds the trademarking of symbols. This tendency of New Mexicophiles has generated what Nancie González (1969:x–xi) has called "The New Mexico Legend," which is suggested by the state's official epithet, "The Land of Enchantment."

The state's investment in commercial symbols is supplemented with a battery of insignias and emblems. An insignia is a graphic symbol of an official entity. The state flag and state seal sometimes serve this function by bringing official sanction to bear upon certain buildings and documents. Emblems are quasi-official symbols; unlike the state seal, they do not mark legal documents, though they have civil or official status. New Mexico has quite a number of these, most of which are commercially exploited: a state gem (turquoise), bird (roadrunner), animal (black bear), fish (cut-throat trout), flower (yucca), tree (piñon) and vegetables (chili and pinto beans). These symbolic emblems are viewed as expressive of the state's natural character, in contrast to its historical-cultural character as expressed in the two insignias, the state flag and state seal. New Mexicans consider them as "capturing the natural essence" of the state.

Occasionally, one of the natural symbols is appropriated as an ethnic symbol, as in the infrequently used term "chili power," a tongue-in-cheek reference to "brown" or Chicano power. But generally the insignias symbolize the civil and cultural environment, while the emblems symbolize the natural environment.

The state flag, designed by the Daughters of the American Revolution, consists of a gold background with a red symbol of the sun originally employed at Zia Pueblo. Red and gold were the colors carried by the first Spanish conquistadors. The new state capitol building is built in the shape of this Zia sun symbol.

The state seal contains a motto, the symbolic ideology of New Mexico: "Crescit Eundo" (It grows as it goes). Above the motto is a Mexican eagle grasping a cactus (an allusion to a tradition regarding the founding of Mexico City). Significantly, this eagle is shielded by a larger, American eagle grasping arrows in its talons.

The state also has three official ritualistic symbols, namely, the singing of "O, Fair New Mexico" and "Asi es Nuevo Mejico," the two state songs, and the reciting of the state salute. The salute reinterprets a natural symbol as a civic, intercultural one: "I salute the flag of the State of New Mexico, the Zia symbol of perfect friendship among united cultures." The theme of perfect intercultural harmony is one that will occupy us in much of the present study. That such perfection is a goal to be achieved, not an accomplished fact, is, perhaps, suggested by the fact that the English-language state song was adopted in 1917, only five years after statehood, while the Spanish-language song was adopted only in 1971. There are no official songs in any of the Indian languages.

The state's symbols are relatively simple forms of emblems and insignias. They may not be the most important civil symbols, but they illustrate in a simple way what will become more complex in this study. As we shall see, symbols become instruments for mediating certain kinds of dichotomies, the most typical of which are (1) regional vs. universal, (2) natural vs. cultural, (3) past vs. present-future, (4) religious vs. civic-civil, and (5) one ethnic group vs. another ethnic group. I can illustrate how these dichotomies are dealt with by referring to one of the most symbol-conscious groups in Santa Fe, Liturgy in Santa Fe.

Liturgy in Santa Fe

Many artists and religious groups live in Santa Fe precisely because they want to appropriate its symbolic richness. Religious groups have come to New Mexico, claiming that they sense it to be "the spiritual center" of the United States. Such remarks have been made by gurus and their followers who find "strong mystical vibrations here," as well as by traditional Catholics who want to tap the symbolic depth of the region.

Liturgy in Santa Fe is both a nongeographically constituted parish and an experimental laboratory in Catholic liturgy. Its philosophical and theological commitments are derived from four primary sources: traditional Catholic liturgy and the writings of C. G. Jung, Mircea Eliade, and J. E. Cirlot. Liturgy in Santa Fe has close ties with Sagrada Studios in Albuquerque, which specializes in Christian iconography. Perhaps the most accurate term one can use for their worldview is "Catholic archetypalism."

Jung and Eliade are both archetypalists, though in somewhat differing senses of the word, and Cirlot's *A Dictionary of Symbols* is dependent upon both Eliade and Jung. Stated in its most basic form, a form advocated by Liturgy in Santa Fe, the archetypalist thesis is that certain symbols, called archetypes, are universal in meaning and therefore independent of cultural, temporal, and spatial variation. Archetypalism has served in various ways as a form of literary criticism (Northrop Frye), psychology (Jung), and religious studies (Eliade). Archetypalism is a child of the interpretive disciplines and ultimately is indebted to Neoplatonic hermeneutics and metaphysics. The archetypalist tends to view cultural symbols as the realization of a limited number of timeless, eternal entities known variously as ideas, types, and archetypes. The archetypalist mind tends to perceive continuities, similarities, and analogies at the expense of discontinuities, particularities, and contradictions.

The archetypalist view of reality is pervasive in large segments of the artistic community of Santa Fe. Mary Forde, one of my student assistants, found that a very large percentage of Santa Fe artists account for both their art and spirituality in Jungian-Eliadian terms. Archetypalism in Santa Fe is not so much a scholarly method as a worldview, with concomitant values and practices. A brochure describing the program of Sagrada Art Studios claims, "In its artistic and religious heritage, Albuquerque-Santa Fe is a primitive Florence of the West." Los Alamos and Santa Fe even had a "Jungian Festival" in October 1973.

Liturgy in Santa Fe modifies archetypalist devotion somewhat by its insistence on using the works of Eliade, Jung, and Cirlot only insofar as they supplement and interpret Catholic Christianity. The community self-consciously tries to resist the ecumenical and secular-relevance themes which mark some liturgical experimentation projects. Although it offers "media concerts" of sacred iconography and music, its worship is not accompanied by either jazz or the guitar but by more traditional and classical music and symbols, the prescribed lectionary readings, and the feasts of the liturgical year. The name of its chronicle indicates its priorities: "Symbol, Season and Heritage."

What is perhaps most important for the purposes of our study is a consideration of Liturgy in Santa Fe's way of handling the universal/regional dichotomy, which in this instance is closely allied with the natural/cultural distinction. Strict archetypalists see an archetypal symbol as having only accidental relations to its sociohistorical context; the archetype is viewed as if it floats above culture and history and only accidentally comes into contact with the flow of time and history. Compared to these "culture free" archetypes, Liturgy in Santa Fe's adherence to Catholicism as unique and normative is tradition-specific in contrast to supposedly culturally-general archetypes. As Catholics, the members of the community lay claim to the historicity of Christian faith; they affirm, rather than deny, history.

Yet if one compares Liturgy in Santa Fe to other parishes in Santa Fe, it appears to be tradition-general, having less concern with the history of the region. Members of Liturgy in Santa Fe explain that they are interested in "universal Christian history." While the core of Santa Fe's public religion is based on the rituals and symbols of La Conquistadora, Liturgy in Santa Fe pays scant attention to the statue. Liturgy in Santa Fe appeals to Catholic tradition, but not Southwestern or Hispano-Catholic tradition. The appeal of Liturgy in Santa Fe's parishioners to what they regard as the broader, more universal Catholic tradition does not attract many of the traditional Hispanos who are devotees of La Conquistadora. And the difference is not merely an ethnic one; it is a matter of views of symbol, history, and time. The fact that Liturgy in Santa Fe is the only nonterritoral parish in the city, along with its neglect of regionally important devotions, means that it is viewed by outsiders as culturally disembodied and spatially dislocated.

But the pressure to identify with the region is great. Liturgy in Santa Fe, consequently, maximally appropriates those symbols provided by the natural environment but only minimally appropriates those provided by the cultural-historical environment. Natural features such as the Sangre de Cristo Mountains and Monte Sol, along with the regional flora, many of which have symbolic Spanish names, dominate the group's use of regionally specific symbols.

This practice illustrates the principle that nature-based symbols tend to express universal or intercultural values while historically grounded symbols tend to express unique identity within some social structure such as an ethnic group or a city. Liturgy in Santa Fe locates its uniqueness in its

Catholic commitment, which is expressed primarily in venerating the saints and observing their feast days—symbols rooted in Catholic *history*. On the other hand, Liturgy in Santa Fe defines its universality in relation to Santa Fe and the Southwest as a region; hence, it expresses its solidarity with other regional groups by employing *natural* phenomena as symbols. The worshipers seldom claim that saints as symbols have a universal meaning, but the sun, water, land, and plants do, they say. Appropriation of the natural environment for symbolic purposes allows them at once to demonstrate their solidarity with all men and with the region without either falling into religious regionalism or becoming simply "religious in general."

Artists and Archetypes

The views of Liturgy in Santa Fe are paralleled in many ways by the views of the artistic community. They tend to share an archetypalism which differentiates their values from the historicalism surrounding the novena-processions and fiesta. In some important respects the Santa Fe artist is what Eric Wolf has called a cultural "broker" (1956:1072). Typically, he considers none of the three cultures as off-limits and feels relatively free to draw on their symbolic resources. The artist is likely to view his own use of these symbols as less ideological, hence less exploitative, than the uses of the civil servant, the businessman, or the priest, because he views art as a universal language which is not a means but is its own end. Many nonartists share this view of art. That it is in considerable logical tension with the sale of art products does not seem to informants an important consideration. The view is given quasi-official sanction by its being displayed prominently on a plaque and a carving at Santa Fe's Museum of International Folk Art. The first reads, "In recognition of the contribution made by the crafts toward universal understanding among peoples." The second reads, "The art of the craftsman is a bond between the peoples of the world."

Whereas politics, commerce, and religion are viewed as divisive, sometimes even villainous and exploitative, the arts are viewed as sources of intercultural harmony. Frequently, artistic symbols, especially those appearing in nonliterary art, are accorded a kind of immunity from partisanship. Perhaps, the only exception is what some Santa Feans refer to as "tourist art" or "airport art." The "fine" arts and "folk" arts are accorded a purity of motive and function which differs radically from special-interest manipulation of symbols. Appreciation, it is held, is not identical with the conflict-inducing business of manipulation.

Because many consider the arts a source of unity between men of other times and other cultures, a kind of devotion to art which construes it as a religious substitute is quite common in Santa Fe. The following paragraphs depict a curator's view of his museum which parallels many artists' views of their studios:

Will museums be the churches of the future? The situation seems probable to . . . the curator in charge of the Museum of New Mexico's Laboratory of Anthropology.

"Through records of the past preserved in museums, a person is able to get some perspective on himself," [he] said. "People seem to be groping for roots today, and through a museum we can make contact with the past and gain some insight about the human condition."

One function of religion traditionally has been to give believers a knowledge that they are part of a larger whole.

"Museums generally take us out of time with the present and the future into the past," [he] said. "Through them we can see ourselves not as isolated but as part of a continuing flow." [2]

[2] George Ewing cited in "Anthropology Curator Notes New Art Interest," *Santa Fe Arts '73*, Supplement to *New Mexican*, July 20, 1973, p. 9.

Mary Forde's interviews, which I mentioned earlier, show that the some twenty-five artists interviewed were generally concerned to elevate regional symbols to archetypal scope and appeal. Many of them understood even their ethnically and regionally specific symbols as speaking to "man as such." Particularly prominent were references to clouds, sky, land, space, and Indians. Indians seemed to be treated as "natural men." Anglo and Hispano figures were mentioned by her informants much less frequently. Getting "turned on to the Indians and nature" seemed to be opposed in their minds to getting turned on to history, as well as military and economic conquest, which was associated with Anglos and Hispanos. Forde found that the majority of artists were critical of Hispanic celebrations like the fiesta because of what they considered their "sentimentality." Yet many artists sold their art during the fiesta, so art has ethnic and economic consequences even though the artist may not have such intentions.

Many artists in Forde's sample describe their living in Santa Fe as a de-intellectualizing process in which both their art and personal values shed the intellectual-competitive-consumer world for a more natural and instinctive world. Art understood in this sense is not merely an occupation but a life style of cultivated innocence. According to this view, which is held by many, the land and cultures of New Mexico seem to respond to art as the most noble paradigm of occupations, because art receives symbols rather than manipulating them—a "more natural," less manipulative form of human behavior.

The plastic arts have comparatively few nonregionalized expressions in Santa Fe. Their ethos is Southwestern. In contrast, the performing arts, such as music, drama, and dance, are characterized by a comparatively overt distinction between regional "folk" forms and the "fine" forms. When the New Mexican published its 1973 supplement on the arts (July 20), articles on regional music, drama, opera, and dance were scarce, while discussions of regional painting, sculpture, and pottery were quite prominent. In the plastic arts the designation "regional" usually implies nothing about its "fineness" or "folkness"; whereas in the performing arts "regional" usually implies "folk" and non-Anglo.

The distinction between art object and artistic performance has another important ramification if we consider the relation between art and the sacred in Catholic, Protestant, and Indian traditions. Protestants claim very little in the way of sacred art with the possible exception of the church edifice and perhaps some stained glass windows. They may even deny sacredness to these, despite their having been consecrated in a ceremony. There is no "Protestant art" (except, perhaps, religious music) in the same sense that there is Catholic art, for example, Jesuit art. Protestants, of course, do art, but only as artists, not as "Protestant artists."

Catholic art in Santa Fe is largely liturgical and typically didactic or illustrative of sacred liturgical actions. Objects directly involved in the liturgy, such as crosses and chalices, are not thought of as art in the same sense that stained glass windows and frescoes are. The former are sacred objects; the latter are objects depicting sacred subject matter. A Catholic icon is only secondarily sacred; it is sacred only insofar as it comes into contact with a holy subject like a saint or a sacred action like the liturgy. The buying and selling of icons are permissible, though not the buying and selling of any sacredness that might inhere in an object. Selling does not desacralize provided one buys with the intention of using the object with faith and devotion.

A Navaho sand painting fixed in glue and sold or a Pueblo dance performed for the public is not sacred. Yet some Navaho sand paintings and Pueblo ceremonial dances can be sacred. A sacred sand painting produces healing and is not an art object; the sand is scattered after its ritual use. Kurath and Garcia (1970:24) classify Tewa Pueblo dances into six categories of descending sacredness. Neither the performances nor the objects used in them are for public consumption. Some of the objects like drums, gourd rattles, and tortoise shell rattles are believed to have supernatural power (p. 40). They are not mere visual aids concerned with sacred things, as a cathedral window might be, but are effective concretions of the sacred, as bread and wine are. The priest with his bread and wine performs a sacrifice. The Navaho singer with his sand paints a healing medicine. The Pueblo dancer with his tortoise shell shakes fertility into air and earth.

Any object can be considered an art object and thus sold to the public. But Hispanos, Indians, and Anglos have differing views on what kinds of objects and performances can be displayed or sold and under what conditions such transactions are possible. For the Protestant all art is profane, even art with religious subject matter; at best such art is only illustration. For Pueblo and Navaho some performances and objects are so sacred that they must be ritually defaced before transactions with outsiders can be carried on. And for the Catholic, sacramental objects release their sacred power only when received by faith, hence exchanges of objects do not necessarily coincide with transactions of sacred power.

Archetypalism and Iconoclasm

A striking feature of a large segment of Santa Fe art and religion is its syncretism. This syncretism, usually explained by appeal to an archetypalist view of reality, is sometimes profoundly offensive to believers of a particular tradition. For example, some Pueblos and Hispanos view the artistic juxtaposition of a *santo* (painting or sculpture of a saint or religious personage), the four sacred vegetables of the Navaho (tobacco, corn, beans, squash), and a plastic egg carton as a profanation in both a religious and a cultural sense. To the traditionalist the effect of archetypalism (which is implicitly syncretistic) is the same as that of iconoclasm: the shattering of the uniqueness and sanctity of the symbol. For this reason archetypalism and iconoclasm in Santa Fe are more closely associated with Protestants and Anglos than with Hispano-Catholics or Indians. Anglos are viewed by others as collectors who gather but do not use ritually what they take from other religions. From the point of view of some traditions collecting objects for museums, books, tapes, or pictures is a form of profanation.

The iconoclastic heritage of the Protestant leads him to archetypalism. Iconoclasm views every symbol as equally nonsacred. Archetypalism views every symbol as equally sacred. The Protestant cannot fully appropriate the myths and rites of American Indian religions (though some try) or Hispanic Catholicism, nor can he fully affirm the myths of his own culture and religion. The result is a meta-system of symbols, which he understands to transcend, and thus include, all three cultures. This is the way of the Protestant-become-archetypalist, a familiar phenomenon in Santa Fe. The result is a profoundly syncretistic art and religion—alternately regarded as naive, mystical, and exploitative.

The archetypalism which apocalyptically declares the brotherhood of man and the synthesis of all symbol systems still shocks traditionally iconoclastic Protestants and offends traditional Catholics and Pueblo Indians, and more usually finds its home in the artistic or new-religious communities. Two striking examples of the power of eclectically combined symbols to jolt traditional associations by appealing to those very traditions are two collages I saw in the same week: Santo Niño de Atocha (the Holy Child of Atocha) accompanied by Batman, and Our Lady of Guadalupe appearing as Adi Shakti (a manifestation of the feminine principle in Hinduism). Traditional Catholicism and Pueblo religion experience twentieth-century syncretism-archetypalism much as their nineteenth-century forebears experienced Protestant iconoclasm, namely, as a desacralization, while the arche-

typalists themselves interpret their own activities as a resa-
cralization of existence. Representatives of Santa Fe's religious and aesthetic archetypalism assert that they do not
want to alienate other religions and cultures but want instead
to include them. One writer has described the art of Santa Fe
as "An Earthbound Iconography" (Pollock 1973). As I have
already suggested, appeals to natural symbols like the earth
are usually accompanied by an effort to emphasize in-
tergroup unity and de-emphasize group uniqueness. Whether
this is the actual effect of the intention is a debatable matter.

Of course not all Anglos in Santa Fe are artists, Protestants, and archetypalists. My argument so far has been simply that archetypalism in Sante Fe is important because of its
association with intercultural activities and ideology, and that
archetypalism seems to be strong among artists, particularly
those of Protestant background.

Protestants, most of the Anglo population, are latecomers
to the state, having arrived only in the mid-nineteenth century. Genealogically, ideologically, and historically, the two
leading non-Catholic Christian denominations, the Baptists
and Methodists, still have close ties with the South and with
Texas in particular. The combination, Anglo-Protestant-
pioneer-from-the-South, is still recognizable in New Mexico,
though less pronounced in Santa Fe, since some Anglo families migrated there from the Midwest and Northeast. Even
though there are Anglo-Catholics and Hispano-Protestants,
the combinations Anglo-Protestant and Hispano-Catholic are
much more common. General Stephen Watts Kearney's
speeches of the mid-nineteenth century, at which time he
was claiming New Mexico for the United States and unseat-
ing the Mexican government, clearly presuppose this basic
division in which distinct versions of Christianity are associated with distinct ethnic groups. American Indian religions have their own identity, but insofar as they are linked
to Christianity, Catholicism has dominated in New Mexico.

Historically Protestant iconoclasm has stood against the prolific use of symbols and rituals by Catholics and Pueblos; sacred symbols have been treated as idolatrous. Whereas Catholics felt they had to save Pueblos from heathen ritual, Protestants felt they had to save both from ritualism. In Lewis A. Myers' *A History of New Mexico Baptists* (1965:31) he points out that Hiram Walter Reed, the first Baptist missionary to reach New Mexico (1849), was said to have assumed the title of bishop in order to influence those Catholics he wanted to convert. And Myers himself incessantly employs terms drawn from Catholicism and used metaphorically, such as "saints" and "requiem," as he describes the work of pioneer Baptists. He feels that Baptists brought enlightenment to New Mexico, the "superstitious arena of Romanism." "Romanism" was far more threatening, and probably still is, than the Indian religions. The virtue of the Baptists was, according to Myers, their introducing "wholesale [religious] competition," which produced the "strongest promise of redemption hitherto known" (p. 37). The competitive, iconoclastic Protestant ethic is still active among New Mexico Methodists and Baptists.

In 1914, New Mexico Baptists described frontier religion thus: "In order to win on the frontier one's religion must be virile, active, resistive toward false doctrines, aggressive, social and spiritual" (p. 632). As late as 1950 some local Protestants, led by Baptists, were protesting a nude terra-cotta plaque, named "Earth," but nicknamed "Miss Fertility," which was being placed in the state capitol. The confrontation between local artists and some Protestants became so heated that the plaque was removed (see LaFarge 1959:393–394).

The Study of Public Ritual

I have tried to illustrate the intensity of popular concern for understanding and appropriating a dense array of public symbols. In Santa Fe archetypalist and iconoclastic interpretations of symbols are not scholarly positions defended in debate but ideologies enacted in dramas and rituals. A major methodological problem in the study of public performances is how we are to articulate the relations between religious, ethnic, civic, and political symbols *as symbols*, that is, how we are to study performances as symbolic actions without reducing them to theologies, psychologies, or sociologies. And a second problem is whether we are to consider symbols as parts of a timeless system or of a temporal process.

Robert Bellah (1968) has popularized the idea of a civil religion as a concept for interpreting mythic, symbolic, and ritualistic forms in the context of government, politics, and civil authority. The merit of Bellah's discussion is that it does not draw arbitrary boundaries between the civil and the religious. Such methodological openness is of considerable use in Southwestern studies, because at least some of the major religiocultural traditions of the Southwest do not agree with the American Protestant's segmentation of existence into discrete areas. Denials of the validity of a church-state or religion-culture dualism are common among both Indians and Hispanos of New Mexico. The rituals and symbols of La Conquistadora, particularly those of the annual Santa Fe Fiesta, are not clearly either religious or civil; they are both. The Santa Fe Fiesta Council is accountable to both the City Council and the Roman Catholic church, albeit on different levels.

Anglos, Indians, and Hispanos all may and do participate in national civil ritual with its "sacred" times (July 4 and Thanksgiving), its sacred rites (inaugurations, swearings-in and pledges of allegiance), its sacred objects (flags, gavels), its sacred edifices and sites (Washington Monument, Gettysburg, the White House), its myths (a world safe for democracy; liberty and justice for all) and its sacred personages (Washington, Lincoln, Kennedy). The civil, federal religion,

Bellah suggests, is a symbol system distinct from that of Christian, Jewish, or other American religions.

The term "public ritual" as used in the present study is somewhat broader than Bellah's "civil religion." I find it helpful to make several distinctions within the area of public religiosity. Public ritual includes civil religion, but it also includes those aspects of non-civil religion, such as Catholicism or Protestantism, which involve the general citizenry and are not restricted in influence to the participants of some particular religion. Christmas is a good example of a public celebration which is not civil in the same sense that Independence Day is. Two Southwestern examples are Native American dances and the Santa Fe Fiesta. Both are public and yet related to specific religious traditions; they are not essentially patriotic. Civil religion, as Bellah develops the concept, denotes those rituals, myths, symbols, values, and holidays perpetuated by political or patriotic interests. But many times a specific religious group or denomination exposes its public face at a civil event, so I find it useful to distinguish between public religiosity and official, civil celebrations. I regard the latter as a subcategory of the former.

I find it helpful to categorize the symbols of Santa Fe in terms of their civic, civil, religious, and ethnic qualities. To indicate that I am speaking not so much about social structures as about symbolic meanings, I use the terms *civitas*, *civilitas*, *ecclesia*, and *ethnos* respectively. The difference between *civitas* and *civilitas* may not be immediately clear; the former designates symbols of city-mindedness, symbols aimed at generating informal cooperation and mutual respect. The latter denotes symbols with political, governmental, or official overtones.

Clifford Geertz's essay "Religion as a Cultural System" (1966:3) defines culture as "an historically transmitted pattern of meanings embodied in symbols, a system of inherited conceptions expressed in symbolic forms by means of which men communicate, perpetuate, and develop their knowledge about and attitudes toward life." If, as, Geertz writes, symbols are the mode of transmitting culture from generation to generation, an inquiry into the symbols of Santa Fe probes the heart of its culture, though, of course, it does not necessarily reveal all of the important institutions which constitute the city of Santa Fe as a society. A study of symbols is not so much a study of social institutions as it is a study of the culture transmitted by those institutions.

The terms "ethos" and "symbol system" are not identical. "Symbol system," a more formal notion, refers to the web-like relations among symbols and between symbols and other nonsymbolic elements. Symbols are like cities on what Anthony Wallace calls "cognitive maps" (1970:15). Symbols crystallize the plans, values, and goals of a people into systems, which Wallace defines as "a set of variable entities (persons, objects, customs, atoms, or whatever) so related that, first, some variation in any one is followed by a predictable (that is, nonrandom) variation in at least one other; second, that there is at least one sequence of variations which involves all of the entities" (1970:27).

That the fiesta and La Conquistadora rituals constitute a public symbol system seems to me unquestionable. However, it would take me far beyond my task to demonstrate predictability, though I will try to illustrate how variation in some symbols evokes probable, if not predictable, responses from other symbols. The Santa Fe Fiesta meets Wallace's criterion of a sequence of activities involving all of the components, which, in this case, are symbols.

The ethos of a people, in contrast to its symbol system, refers to "the tone, character, mood and quality" (Geertz 1966) of their life. The term "ethos" is a holistic way of referring to a people's style, which, of course, is reflected in its symbol system. The ethos of Santa Fe is its ambience, its milieu, the affective outcome of its symbols.

No culture is ever fully consistent. Not all of its units are fully articulated, nor would they be mutually consistent if they were. Cultural systems, like sentences, often contain contradictions. Feelings can be contradicted by actions, and symbols, particularly those of public rituals, often mask these contradictions. Undoubtedly, this accounts in part for the typical defensiveness we usually have with regard to our rituals. This also accounts for the secrecy which sometimes clouds symbol systems, even public ones.

Particularly in public ritual, participants are likely to deflect scrutiny away from symbols that hide social and religious contradictions by insisting on the simplicity and obviousness of the symbols' meanings. Public ritual, despite its public nature, or perhaps because of it, is seldom probed for its meaning. Participants are sometimes surprisingly inarticulate about their rituals; they simply do them without question. We do well to beware of too obvious meanings, especially when we find that one informant discusses the "obvious" meanings of the same symbol in ways that contradict the "obvious" meanings offered by another informant. We surpass the obvious, not by psychoanalyzing our informants or appealing to unconscious meanings, but by systematically imagining and thinking through implications until implied systemic lines either meet or fail to meet. Only when a collection of symbols is viewed as if it were a potential system can we discover what relations a ritual-cycle facilitates and what relations it prohibits.

Treating a group of symbols as a system of forms and meanings is not without its problems. The fundamental problem is whether symbols are best understood systemically in terms of their contemporary relations to one another or chronologically in terms of their historical development. In other words, should we regard these symbols as constituting a symbol system or a ritual process? Sometimes the question is raised as the familiar debate over synchronic systems vs.

diachronic processes, or the sociology vs. the history of religion. My own approach is to treat the public ritual cycle as an evolving system; hence I try to combine a concern for system with a concern for developmental processes. As my concluding summary chart (p. 264) suggests, however, my most basic intention is to isolate the fundamental pattern which is Santa Fe's public ritual system. Yet, despite my interest in the systemics of ritual, I choose to focus on one year, 1973, of a cycle which is already undergoing some obvious changes. One simply cannot describe everything that occurred in 1973 in the present tense as if it were an eternal present. Even though a charting operation may seem to isolate eternal verities, it does not. At best a symbol system is but a slowly evolving pattern against which one plots the course of a more rapidly changing ritual process.

The very mention of change implies something against which one measures or plots the course of movement. A symbol system, then, is not a set of immobile archetypes whose relations and meanings remain static. Rather it is a patterned set of symbolic actions and transformations. The history of the Santa Fe Fiesta amply illustrates that the interchange between symbol-complexes is a process thoroughly immersed in historical time. A study of a single year's ritual cycle is at best exemplary, not definitive or normative.

How one views the tensions between structure and process greatly affects one's interpretations. Most written sources on Santa Fe stress historical methods, and most of my informants interpret the symbols of the fiesta and novena-processions in historical terms. But history, like ritual, may be viewed as a static entity or a process.

The "Monument Controversy"

Some observers have criticized Santa Fe as a city which tries to live in the past, as if time and change were realities to be minimized. More than one informant has said to me,

"Things haven't *really* changed here." This may sound like a very strange comment coming from a people so concerned with history, which is nothing other than an interpretive record of change. How can one be at once an historiophile and remain oblivious to change?

A love for history, when it becomes preoccupied with history-as-model rather than history-as-process, may represent an effort to flee the ravages of time. One can study and recite history for the same reason men in some cultures recite myths, namely, to escape recognition of time. The line which separates escaping into the past from a legitimate refusal to be cut off from one's roots is not easy to draw. In both cases the assumption is that men and cultures have an integral relation to their origins. But in one instance a group consults the past in order to repeat or preserve it and thus inhibit change, while in the other, it reconsiders and reinterprets the past in order to derive power for determining the direction of the present. Historical study and historical pageantry may function either to relieve the pressure of the present or to operate as levers for exerting pressure on the present. They can be the sources either of stasis or continuity in process.

A particularly revealing debate occurred during my field study in Santa Fe. The "monument controversy" illustrates that the structure/process debate is not restricted to forums of scholarly argument but is a public problem as well.

A monument erected in 1866–1868 stands at the center of the Santa Fe Plaza. One of its inscriptions reads, "To the heroes who have fallen in various battles with savage Indians in the territory of New Mexico." At the instigation of AIM (American Indian Movement) and following a letter from the governor, the City Council voted unanimously to seek removal of the monument. Upon announcement of this decision, the controversy became so heated that the decision was reversed and an explanatory plaque added instead.

The Santa Fe Historical Society suggested it would go to court to stop removal, in part because the plaza could lose its status as a National Historic Landmark, and thus its right to receive federal aid. But an important historiographic principle became the central ideological issue. Stated simply, the argument which won followed the editorial lines of the *New Mexican*, which argued, "You can't rewrite history" (July 30, 1973). The overwhelming majority of letters and opinions supported the state historian and the newspaper editors in their contention that the offensiveness of the word "savage" should not cause people to censor history. Some typical comments were as follows:

"To remove the word 'savage' from American history would involve a book-burning spree equal to Hitler's."

"Any monument is an anachronism ten years after it is completed. It's simply a visual, historical record of a specific time and place."

"The word 'savage' does not refer to New Mexico Indians [i.e., Pueblo Indians], but to Navahos, Comanches, and Apaches."

The monument refers to "savage Indians," it means exactly what it says, and furthermore, the term is accurate. I know of no recorded case of Comanches killing anyone with kindness." (See especially the *New Mexican*, July 27, 1973, pp. 1, 7.)

Most of the opponents of removal based their positions on a what-is-done-is-done argument, thus disavowing any connection between contemporary and historical meanings of the monument. But others saw the symbolic dimension of the monument quite clearly and treated the monument not as a dead historical fact but as a symbolic continuation of the past into the present. A symbolic continuation is not, of course, the same as a literal one, but it is nevertheless a continuation. Hence, a prankster glued a sign over the monument so it read "savage conquistadors" instead of "savage Indians." The next day's paper contained a picture of a policeman tearing off the sign. Almost every argument for leaving the monument could have been used to defend leaving up the pasted sign, but, of course, no one used such arguments.

One letter to the editor noted, "Each year we celebrate the 'peaceful reconquest'. . . by the Spaniard De Vargas of Indian lands and La Conquistadora is its focus. After all the emotionalism is set aside just what is the difference in these two objects?" (*New Mexican*, August 1, 1973). This comment implicitly recognizes that neither La Conquistadora nor the monument is a mere dead fact of the past. Both are facts-become-symbols whose meanings are partially determined by their use in the present. To be sure, one cannot change the historical facts, but facts are always embodied in interpretations. One cannot rewrite history insofar as it is a process of human interaction, but history as an interpretive account of that interaction is always being rewritten or reinterpreted. Removing a symbolic object, like an obelisk, would not haved changed the facticity of history, but it would have changed the value and meaning of that facticity in the present. The monument is located in a symbolic place of honor, the center of the city. Placed in a museum it would mean one thing; left in the center of the plaza it meant another. Symbolic objects develop meaning in terms of what one does with them. Not every historical event is of symbolic value, but those that are we preserve with symbolic forms like monuments, rituals, myths, and pageants. The monument apparently still has symbolic value for some Santa Feans. They not only want it preserved but want it preserved publicly in its present location. One might ask what is the meaning of this gesture of public preservation. Knowing the answer to this question would tell us more about Santa Fe than the proposed explanatory plaque which read:

Monument texts reflect the character of the times in which they are written and the temper of those who wrote them. This monument was dedicated in 1868 near the close of a period of intense strife which pitted northerner against southerner, Indian against white, Indian against Indian. Thus we see on this monument, as in other records, the use of such terms as "savage" and "rebel." Attitudes change and prejudices hopefully dissolve. [*New Mexican*, October 16, 1973, p. 1]

Of immense significance to the future of Santa Fe's public symbols and rituals is the view of history and change embodied in them. If Santa Fe views its history as either a sheer paradigm or an entity to be repeated uncritically in drama and ritual, the rituals will either die for lack of contemporary meaning or ossify into museum relics. If, however, the rituals are understood as a selecting of symbols whose meanings evolve—whose meanings are neither mere facts (or artifacts) nor mere reduplications—they will continue to be of immense significance as a microcosm of the city's growth and development.

CHAPTER 2

Sacred Space and Symbolic Transformation

I state that in the name of the most Christian king, Don Philip, our lord, sole defender and protector of holy mother church, and its true son, and for the crown of Castile and the Kings of his glorious lineage who may reign there, for and on behalf of my said province I take and seize tenancy and possession, real and actual, civil and natural, one, two, and three times, one, two, and three times, one, two, and three times, and all the times that by right I can and should, at this said Rio Del Norte, without excepting anything and without limitations, including the mountains, rivers, valleys, meadows, pastures, and waters. In his name I also take possession of all the other lands, pueblos, cities, towns, castles, fortified and unfortified houses which are now established in the kingdoms and provinces of New Mexico, those neighboring and adjacent thereto, and those which may be established in the future, together with their mountains, rivers, fisheries, waters, pastures, valleys, meadows, springs, and ores of gold, silver, copper, mercury, tin, iron, precious stones, salt, *morales,* alum and all the lodes of whatever sort, quality, or condition they may be, together with civil and criminal jurisdiction, power of life and death, over high and low, from the leaves of the trees in the forests to the stones and sands of the river, and from the stones and sands of the river to the leaves of the forests.

Don Juan de Oñate, Act of Taking Possession of New Mexico, April 30, 1598 (Hammond and Rey 1953:334–335).

All of the rituals and symbols of La Conquistadora involve metaphors of royalty such as "queen," "coat of arms," and "court." But for purposes of interpretation, it is helpful to separate the summer processions and novena from the fall fiesta, because certain "democratic" metaphors associated with the fiesta are atypical of the royal rituals. In this chapter we shall be concerned particularly with coronations, Masses, and processions.

La Conquistadora has been crowned more than once, though, whenever the coronation is referred to, devotees assume that it is the papal coronation. The statue was crowned in 1954 by Francis Cardinal Spellman. The episcopal coronation occurred during a celebration of this Marian Year which marked the centennial of the promulgation of the Dogma of the Immaculate Conception. In 1960, La Conquistadora was crowned again. This time the rite was a papal coronation performed by an apostolic delegate of Pope John XXIII. During the period of the present study she was crowned yet again, by the fiesta queen, in a special ceremony.

The meaning of these three coronations is more complex than it appears. In one sense La Conquistadora was queen and patroness of the Espanoles-Mexicanos long before she was so recognized by papal authority. In another sense she only became officially regal at the moment of her recognition by the Holy See. And the fact that she can be crowned from above by the pope or from below by the fiesta queen indicates that the authority for La Conquistadora's queenship is both popular and sacred, hence legitimized by symbols of *civitas* and *ecclesia*. La Conquistadora was not crowned once for all, but is crowned repeatedly to promote devotion. As in the eucharistic celebration of the Mass, a paradigmatic act is ritually reenacted as a mode of continuation. La Conquistadora was crowned paradigmatically by a papal delegate in recognition of the regal standing which she has among Hispanic people, but that queenship is continued by subsequent coronations.

The devotees of La Conquistadora arranged to have the papal coronation coincide with the 350th anniversary celebration of the founding of the City of Santa Fe. This celebration, called Siglos de Santa Fe (Centuries of Santa Fe), was the occasion for a dramatic pageant that depicted the history of the past three and a half centuries. The celebration began on June 17 and ended on June 26, 1960, the day of the papal coronation.

The coronation not only reflected the centuries of devotion necessary for such an honor, but it also illustrated the close alliance of civic and religious interests typical of La Conquistadora devotion. An article in the Catholic periodical *St. Anthony Messenger* described the coronation as "without question the most stirring exhibition of the Catholic Faith in the United States" (May 1961, p. 31). Estimated attendance at the coronation was 15,000, with 8,000 participating in the procession.

Prior to the coronation Fray Angélico Chávez, a local Franciscan and historian, had written the only book-length treatments of La Conquistadora, *Our Lady of the Conquest* (1948) and *La Conquistadora: The Autobiography of an Ancient Statue* (1954). In 1956 the archbishop had directed the reestablishment of the Confraternity of La Conquistadora, which had died out in the previous century. The prime movers in doing the groundwork for such a reorganization were Chávez, Pedro Ribera-Ortega, present *mayordomo* of the confraternity, and Aileen O'Bryan, the daughter of a former governor.

The papal coronation followed the reestablishment of the confraternity by only four years, indicating the intensity of effort exerted by devotees. The coronation was preceded by a year of intensified prayer and devotion at the direction of the archbishop, who wanted the people prepared for the event. As evidence of their devotion, devotees and friends gave gifts of gems and precious metals which were worked by a local artist [1] into a crown used for the coronation. The crown included sixty-five precious stones. One stone was a three-carat diamond sent taped to a card in a plain envelope by an anonymous donor; it became part of La Conquistadora's pectoral cross. In 1973 the cross was valued at $75,000 and the crown at $25,000.

An interpretation of the crown was published in the *New Mexican* (May 29, 1960). The crown has three colors of gold—rose, gold, and green. On top is a cross made of silver

[1] The crown was designed by Maurice Loriaux of Santa Fe Studios of Church Art; it was made by Karl Larsson.

and turquoise to suggest the Southwestern character of La Conquistadora. The cross is said to represent the kingship of Christ on earth. Twelve robin's-egg turquoise stones surround the crown to symbolize the twelve apostles. Four of the points are stylized blooming lilies meant to suggest the four evangelists. At the junctures between the points are rubies representing the drops of blood shed by Jesus at his crucifixion. The diamond at the center of the front part of the crown is "the light of life," and the orb is banded by three gold circles which stand for the Trinity.

In 1973 most devotees knew none of the intricate symbolism supposed to be embodied in the crown. If these meanings published in 1960 were ever learned, they were forgotten for the more general symbolism of the coronation rite. For devotees the crown symbolizes honor and regal dignity. It does not symbolize the Trinity plus the four evangelists plus the blood of Christ, etc. The symbolism of the crown is a good example of a case in which one must distinguish the popular meanings of symbols from meanings applied or attributed by clergy, artists, and other professionals, though the two kinds of meanings are not completely different. Symbolic meaning is not necessarily coincident with intended meaning. We must always ask, "Symbolic for whom?" if we are to discover fine shades of meaning.

In the coronation sermon the apostolic delegate to the United States made a suggestive link between two kinds of conquest, that of love and that of democracy. To quote from a bulletin of the Confraternity of La Conquistadora:

In his sermon, the Papal Delegate asked all present to give their hearts to the Blessed Virgin as a conquest of love and faith in the victory of the principles of the Gospel and of democracy in the world.

And it must be remembered, always, that the center of all Marian devotion is Christ. Our Lady of the Conquest in New

Mexico was an instrument in the hands of God for the conversion of the Land of Enchantment to Christ.   [July 3, 1960]

This interpretive report of the delegate's message shows a close association of Christian faith with democratic ideology; the victory of the one implies the victory of the other. The tension between the metaphors of royality necessary to a ritual coronation and democratic ideology are apparent throughout the novena-processions, and I shall consider the tension more fully when I discuss the Mass. The royality is, of course, metaphoric, not literal, therefore the devotees usually see no contradiction between royal rituals and their democratic social context. Both the democratic ideology and the royal metaphors can at least agree on the goal: a Christian, democratic victory.

The coronation established La Conquistadora by an act from the highest rungs of the Roman Catholic hierarchy, thereby lending her an official scope not restricted to Santa Fe alone. One should not assume, however, that official or formal recognition automatically results in a popular internationalizing as, for example, Our Lady of Lourdes has. Devotion to La Conquistadora is quite regionalized in comparison to that of Lourdes or Fatima. Devotees try to extend La Conquistadora's ritual domain though, and an archbishop wrote in his episcopal letter announcing the coronation, "She belongs to everyone in our archdiocese; she belongs to every heart in New Mexico" (*New Mexico Register*, March 11, 1960).

Interviews and written documents suggest that La Conquistadora's metaphoric kingdom consists of a series of concentric circles of lessening intensity: (1) her confraternity, (2) Catholics of Santa Fe, (3) Catholics of the archdiocese, (4) non-Catholics of Santa Fe, (5) citizens of New Mexico, (6) Southwesterners, (7) all Christians, and (8) all people. Each of these, and sometimes combinations, are mentioned by devotees as composing La Conquistadoras's "kingdom."

The international appeal of La Conquistadora, to which devotees refer only infrequently, reaches into Mexico and Spain. Devotees typically emphasize the latter connection. A letter from the present *mayordomo* (president) is particularly instructive. He writes regarding the attendance at the coronation by two of Don Diego de Vargas' seventh-generation descendants:

Typically Spanish, the two guests made it a point to emphasize that their presence at the Papal Coronation was the highlight of their trip, since it added yet another star to their family crown: La Conquistadora and Don Diego, the Reconqueror of New Mexico, are periods in their family history which they cherish, coupled with the fact that three other canonized saints preceded them: San Ysidro the Laborer, a share-cropper on their estate and the patron of aristocratic Madrid (12th century); Saint Teresa of Avila, who is a blood relation to the De Vargas' (16th century); and our own city patron, St. Francis of Assisi, who obtained land for his first Spanish monastery on De Vargas property. [Letter of June 10, 1960]

The importance of this excerpt lies in its crystallizing so many values crucial to La Conquistadora devotion. It illustrates how important the institution of the family is. The statue's coronation is a "star" in the "family crown." The expected imagery, namely, the family as a star in La Conquistadora's crown is reversed. The De Vargas family is central; La Conquistadora and the saints are the circumference. A systemic web, resembling a family tree or a royal hierarchial ladder, yokes together a statue, a heavenly personage, a soldier, a sharecropper, a mystic, the founder of a mendicant order, and the two sisters, to the people of Santa Fe. The ties are at once historical, mythic, economic, political, and familial. The presence of the De Vargas descendants is as important to the celebration and coronation as the presence of the apostolic delegate. The former establishes historical and cultural legitimacy, while the latter establishes religious legitimacy. The notion of descent is of utmost importance in the La Conquistadora ritual cycle, because her followers tend to identify authenticity and legitimacy with "having descended from" in a hierarchical-ecclesiastical sense, as well as a genealogical sense. Genealogical descent is frequently taken as a symbol of spiritual and cultural descent. Something is authenticated by tracing its lineage to a valued origin.

The same letter from which the passage above is taken speaks of La Conquistadora as "Christ's Mother, our Queen and Patroness." The first metaphor is familial. The second is royal-political. And the third is socioeconomic. And each implies a descendancy—a hierarchy, an above and a below. This coordination of heavenly and social ascendancy and descendancy is crucial to the public ritual of Santa Fe.

The Novena-Processions

Coronations are special occasions in the ritual-cycle of La Conquistadora and Santa Fe, but they lend legitimacy to the annual celebrations of the novena-processions and fiesta. Virtually all informants begin their accounts of the novena-processions with the Corpus Christi celebration, which normally occurs on the Sunday preceding the novena-processions and serves as a prelude to the much more popular, and much more public, La Conquistadora processions. The local Marian celebration receives much more attention than its more universally Catholic, more Christocentric, prelude. One informant, for example, remarked during the Corpus Christi procession, "Just wait until next Sunday. Then you will see a *real* procession." It seems to be a principle in almost any kind of religious observance that the more specifically local its idiom, the more popular.

Structurally, the Corpus Christi procession is similar to the La Conquistadora processions. The processions are ordered almost identically, and both are rituals involving the same basic human actions: sacred display, worship and praise, the reception of divine grace and favor. They are both modes of showing, giving, receiving, and moving through space in a symbolic manner. The La Conquistadora processions, however, are an expression of *civitas*, as well as *ecclesia*, while Corpus Christi is characterized primarily by *ecclesia*. Officially, the celebration of Corpus Christi is left to individual parishes, but unofficially, many join the cathedral in its celebration—an anticipation of the city-wide processions which follow a week later.

The La Conquistadora celebration begins at the cathedral on July 1 with a vespers service in Latin (see Figure 2). The use of Latin suggests the solemnity of the occasion of La Conquistadora's trip from St. Francis Cathedral to Rosario Chapel. Following the chanting of vespers, a procession, bearing the statue of La Conquistadora on a palanquin carried by the Caballeros de Vargas, winds its way through Santa Fe's central plaza and ends in Rosario Chapel, a mile away in Rosario Cemetery. Before 1970 the statue was carried by the Niñas de María (Daughters of Mary), but now the men of the Caballeros de Vargas are her official escorts and bearers. The following processional order, though not rigid, is traditional and does not vary greatly in any of the processions of the La Conquistadora cycle:

1. Santa Fe Police motorcycles
2. Cross bearer
3. Candle bearers
4. Color guard (papal and American flags)
5. De Vargas figure and staff
6. St. Anne's Parish
7. Our Lady of Guadalupe Parish
8. Cristo Rey Parish
9. Catholic Daughters of America
10. St. John's Parish
11. Sacred Heart League
12. Third Order of St. Francis

Figure 2. Adoration of the statue of La Conquistadora in St. Francis Cathedral

13. Tesuque Mission
14. St. Francis Cathedral
15. Holy Name Society
16. Choir
17. Flower girls
18. Confraternity of La Conquistadora
19. Fiesta queen and court
20. Caballeros de Vargas, bearing La Conquistadora
21. Santa Fe Police Guard
22. Clergy

According to a Caballero ("Knight" of De Vargas) who usually organizes the processions, the order of the procession is dictated by two principles. Places of highest honor go to the oldest organizations or parishes and to males. The place of highest honor is at the end of the procession, where the sacred object, either the Blessed Sacrament or the statue of La Conquistadora, is located. If one actually studies the order in the light of these two suggested principles, he discovers that at best they apply only to numbers 6 through 15, and even then there are exceptions. If, in fact, the placing of the queen and court, on the one hand, and the De Vargas figure and his staff, on the other, indicates relative positions of honor, the ranking in the procession contradicts claims that the higher honor is De Vargas'. Most informants simply state that tradition determines the order without specifying any organizing principles; clearly the old organizing principles determine the order of only a few groups.

The procession to Rosario Chapel is in many ways like the Corpus Christi procession; people walk, meditate, carry and say rosaries, and sing *canticos* (devotional songs). There are no stops and no benedictions on the way to the ritual enthronement of La Conquistadora. Before the enthronement of the statue on her platform in front of the central reredos, all of the banners used in the procession are posted in a rack to the right of the altar. During the enthronement, flags are alternately raised and lowered at the commands of the color guard. Both the altar and statue are incensed and circumambulated, and a Benediction of the Blessed Sacrament is performed before the statue is actually enthroned by the *mayordomo* of the Confraternity of La Conquistadora. Flowers are presented by the fiesta royalty; they are placed at the base of La Conquistadora's pedestal while she is still on her palanquin. People reach out to touch both La Conquistadora and the velvet costumes of some of the fiesta royalty. Whereas the language at the Cathedral on this occasion is primarily Latin, it is both Spanish and Latin at Rosario Chapel. The Church has no enthronement rite per se, so participants use a continuation of vespers, an incensation, and the Benediction of the Blessed Sacrament instead—all of which function to create a ritual context for the simple act of placing La Conquistadora on her platform-throne.

On Monday, following Sunday's procession and enthronement, a series of Masses begins in La Conquistadora's honor. Mass is celebrated at Rosario Chapel twice daily (6:00 A.M. and 5:15 P.M.). The novena of Masses continues through the following Monday, even though the procession that returns La Conquistadora to St. Francis Cathedral occurs the day before; two novena Masses occur on the Sunday of the statue's return. The return procession concluded in 1973 with a Mass accompanied by mariachi-style music preceded by a coronation of the statue and a rededication of New Mexico to La Conquistadora.

The Corpus Christi and La Conquistadora processions are relatively simple. Neither the actions nor interpretations of these actions is complex: one merely walks reverently from one place to another, carrying a revered object. Most indigenous interpretation is historical. If one asks the meaning of these rituals, the responses are narrative, not theological, in form. Questions about contemporary meaning are met with stories about the origin of the processions, as if reciting the story of origin were itself sufficient reason for continuation of the ritual in the present. The reason most frequently offered for participating in the processions is the continuation and fulfillment of De Vargas' vow.

Important genealogical, historical, and cultural lifelines run back to De Vargas, and either he can serve as a static, but potent image, or, more typically, he can be a dynamic actor in a narrative-drama which Hispanos insist is still being acted out in contemporary Sante Fe. That side of De Vargas which is peculiarly religious is embodied in the icon of La Conquistadora; she has the dominant role in the novena-processions, while De Vargas overshadows her in the fiesta. Telling the story is explanation enough for many participants because the conclusion of the story is, "And here we are, adding another chapter today." But it would be wrong to suppose that the "plot" merely goes on, leaving earlier episodes behind. Modern episodes are resonances of the earlier ones.

Procession and Pilgrimage

One way to interpret a procession is by selecting and reciting a story—a historical or mythical narrative. Another way is to examine it in terms of its most general structures. Stated most generally, a procession is a ritualistic movement through space, so comparing the La Conquistadora processions with other symbolic modes of moving through space ought to supplement the indigenous historical mode of interpretation.

The typical activities involved in processions are walking, carrying, showing, viewing, praying, singing, and being seen. In a procession these ordinary human actions take on an extraordinary symbolic significance. Processions and kindred ritualistic movements like pilgrimages are important to many peoples, especially to those of Spanish descent. It is no accident that Saint James, the patron of Spain and the saint whose name ("Santiago" in Spanish) was shouted by De Vargas as a battle cry, is usually depicted wearing pilgrim's clothing. Images of pilgrims, whether on foot carrying staffs, or on horseback as pilgrim-knights in quest, are still important in Spain, Mexico, and New Mexico. Any human gesture can become ritualized; therefore emphasis on one gesture rather than on another tells us something vital about the people using that gesture.

B. I. Mullahy, who notes that religious processions in the history of religions are most commonly related to enthronements, new year's celebrations, the aversion and propitiation of calamities, and triumphant entries, suggests that processions are theologically associated by Christians with the pilgrimage [Exodus] out of Egypt, following Christ on the road to heaven, and the church's pilgrimage on earth. Prayer to the pilgrim, he says, is "walking with God" (1967:819–821).

None of the participants interviewed was so full in his interpretive associations as this, but certainly Mullahy's description would not contradict the viewpoint expressed in the iconography and mythology of the regional Catholicism of New Mexico. The Virgin Mary is not only the object of pilgrimages and the focus of processions, she is herself regarded as a pilgrim. De Vargas refers to her as "both pilgrim and patroness" (Espinosa 1940:107). In this respect, La Conquistadora is an image of the people themselves. They are pilgrims; she is a pilgrim. One prominent Franciscan devotee declares that processions satisfy a basic human need to incorporate one's entire being into religion. The Mass, he reflects, is full of "little processions."

The attractiveness of pilgrimages and processions to some Catholics is obvious when theologians incessantly have to warn against abuses. Two prominent abuses of Corpus Christi processions, according to some theologians, are valuing the procession over the Mass and giving more ritualistic solemnity and dignity to the procession than to the Mass.

Liturgists are careful not to give free rein to the procession-pilgrimage impulse lest it overshadow the central ritualistic act, the Mass.

After Cardinal Spellman crowned her, La Conquistadora herself became a pilgrim during her *visitas* (formal visits) of 1954 as she traveled around New Mexico and to the Midwest and East, as well as Mexico, thus recalling her various "pilgrimages" up and down the Rio Grande during the Hispano-Indian conflicts of the seventeenth century. La Conquistadora had not ritually left Santa Fe since her return with De Vargas in 1692, except in 1954. Her reason for undertaking the pilgrimage in 1954 was, according to one unidentified written source, "to make a shrine of every parish and of all hearts!" During this time, Fray Angélico Chávez became "La Conquistadora's Bard" as he accompanied her on her visits and wrote poetry venerating her. Newspapers chronicled her pilgrimage; the result was a kind of "travelogue of the sacred." Although processions bearing statues are far from extraordinary in the United States, the frequency and intensity of La Conquistadora's travels through the streets of Santa Fe are unusual. In being episcopally crowned by Francis Cardinal Spellman and then attempting to visit every parish in her "kingdom," La Conquistadora began to push at the boundaries of her domain. Proponents of her veneration now insist that her domain is not limited to Catholic Santa Fe.

During the visit of La Conquistadora, the pilgrim virgin, to Las Vegas, New Mexico, in 1954, prayers were offered for the conversion of Russia. Everywhere she visited there were banners, processions, Masses, sermons, and speeches—many of them in the form of combined religious-civic gatherings. Devotion was generated and intensified. The abbess of the Poor Clare Monastery of Our Lady of Guadalupe in Roswell, New Mexico, describing the event almost twenty years after its occurrence, writes:

When our Mother M. Immaculata and Sister M. Annuntiata came to found the monastery in 1948, they passed through Santa Fe, and saw the ancient statue [of La Conquistadora] in her own chapel. The rest of us had only seen small pictures which did not prepare us for the real loveliness of this Marian image. Late in the evening of May 31, 1954, Fray Angelico Chavez, O.F.M., who was taking the statue on pilgrimage for the Marian year, arrived at our chapel. We received the statue at the door which connects our choir with the chapel, and four of us carried her on a kind of litter which Fray Angelico provided into our chapter room. We sang the "Salve Regina" . . . and a few other hymns, and then retired. It was about 10:30. Two hours later we rose as usual for the night office of the Church, which we chanted that night in the chapter room before the ancient statue. Fray Angelico celebrated our early morning conventual Mass, with Our Lady enthroned on our cloister altar. Afterwards, we sang about a dozen hymns, and he then received her back to continue her journey. It was a brief visit, but the memory of it will always be a precious one. We keep her framed picture in a place of honor in our chapter room. [Mother Mary Francis, P.C.C., letter of September 19, 1973]

So important were these Marian Year travels that members of the experimental La Conquistadora Farm at Dilia, New Mexico, commissioned a special medal and plaque in commemoration of the event. The medal became the confraternity's official one.

For devotees of La Conquistadora, as for their ancestors, one conquers and cultivates, in both an agricultural and cultural sense, by moving through space. To exist is to move, to visit, and to visit is to take possession of, thereby making visited space home space. Space is symbolically and geographically such a pervasive and vast force in the Southwest that the failure to traverse it results in the dissolution of the relations which constitute life itself. Symbolically, the exploratory wanderings and long expeditions of the conquistadors are still being enacted in processions, parades, and pilgrimages in the Hispanic Southwest as a means reaffirming the vital connection between life and space.

Victor Turner's important survey article on pilgrimages (1973a: 191–230, also in 1974:166 ff.) draws much of its material from Mexico. A comparison of these Mexican pilgrimages with the New Mexican processions of La Conquistadora can help set into relief the continuities and contrasts between the two forms of ritualistic movement.

For Turner, pilgrimages are liminal phenomena; they occur in the interstices between the structures and processes of ordinary cultural reality. Turner finds in the pilgrimage a spirit of *communitas*, that is, a spirit of unmediated relationship between individuals, which is characteristic of the transitional phase of certain rites of passage in preindustrial, tribal societies. Pilgrims immerse themselves in a ritual movement through space which, in relation to their ordinary routines, is destructured, sacred, devoid of hierarchical distinctions, and characterized by voluntary promises and obligations. Of course, any liminal situation has a tendency to revert to its structured opposite, that is, the status system. Turner describes his own view: "I myself tend to see pilgrimage as that form of institutionalized or symbolic "antistructure" (or perhaps metastructure) which succeeds the major initiation rites of puberty in tribal societies as the dominant historical form. It is the ordered antistructure of patrimonial-feudal systems" (1973a:204).

Turner points out that a "ritual topography, a distribution in space of permanent sacred sites," is not usually identical with the political topography (1973a:206). Furthermore, the two kinds of spatial organization are grounded on different principles. Political structures tend to stress group divisions of power and exclusiveness, while cults built around earth shrines tend toward shared interest, unity, and inclusiveness. In pilgrim centers, he suggests, complex societies "look for the topography of the inclusive, disinterested and altruistic domains" (1973a:208). Turner's study of Mexican pilgrimages suggests that the sites are usually those of some hierophany, that they are usually characterized by images rather than relics, and that they are liminally located beyond the centers of cities and towns and beyond the centers of economic, political, and ecclesiastical power.

Viewing a Mexican pilgrimage alongside a New Mexican procession is instructive primarily for the contrasts it provides.[2] Though they are both symbolically laden movements through space, a pilgrimage is not a procession, nor is Mexico, New Mexico. The space through which pilgrims move is liminal; it is "betwixt and between" both geographically and symbolically. Such a characterization could be applied to the La Conquistadora processions only in a limited sense—perhaps only inasmuch as devotees process down the middle of streets in which normal occurrences such as traffic have been temporarily suspended. The fact that the La Conquistadora processions move from the center of Santa Fe to the edge of Sante Fe, from a cathedral to a cemetery chapel, might be construed as a movement from the symbolic status system of the center to the symbolic liminality of the boundary, but other factors must be considered.

The processions inevitably pass through the central plaza of the city, and informants often speak of the plaza as the center of town, whether or not this is an accurate geographical judgment. Passing through this center usually symbolizes, and requires as a prerequisite, the sanction of civil authorities, many of whom actually participate in the processions. The status system is intensified, not temporarily

---

[2] Incidentally, J. Manuel Espinosa argues convincingly that cultural contact with Mexico can account for the existence of a procession with a *conquistadora*, or *conquista*, and a chapel in her honor. Many of the Santa Fe traditions, including the story about La Conquistadora's growing heavier on the return journey to St. Francis Cathedral, can be paralleled in Mexico (cf. J. Manual Espinosa 1936).

suspended, by this ritual passage through the city's center. Furthermore, Rosario Chapel, the destination of the processions, is a sacred center in its own right. It is the place De Vargas is said to have camped in 1692, and it is where the ancestral dead are. "Going out to Rosario" is not a movement from status system to liminality so much as it is an extension of the domain of the status system to include those "above" and those "out there." A ritual journey is not necessarily mapped through a liminal zone, especially if the ethos of the journey is that of conquest rather than search or reaching a sacred goal. A ritual journey may simply be an extension of the normative status system. In this sense the La Conquistadora processions are ritual extensions of the reconquest. They symbolically take possession of what already "really belongs to us." Moving through the civic center of town, the plaza, is a way of declaring symbolically that the event is of citywide, not merely churchwide, significance.

The nonliminal, status system ethos of La Conquistadora and her processions is strong. The statue's home is the seat of the archbishop; she is at the heart of ecclesiastical power and order. And in her processions a definite hierarchical order maintains. Though some of the civil authorities who participate insist that they do so as devout individuals, not as community officials, the average participant still views them in terms of their statuses. Unlike the Virgin of Guadalupe, La Conquistadora does not represent a hierophany, if by this term one means a miraculous appearance of the holy, such as a vision or an audition. Virtually no miracle tradition is connected with her. Many come to Santa Fe to visit her, but few stories of healing or miracles surround her. The *mayordomo* of her confraternity takes this as a sign of her uniqueness. "Perhaps," he says, "she has performed a greater miracle—she maintained our faith under conditions which ordinarily would have destroyed it. Our faith is her miracle."

Far from tending toward "antistructure," La Conquistadora processions crystalize the status system in both its religious and civic forms. The political and sacred topographies of Santa Fe overlap at crucial points, most of which are in some way related to La Conquistadora. It is no accident that the mayor and a U.S. senator, to take two examples, were members of the Caballeros de Vargas in 1973.

Unlike a pilgrim, a processant in Santa Fe's public ritual seldom undergoes strenuous physical activity in reaching faraway places, nor does he tolerate the anxiety of being on foot in a strange land. The processant seldom forms close or lasting relationships solely on the basis of his participation with others in the procession. Typically, he knows many of those in the procession; they are his family and friends. But intimate chatting or sharing of food, as pilgrims might do, is suspended for the formality of marching quietly or singing and praying. There is neither the time nor the necessity for what Turner calls *communitas* and what Martin Buber calls I-Thou relations. Processants do not eat, sleep, and suffer together; they simply walk and pray together. Processions do not demand devotion and commitment the way pilgrimages do; processions are considerably more open to spectators, tourists, and curious bystanders. If one makes a pilgrimage, he at least has to be serious enough about it to pay the money for plane or bus fare. Processions, according to participants, are for praying and singing, and the praying and singing are for the purpose of bearing witness. But bearing witness, when secularized by the perceiving eyes and ears of spectators, easily becomes entertainment. This is especially true in Santa Fe because of the high tourist population in the summer. The process by which processions become secularized into parades is simpler and more obvious than the process by which pilgrimages become family vacations and tourism.

Whereas a procession is a sacred display either of an object, such as the communion Host, or of one's devotion, a pilgrimage is an accomplishment. A pilgrimage is goal-oriented;

it is teleological in tone, hence its link to quest myths such as that of the Holy Grail. And its goal is to get from here to there, from near to far. In a procession there is no geographical goal but a symbolic activity which is its own reason for being. Instead it has a procession route, which is circular. Processions do not involve the elaborate apparatus of penitence and self-denial characteristic of pilgrimages, therefore they are much more likely to involve the central rather than the liminal, the middle rather than the edges of a city.

One need not search as far as Mexico for relevant comparisons to the La Conquistadora processions. One might compare them to the pilgrimages to El Santuario de Chimayó, located thirty-eight miles northeast of Santa Fe, or to a secular parade like the Rodeo de Santa Fe.

Pilgrimage to Chimayó

The small village of Chimayó, sometimes referred to as the "Lourdes of New Mexico," is probably the most important pilgrimage site in New Mexico. Pilgrims can be found there at any time during the year, but crowds estimated to be as large as ten thousand arrive on Good Friday. The shrine is particularly important as a site for healing and intercession for victims of war. The fact that the largest attendance at El Santuario is on Good Friday rather than Easter Sunday indicates the strong Penitente influence in the area. The Penitentes are lay Catholic men devoted to mutual support and the observance of penance during Holy Week, at which time they enact the *via cruxis* (way of the cross) with flagellation and sometimes a crucifixion of one of their members. The Santuario de Chimayó displays on its main altar the black Christ known in New Mexico, Mexico, and Guatemala as Our Lord of Esquipulas. In Chimayó there are two popular pilgrim-figures: Santiago, the equestrian pilgrim, and Santo Niño Perdido, the "lost" Christ child who travels during the night, wearing out the shoes laid by pilgrims on the altar.

Stephen F. De Borhegyi (1956:21–22) argues that Santo Niño Perdido is really Santo Niño de Atocha under a mistaken title. The attribution of lostness (*perdido*) occurs, he argues, as a result of the tradition that the Holy Child is gone from the church at night. Santo Niño de Atocha is also frequently assimilated to the Holy Child of Prague. The conflation of three different forms of the Holy Child produces some interesting variants of the traditional stories associated with each title.

Pilgrimlike figures are important to Chimayó and to the Santa Feans who make pilgrimages there. Since ritual movement through space is important to the Santa Fe area, it is not surprising to find that the land is symbolically valued. Many pilgrims go to Chimayó to obtain sacred dirt. Thousands of pilgrims a year visit a hole which is said never to be empty of miraculous soil. Pilgrims carry away the dirt in jars, eat it (geophagy), and use it with saliva to make the sign of the cross on children's foreheads. In addition to the healing power of this *tierra del Santo* (sacred soil) and the pilgrimage to El Santuario, a third spatially significant feature attracts pilgrims. Just around the corner from El Santuario is the Church of Santo Niño de Atocha. According to the tradition, Santo Niño de Atocha visited Spaniards who had been imprisoned by the Moors. He carried food to them when no one else was allowed to visit. As part of a rivalry between the two neighboring shrines, El Santuario now has its own Santo Niño de Atocha.

Each of these popular symbols of Chimayó—pilgrimage, soil, shoes—is related to sacred space and passage through it. And insofar as space becomes objectified as land, one can "carry space" back with him in the form of a jar of dirt. The primary difference between the Santa Fe processions and the Chimayó pilgrimages is that the former is a movement through space which is a display of pure faith that does not depend upon reward nor claim to possess its object; one looks at the Host or La Conquistadora but does not own them or control them with prayer-requests. The Chimayó pilgrimages represent a task-oriented faith. One goes there to accomplish some spiritual or physical deed such as healing, and one carries back, and thus to a certain extent controls, sacred power.

In almost every respect the understanding of sacred space reflected in pilgrimages to Chimayó parallels the Mexican pattern described by Victor Turner (1973a). Both are connected to natural, geographical features; both are on or near probable sites of pre-Christian worship; both are composite shrines typified by a cluster of sacred sites. The only important differences seem to be that in Mexico there are sacred way-stations along traditionally established pilgrim routes.

Keeping in mind that a large percentage of the Good Friday pilgrims to Chimayó are Santa Feans who also participate in the La Conquistadora processions, one cannot generalize about the kinds of people who participate in processions in contrast to those who go on pilgrimages. The same person often does both. However, it does seem that urban Santa Fe provides less fertile ground for the miracle traditions typically associated with pilgrimage sites. The public, civic nature of her rituals seems to focus too strong a light on her, which inhibits the development of a strong miracle ethos.

I do not wish to overemphasize the differences between processions and pilgrimages, because both are, after all, ritualistic modes of demarcating sacred space and organizing movement through it. The most important difference is one of emphasis. For the pilgrim, reaching the destination, with its attendant self-denial, offerings, and cures, is everything. For the processant the act of witnessing by walking, displaying, and carrying is everything. Processions other than funerary ones are typically circular in their spatial orientation. Employing stylized gestures of walking and carrying, a procession leaves and returns, but neither the leaving nor the returning place is very important in comparison with the circular process of movement itself. This contrasts with the arrival-orientation of the pilgrim; he has arrived at the moment he views his goal from the *mons gaudii*, the hill from which one first sees the shrine. Returning home is of little significance in comparison. The pilgrim draws near the sacred space, the "center out there" (Turner), while the processant carries what is sacred with him, thereby generating sacred space as he walks. Processions are more firmly grounded in *civitas* than are pilgrimages. They are, therefore, more likely to become imbedded in the practices of public religion and civic ritual, thereby becoming more open to evolving into parades.

Parades in Santa Fe

Parades are secularized processions. Processions are not typical of communities in the United States, but parades are still quite common. In the United States parades are usually organized and supervised by civic leaders and civil authorities, whereas processions are instigated and conducted by ecclesiastical institutions. Parades are typically for either sheer entertainment or the displaying of patriotic sentiments and military power. But patriotism can become just as absolutistic in its claims as religion can. The civic and civil virtues symbolized in parades can bring strong sanctions to bear on the enforcement of social values. In this respect they are as binding and therefore as "sacred" as religious values. Just because parades are enjoyed and utilized for commercial and political purposes does not mean that we should minimize their impact and meaning for a community.

A rather full cycle of parades characterizes the public life of Santa Fe, especially during the summer months. The symbolic importance of parades is obvious if one looks at a sampling of the kinds of groups which participate. The governor of the state of New Mexico was present on horseback at the Santa Fe Rodeo Parade of July 12; so was the mayor of the city. The parades averaged between fifty and seventy-five entries. In addition to mariachi bands and clowns intended simply for entertainment, the following kinds of groups were represented: law enforcement (police, sheriff, mounted patrol, sheriff's posses), military (Army, Marines), quasi-educational (school bands, cheerleaders, twirlers), commercial (resorts, auto sales, restaurants), civic (Lions Club, Cub Scouts), paramilitary (Civil Air Patrol, R.O.T.C., Young Marines), civil (governor, mayor, city council), recreation and sports (Little League, drama groups, dance groups, riding clubs), quasi-royalty (queens of rodeos, cities, fiestas), special interest and protest groups (Boycott Safeway, Women's Liberation, satirical entries), church groups (Presbyterian and Methodist bell ringers).

Parades, like processions and pilgrimages, are ritualizations of space, but parades do not issue from promises and vows as pilgrimages often do, nor are they a bearing witness as processions are. Although parades, like processions and pilgrimages, instill certain values and extol certain virtues, their primary purpose is to be seen. Though processions bear witness, the ones for whom the witness is borne need not be different from those participating in the procession. Parades demand distinct audiences and participants; processions do not. Even though a procession typically has an audience other than those participating, it does not require spectators. And pilgrimages need spectators even less. But a parade fails unless it is a spectacle, unless it is seen. Some individuals participate in parades by riding horses, driving cars or whatever, for the sole purpose of being in the public view. A parade is a show, not a sacred display nor a journey to a sacred place.

Sacred Space

The centrality of three kinds of ritual movement (procession, pilgrimage, and parade) in Santa Fe gives us some im-

portant clues to interpreting public ritual in the city generally. To invoke Kenneth Burke's dramatistic "grammar," the
scene-act "ratio" is of utmost importance in Santa Fe (Burke
1969). Of any act Burke would have us inquire what is done
(act), the context or locus of doing (scene), how or with what
means it is done (agency), what is its goal (purpose), and who
performs the act (agent). The scene-act ratio is the relation
between action and context. Specifically, we have been concerned with ritualistic, or symbolic, actions such as walking
and displaying in the context of civic-sacred space. Spatial
considerations and scenic interpretations are of special significance in New Mexico, as is illustrated by its long and continuing land controversies. The human actions which have
developed "in ratio" to this scenic preoccupation are those of
travel and transportation, as is illustrated by the unusual
amount of attention paid to rituals of mobility, namely, parades, processions, and pilgrimages. New Mexicans view life
as dependent upon mobility. In the nineteenth century stealing a man's horse was a capital offense. In the twentieth century New Mexico's governor was the first to object to a
federally proposed fifty-mile-an-hour speed limit, insisting
that New Mexico be excepted from this limit, as well as from
any ten-gallon-a-week fuel ration. Calvin Ross, in his "Sky
Determines" thesis (1934), suggests that New Mexicans
frequently view scene, or space, as if it were agent; the sky
itself is prime actor.

Relationships between Hispanos, Anglos, and Pueblos in
the Santa Fe area are in large measure reflected in their contrasting modes of handling symbolic space. Their views of
land and mobility are sometimes quite different. Alfonso
Ortiz, for example, argues that the Tewa Pueblos classify
human existence in terms of a hierarchy of six categories, all
of which are linked to six geographical categories (1969:9).
The Tewa worldview posits a world boundary consisting of
four sacred mountains; on top of each is an earth navel (*nan
sipu*). Within this tetrad is another, associated with flat-

topped mesas and inhabited by Tsave Yoh, masked supernatural whippers who live in the caves and tunnels there. The third tetrad consists of shrines, often in the form of piles of stones associated with the cardinal directions. The innermost tetrad is linked to the plazas in the villages themselves. At the center is the navel of mother earth (1969:19–21).

The spaces depicted in Ortiz' schema of concentric tetrads are, of course, conceptual and symbolic. The center may or may not be at the exact geographical center of the pueblo. Ortiz says that the sacred power of blessing flows inward from the mountain earth navels and outward from the central, mother earth navel; center and circumference are joined in this process. The earth navels serve as orientation points, as well as contact points between the above, middle, and below.

The Tewa world, as described by Ortiz, is bounded by definable limits; power flows inward and outward within this sacred world. This conception of sacred space is quite different from that of either Hispanic Catholicism or Anglo-Protestantism. In Catholicism there is no sacred world which coincides with some organically articulated natural boundaries. There are sacred places, but these are prolongations of a vertically extended, hierarchically organized sacred world. For Catholics sacred space appears in the form of pilgrimage sites, cemeteries, cathedrals, shrines, and finally, Rome. What unifies these into a whole is not a set of natural boundaries like mountains. Rather it is the performance of a common consecrating rite.

For many Protestants the notion of sacred space has become secularized into the concept of private property. Church buildings and cemeteries are not especially sacred; they are simply the practical necessities of religion. Churches are "meeting houses." What is sacred is the space occupied by individuals; it is "body space." Neither the land nor the mountains nor edifices set aside for worship constitutes the ultimate "scene" in which human beings act.

Hispano-Catholics and Anglo-Protestants have, however, shared an essential Christian concept which continues to influence their view of space. Especially between the sixteenth and nineteenth centuries both considered the movement through and possession of space a sacred duty. Their mission was the extension of the kingdom of God and church, or else the opening up of a new world full of eschatological and utopian possibilities. For Protestants the settlement of the West, and westward movement generally, was the preparation of new grounds for an eschatological kingdom. The movement westward was a movement toward sacred renewal of the destiny intended by Providence. These Anglos met Hispanos in New Mexico, and for the latter, the movement north from Mexico was a holy conquest for "both Majesties."

If one looks for the epitomizing ritual of mobility for each of the three groups insofar as they perform public rituals in Santa Fe, he finds Catholics dominating processions and pilgrmages, Protestants dominating parades, and Pueblos dominating dances. Whereas the two Christian groups ritually move through space, the Pueblos fill space by dancing sacredness into the earth. These differing ritual styles are metaphors of much larger value-symbol complexes which sometimes become the source of intense conflict. The symbolic, spatial models do not always synchronize. Pueblos move inward and outward within the bounds of concentric sacred space. Hispanos process through civil-civic space on their way to the sacred space of Holy Church, which is owned by no man. And Protestants go to their semisacred edifices to reaffirm the worth of the individual before God. To live in Santa Fe, then, is often to find that one is not sure where he is—in what scene he is acting. There is both fusion and confusion of worlds, and the maxim, "When in Rome . . ." is of no help when one is not sure where Rome stops and Greece begins. It seems that the only space which is ever organized and shared in common is civic space. For Santa Fe this is the space of the plaza, and precisely for this reason the plaza became the locus of the interethnic "monument controversy" mentioned earlier. One thing is clear though: the public rituals of the plaza, not those of *kiva* (sacred edifice of the Pueblos), *morada* (the meeting place of Penitente Catholics), cathedral, or church, generate a symbolic space which at least has the possibility of being a shared space.

The La Conquistadora Masses

So far I have considered only the most regionally distinctive phase of the early summer rituals. The processions mark the beginning and culmination of a novena of Masses, and the Mass is far more universal in Catholic Christianity than processions are. One does an injustice to the public ritual of Santa Fe if he considers regional symbols and practices in isolation from more universal ones.

Catholic theology maintains that the Mass constitutes its ritualistic center. Pope Pius XII in *Mediator Dei* refers to it as "the culmination and center, as it were, of the Christian religion," and Paul VI in *Mysterium Fiedei* speaks of it as holding "first place in the life of the Church." No devotee would imagine a fiesta or the novena-processions without the Mass. The Mass may not generate the most enthusiasm or attendance, but it religiously legitimizes and lays the foundation for everything else that is done. In this sense it is the chartering enactment.

Catholic Christianity has a finite number of rituals, but an almost infinite number of variations in sociocultural context. The church meets varying conditions in a variety of ways: (1) by developing different rituals for different occasions, for example, marriage, baptism, birth, death, (2) by allowing a controlled adaptation and modification of prescribed rituals, (3) by allowing the growth of paraliturgical devotions which derive their legitimacy from the central rites, particularly the Eucharist, and (4) by allowing the combining of ritual fragments, or modules, into "new" rituals.

On at least three specific occasions during the period of my study local situations created a need for rituals that do not exist in any current liturgical text: the enthronement of La Conquistadora at Rosario Chapel, the coronation of La Conquistadora by the fiesta queen, and the coronation and knighting of the queen and De Vargas figure. In each case a ritual was created by a combination of elements from the rite for blessing objects, vespers, the Benediction of the Blessed Sacrament, music and prayers from the Mass, and gestures of courtly etiquette. Parts of these rituals are used as modules linked together into a ritual to fit occasions with no prescribed rituals. The modules, along with a few interpolated phrases and perhaps some interpretive remarks by an officiant, become the materials for constructing rituals. Any ritual, therefore, can be studied not only as a unitary performance but also as a source to be used by other rituals. Rituals do not exist in vacuums, but in systems, and the center of the Catholic system is the Mass, even though processions and saints elicit more conversation than Masses do.

Along with structurally stable, relatively unchanging elements, the Mass has flexible aspects which the church intends to reflect the temporal and regional commitments of the people. An excellent example of adaptation is the mariachi Mass, used on at least three occasions during 1973: (1) the return of La Conquistadora after the theft of the statue early in the year, (2) the return of La Conquistadora to St. Francis Cathedral at the end of the novena-processions, and (3) the Solemn Pontifical Fiesta Mass ("Misa Panamericana"). These were occasions for simultaneously heightening *ethnos* and *ecclesia*. During mariachi Masses on these occasions non-Catholics, and even Catholics of non-Spanish descent, tend to become fascinated spectators rather than active participants.

Though the choir director for the mariachi Masses considered the term "mariachi" inaccurate, because mariachi style music is really Mexican, and the music of this Mass had been modified sufficiently to make it "northern New Mexican," the term persists. The Mass originated in Cuernevaca, Mexico, but had been modified subsequently. The use of mariachi-like music is considered by many, especially older participants, to be experimental and innovative, so the mariachi Mass should not be viewed as a traditional form of folk celebration. This "indigenization" of the Mass is a post-Vatican II phenomenon, not the survival of an old La Conquistadora tradition. Some older people say they enjoy mariachi music but regard it as too distracting for worship.

A good example of ritual construction and adaptation is the Mass following La Conquistadora's return to St. Francis Cathedral after the novena at Rosario Chapel. Most informants regarded as a unit the procession-coronation-rededication-Mass which occurred on July 8, 1973.

The ritual begins with a procession from Rosario Chapel essentially like the procession to the chapel a few days before. As participants reach the cathedral, they begin to sing "Las Mañanitas," [3] a striking song in this context, because it tells the story of Our Lady of Guadalupe to a tune used in New Mexico on personal birthday–saint's day celebrations. No one seems bothered that Our Lady of Guadalupe is praised rather than Our Lady of the Conquest; "she is still Our Lady."

Following the processional entry during the hymn, the *mayordomo* of the Confraternity of La Conquistadora set the tone for a coronation with the following words spoken from the Gospel side of the altar:

Brothers and sisters in Christ, from the sacristy will come a simple procession of the fiesta queen and her princesses, De Vargas and his captains. They will represent the people of Santa Fe, of New Mexico and of the Southwest. Father Austin, the chaplain of the

[3] I am indebted to Paco Ramirez for his help in translating the Spanish of mariachi and novena masses.

cofradiá [confraternity], will represent the church. Mayor Valdes will represent the City of Santa Fe. They will march from the sacristy of the church with the papal crown. Our Blessed Mother will be crowned by the fiesta queen after a blessing of the crown and the incensation of the statue of Our Lady. The reason for this unusual ceremony today is because we are grateful to almighty God for the return of Our Lady to her proper place in the Cathedral. She represents not only the queenship of Santa Fe, but of the entire Southwest. And today, as we have done in the past, for example in 1771 in the Santa Fe Fiestas, when in the processions Our Lady was venerated—given more glory and honor for Our Lady. In commemoration of those days when the people realized that periodically they would consecrate themselves to Our Lady . . . In memory of those days we will consecrate the Kingdom of New Mexico and the city of Santa Fe to its queen, La Conquistadora. [from a tape recording]

This introductory address shows that the civil aspects of the La Conquistadora rituals are not restricted to the fiesta, but are present even in the summer novena-processions; the mayor of the city is present, representing the City of Santa Fe in a religious function. This particular mayor was a member of the Caballeros de Vargas, the Confraternity of La Conquistadora, and the Roman Catholic church, but according to this address, his participation is not dependent upon these affiliations so much as upon his position as mayor.

The speech also suggests that De Vargas and his staff and the queen and her court represent all of the people of the Southwest. The notion of "representing" here is quite unlike that implied, for instance, in a representative government. The "royalty" are not *elected by*, but are *symbols for*, Southwesterners. The representing that they do is from the point of view of a Hispano devotee.

Another important fact about the speech is that La Conquistadora is interpreted in terms of a regal metaphor, which in turn implies that her followers see the state of New Mexico in terms of the metaphor of a kingdom. Later, at the moment of the statue's crowning, the *mayordomo* announces that the act is in the name of "all people of the kingdom of New Mexico and the Royal City of Santa Fe." In Christian imagery God has his kingdom, but this has nothing to do with actual forms of governance in specific nations. La Conquistadora also has her kingdom, but this metaphor only symbolically contradicts the empirical fact that Santa Fe and New Mexico are democratically, not royally, governed.

The procession announced in the *mayordomo*'s introduction comes down the center aisle of the cathedral, bearing the crown during the singing of the Sanctus in Spanish. The clerical leadership proceeds to the Gospel side, and the civil and civic members to the Epistle side of the altar, where the statue is located. The Sanctus normally signals the most sacred part of the Mass, the Eucharistic Prayer. The Sanctus itself suggests this with its opening words, "Holy, holy, holy. . . ." The fact that it occurs here, outside the context of the Mass proper, indicates how highly this coronation is esteemed. This conclusion is not drawn merely from the recurrence of the Sanctus here and again at the middle of the Mass. Later De Vargas, the queen, and one of the Indian princesses all referred to the special nature of this moment. One said that they were on the verge of tears. Another said this was the moment they realized "that our roles were not just fun and games but had a serious, religious purpose." The sanctity of the moment is heightened considerably, according to the reports of the participants, by the fact that they are carrying a priceless gold crown studded with jewels. The words of the Sanctus are most theologically appropriate at their usual place in the Mass. Their being used here is probably not a result of their conceptual content so much as their association with peak moments. Consequently, their message here is simply, "This civic moment is of special, sacred significance."

Following the Sanctus the crown and statue are incensed by the priest after the fiesta queen has placed the crown on the head of La Conquistadora. Precisely why the queen and not, say, De Vargas, a priest, or someone else is chosen to do the coronation could not be determined by interviewing participants. Their responses usually take the form, "Well, I don't know. She just seems to be the natural one to do it." This kind of response is part of a more general indigenous difficulty in interpreting the queen's role, a problem I discuss more fully in the final chapter.

After the coronation and incensation a prayer, written by Pius XII for the Marian Year 1954 and modified slightly for this occasion, is read as an act of reconsecration of the "Kingdom of New Mexico," an act last occuring in 1771. The prayer petitions Mary as Immaculate Mother of Jesus for peace, purity from sin, and the "impregnation of our hearts with your celestial perfume," after having praised her for her purity and presence in difficult times. Mary is asked to receive this fervent prayer in reconsecration of New Mexico and Santa Fe and to hear the hymns which rise to her altar and image.

The sheer fact of such a reconsecration preceding the Mass is an unusual combination of historical reenactment and symbolic gesture. On the one hand, the reconsecration of the kingdom is akin to the Entrada pageant celebrating De Vargas in the fiesta (see Chapter 4). It refers to New Mexico as a kingdom, yet it is not merely a mimetic reenactment of the past because it is offered as an act of devotion in the present—as a response to the very contemporary event of the theft of La Conquistadora earlier in the year (see below, page 130). The reconsecration is at once mimetic and ritualistic.

For most participants the transition from the coronation-reconsecration to the Mass is hardly perceptible, the only indicator being a movement by the priests from the side of the nave to the center of the sanctuary. The center of symbolic enactment, and thus of attention, shifts from the now popularly crowned Marian image to the more ecclesiastically and Christologically centered rite of the Eucharist. Although the priest has incensed and blessed the crown during the coronation, he was not the chief actor; laymen were—specifically, the fiesta queen and the *mayordomo* of the confraternity. They performed the sacral acts of crowning and reconsecrating respectively. If we were to view hierarchy as triangular in shape, then we would have to say they receive their authorization from the broad base of it, from the people. In contrast, the sacral officiant of the Mass receives his authorization form the pinnacle.

There is no need to describe the Mass except to note that it includes thematic interpolations which link the standard order of the Mass to La Conquistadora. However, I do wish to say more about the ritualistic structures and processes embodied in the Mass. The Mass has a hierarchical structure in which occurs a process of exchange and transformation. The Mass creates the ritualistic conditions under which worshipers can approach God with gifts of bread, wine, money, praise, and repentance. The condition under which these can be transformed into effective spiritual power is that they be offered by the worshipers mediately through the hierarchy. The gifts are offered "up" through the ranks. They are transformed and given "down" to the people. The hierarchical movements of ascent and descent parallel those of the processions, except that in the case of the Mass, "space" is metaphorically "vertical." If in the processions devotees symbolically "take possession" of what is "horizontal," in the Mass they receive (rather than take) what is "given down."

Insofar as public rituals are embodiments of *civitas* they tend toward egalitarian metaphors, and certain symbols, particularly that of the fiesta queen, represent the people at large—the public without distinction of rank. But insofar as public rituals embody *ecclesia*, they tend toward royal or hierarchical metaphors. The problem, of course, is how to bridge the chasm between *civitas* and *ecclesia*. As the Mass moves away from dedications of the *civitas* to Mary and toward its own Christocentric act of transformation, symbolic gestures multiply and become more elaborate. Initiative shifts from laity to clergy. Some of the words and gestures are so priestly that they are not entirely audible or visible to lay participants. The distance between laity and clergy becomes most intense during the Liturgy of the Eucharist, the central section of the Mass. The Liturgy of the Eucharist is the least flexible part of the Mass, the least adaptable to local situations. Within it is the canon, the rule, the norm of *ecclesia*. In the Liturgy of the Eucharist laymen's actions are essentially two: the offering of gifts and the reception of communion. But the gifts return as the "medicine of immortality" only through the mediatory, consecrating act of the priest. The priest becomes, as it were, the broker between heaven and earth.

The Mass is sometimes spoken of as the "sacrifice" of the Mass. But sacrifice is a mode of transformation that is by no means simple. Several sacrifices are implied by the Mass: (1) Christ's sacrifice of himself on the Cross, (2) the priest's sacrifice at the altar, (3) the people's sacrifice of bread, wine, water, and money, (4) the church's sacrifice of itself—its very mode of being, (5) the "sacrifice of praise and thanksgiving."

The complexity of ritual exchange and transformation, is complicated further by a subtle notion of receiving. The bread the people symbolically offer is not simply whisked away, taken up, or burned. Actual shedding of blood or consuming by fire is not involved. Rather the gift is returned to the believer in a transformed mode. What is given away bread is returned as Christ's body. What is given away wine is returned as Christ's blood. Christ offers himself as a sacrifice; the priest offers him again; and the people join the priest in a perpetual sacrifice of Jesus, the Victim. This cycle pre-

cipitates difficult questions: Who offers the gift? What is offered? To whom is it offered? Who receives what is offered?
What happens to what is offered? What are the conditons of
receiving divine gifts? The crux of Catholic theology and ritual lies in the answers to these questions.

The Hierarchy and the Public

We will not become involved in theological controversy
here. My question is not about theology but about the relation of ritual to culture. The question is, "What is the relation between the hierarchically ordered rituals of symbolic
acquisition (the processions) and transformation (the Mass)
and the publically or democratically ordered symbols of the
Santa Fe *civitas?*" In other words, how are "royal" symbols
related to civic ones? The royal, hierarchical rituals contain
elements of exclusivity characteristic of the *ecclesia*, yet they
are included in a cycle that aims at inclusivity of the entire
public. The function of a ritual that includes procession, coronation, rededication, and the Mass as modules is to bridge
the chasms separating religious observances from civic ones.
Hence, the Mass, normally a celebration among the faithful,
is made to serve on such occasions as the religion of Santa
Fe, the ritual of the *civitas*.

Informants say the Mass is open to everyone. Nevertheless, non-Catholic informants sometimes say they feel out of
place in the Mass. Even though some Catholic informants
express reservations about non-Catholic participation in the
actual communion, most of them take a more pragmatic attitude. Their argument is, "Nobody will ever know whether a
communicant is Catholic anyway, so anyone can participate
who wants to." Some non-Catholics do attend fiesta and novena masses, though the ones I could identify generally did
not participate in communion. The novena Masses are attended almost solely by Catholics, whereas the fiesta Masses
have a substantial number of non-Catholic participants. The

public is invited to fiesta Masses but is simply informed that the novena Masses are occurring.

The Santa Fe Fiesta Council describes the fiesta as open to everyone regardless of language, cultural background, or religious affiliation. But the council has not had to face the problem inherent in this kind of public celebration. The public religion of Santa Fe is hardly nondenominational or fully ecumenical. No requirement states that the members of De Vargas' staff or the queen's court must be Roman Catholic, yet all of them are expected to participate in Catholic Masses and processions, and they are crowned or knighted in a Catholic ceremony at the cathedral. The problem of a public, Catholic religion is still only a conceptual one, not yet a practical one, since, as far as I can determine, there have been virtually no non-Catholic participants among the court or staff members. The implicit assumption seems to be that contestants for these roles are Catholic because they are usually Hispanic. I am told that there have been a few non-Hispanic participants on the staffs and courts of past years. These seem to be more frequent than non-Catholic participants.

The problem of denominational affiliation has not arisen either because the participants are not conscious of the problem or because non-Catholic participants view their participation as a cultural, rather than religious, affirmation. Despite the very open attitudes of fiesta officials regarding non-Catholic participation, structurally the fiesta militates against the presence of non-Catholics in the court and staff. If a non-Catholic were elected, to participate in the fullest sense he or she might be forced to choose between disrupting fiesta rituals or compromising any exclusive claims his denomination (or even his atheism) might make. Full participation in a royal role presupposes, not general religiosity, but specifically Catholic religiosity.

The question of the public nature of the Mass is not lim-

ited to Santa Fe's public ritual. It is a concern in recent ecclesiastical documents on the ritual of the Mass. The *Constitution on the Sacred Liturgy* of the Second Vatican Council
(1964:40) declares that "every Mass has of itself a public and
social nature" (article 27). But the interpretation offered by
Pope Paul VI in his encyclical, *Mysterium Fidei* (1965:39),
implies that the public/private issue is not to be equated with
the Catholic/non-Catholic issue. The Mass is public, he
suggests, in the sense that a Mass celebrated by a priest
without a congregation is still a corporate act. A Mass celebrated without a congregation is still "an act of Christ and
the Church" (article 32). Even though he declares that the
Mass is for the benefit, not just of the church, but the whole
world, that is, the public, the participants in the Mass are
still defined as "the faithful."

Whereas the participants whom I interviewed on the question about who can or should participate in fiesta and novena
Masses consider the question irrelevant because it has never
become an issue, the church hierarchy invests the question
with considerable meaning. Article 26 of the *Constitution*
views the Mass as a sign of the unity of the church: "Liturgical services are not private functions, but are celebrations of the Church, which is the 'sacrament of unity,'
namely, the holy people united and ordered under their
bishops." This statement is paralleled by the first sentence of
the "General Instruction" in the *Roman Missal*, which reads,
"The celebration of Mass is the action of Christ and the people of God hierarchically assembled" (article 1).

Despite the theological problem implicit in the La Conquistadora cycle, the primary symbols of the cycle permit a
successful ritual transcending of the issue. It is useful to
identify the personages which stand for the ecclesiastical,
civil, and civic arenas. The celebrating priest symbolizes *ecclesia;* the mayor, *civilitas;* and the queen, *civitas.* In the particular performance we have been considering (July 8) it is

significant that the mayor is merely present; he performs no ritual act other than simply being visible. The mayor is a symbol of civil power, which is essentially inoperative during the novena-processions but quite active during the fiesta. The fiesta queen, however, represents the people in a way different from that of the mayor. She is their civic representative—a symbol of the cooperation which results from good will or economic motives rather than legal-political structures. The queen is a representative figurehead without coercive power. A few Hispano informants regard this ritual and others in the cycle as the wedding of church and state. But Santa Fe is essentially Catholic in the same way that some other American cities are Protestant, that is, in terms of ethos rather than official status. These rituals are not an example of the wedding of two institutions, church and state, but of two different kinds of symbols, namely those of *ecclesia* and *civitas*. A marriage of symbols is not identical with a marriage of institutions, and, in fact, the former may be a substitute for the latter. The marriage of ecclesiastical with civic symbols is a joining of royal and civic metaphors.

Renato Rosaldo explores the relationship between ritualistic and social hierarchy in Catholic rituals associated with Our Lord of Esquipulas. He finds that, "the main subject of ritual performed by members of the religious hierarchy is hierarchy itself." "At the same time, this ritual reflects and reinforces patterns of hamlet life; much of the ritual action is a condensed elaborate version of daily social intercourse in Zinacantan, in particular of the various ways in which individuals signal their recognition of difference in age" (1968:526).

Rosaldo's study concentrates on a system used for ranking participants in a flower-changing ceremony, and his conclusion resembles my earlier observation about the Mass: "Elaboration of metaphors for hierarchy corresponds to increased 'sacredness' in ritual action" (p. 533). But an important dif-

ference between his findings and mine is that the ritual hierarchy of Zinacantan reflects a social hierarchy, while the hierarchy of the Mass does not reflect a corresponding hierarchy
in Santa Fe. He finds a structural congruity; I found a structural incongruity.

Certainly, the City of Santa Fe has its chain of authority;
it is a city council–mayor–city manager type of government.
But *de jure* power resides at the broad, popular base, not in
divine or quasi-divine figures at the pinnacle. The structural
incongruity of a royal *ecclesia* and a democratic *civitas* would
become obvious if, for example, someone were to propose
that the state legislature adopt a state saint to accompany the
state flower and state bird. The move would be crushed by
Protestants, perhaps even by Catholics. Separation of church
and state is maintained in New Mexico, though nothing prevents a ritualistic orchestration of civil, civic, and ecclesiastical symbols. Church and state are not allied as they were
when De Vargas carried an official banner with the Virgin
on one side and the Spanish coat of arms on the other, but if
a civil-ecclesiastical alliance is now impossible, a civic-
ecclesiastical alliance is quite possible. And ethnic structures
serve as the essential link between ecclesiastical and civic
structures.

In the ritual we have been using as an example the process
follows this order: the City Council (a civil body) authorizes
the Fiesta Council (a civic, quasi-civil body) to choose a fiesta
queen ("Miss *Civitas*") from nominees made by the public.
She in turn crowns La Conquistadora (a symbol of *ecclesia*
with ethnic and public overtones). And finally, in honor and
in the presence of La Conquistadora is celebrated a Mass, a
theologically nonpublic ritual of *ecclesia* which invokes other
ritual prerequisites such as ordination, confirmation, and
baptism. Hence a chain of symbols links *civilitas* to *ecclesia* via
intermediate *civitas* and *ethnos*. These form an ethos which
generates the symbol system of public religiosity in Santa Fe.

CHAPTER 3

Organizing and Symbolizing Power

> Wherefore, when about to ascend to His eternal Father, He left as His earthly vicar and substitute, Saint Peter. . . . To his successors, servants, ministers, and vicars, Saint Peter left not only ecclesiastical jurisdiction and spiritual dominion, but also, forever, temporal jurisdiction and power, double-edged authority, in order that by themselves or through their children the emperors and kings, whenever and in what manner they deemed it convenient or necessary, could transform this jurisdiction and temporal power into action; that later, as occasion and necessity arose, they might exercise it, availing themselves of the all-embracing temporal authority of the secular power, both by itself, with armadas and armies, on sea and land, in their own and in the various barbarous nations, with their imperial pennants, banners, and flags of the cross, subduing the different barbarous nations, smoothing the way for the evangelical preachers, safeguarding their lives and persons, avenging the offenses they might receive after these spiritual advisers had been accepted, restraining and checking the bestial and savage ferocity of the natives; and the friars, in the name of Almighty Christ God (who ordered His gospel preached throughout the world), were extending by His authority and right, the limits of the Christian fold and broadening His empire, aided by the hand of His children, the emperors and kings.
>
> Don Juan de Oñate, Act of Taking Possession of New Mexico, April 30, 1598 (Hammond and Rey, 1953:331–332)

The Santa Fe Fiesta, in which the De Vargas figure plays a role more prominent than that of La Conquistadora, occurs in the late summer, usually on the Labor Day weekend, and is attended by crowds much larger than those attending the novena-processions. The fiesta is best understood as a ritualizing of the power necessary for *ethnos* to determine the mode of relation between *civitas*, *civilitas*, and *ecclesia*. The problems its organizers face are how to relate a hierarchically constructed *ecclesia* to a democratically inclined *civilitas* and how to relate three different traditions of *ethnos*. The events of this four-day celebration include the Entrada pageant, the candlelight procession to the Cross of the Martyrs, Indian

dances, the Solemn Pontifical Fiesta Mass, the fiesta proclamation and De Vargas Mass, the burning of Zozobra (Old
Man Gloom), the knighting of the De Vargas figure, the
crowning of the fiesta queen, the fiesta melodrama, and
various parades and performances (see Appendix B).

Though the term "fiesta" is gradually being secularized, it
still retains much of its religious meaning for Hispanic, and
even some non-Hispanic, residents of Santa Fe. Originally,
the term designated a feast day for a saint, usually a patron
saint, though this religious usage is now stronger in rural
areas of northern New Mexico than in the city itself. One
frequently hears the plural, "fiestas," and some even insist
that the plural form alone is proper because of the plurality
of events and days involved. The use of the singular form of
the noun probably represents an Anglicization of the terminology, but it is the form found most often in Fiesta Council
usage, so I have used it here.

The Taos Fiesta, held on the feast day of Saint James
(Santiago), the patron of Taos' early Spanish settlement, and
the Fiesta of Oñate in Española, New Mexico, both occurring in the latter half of July, have elements that resemble the
Santa Fe Fiesta. A certain amount of competition, borrowing, cross-fertilization, and imitation goes on among the three
in areas such as the crowning of queens, tricultural rhetoric
and costume, balls and dances, historical pageants and parades. These three fiestas, especially those of Santa Fe and
Taos, differ somewhat from those taking place in more rural
or less populous towns because of the influx of tourists and
money and simply because of the semiurban ethos and high
proportion of artists and writers in the two towns.

The adjectives most frequently used to describe the Santa
Fe Fiesta are "civic," "religious," "traditional," "Spanish,"
and "celebrative." No one of these terms alone will suffice;
any one by itself tends to distort the picture. Strong disagreement has sometimes characterized discussions and

power struggles concerning the balance between some of these elements. A cartoon that appeared on an editorial page near fiesta time with the caption "They're all a part of fiesta—Viva la Fiesta!" (*New Mexican*, August 31, 1973) depicted an Indian, a Spanish conquistador, a Mexican, and a tourist picnicking together as Zozobra is burning and people are forming a procession to the Cross of the Martyrs in the background. This is a typical, graphic attempt to summarize the fiesta.

One must be rid of biases against syncretistic, public, and commercialized rituals to see clearly how important such enactments are to Santa Fe. Clifford Geertz offers an important observation:

However, though any religious ritual, no matter how apparently automatic or conventional (if it is truly automatic or merely conventional it is not religious), involves this symbolic fusion of ethos and world-view, it is mainly certain more elaborate and usually more public ones, ones in which a broad range of moods and motivations on the one hand and of metaphysical conceptions on the other are caught up, which shape the spiritual consciousness of a people. [1966:28]

Neither cartooning nor salesmanship necessarily contradicts the claim that one can understand religion and its role in the intercultural life of Santa Fe by studying fiestas.

The fiesta has grown increasingly public in recent years. The influx of both new residents and tourists has led some natives to complain that the fiesta has lost its essential religiosity, as well as its local-regional character. Some have expressed desires to curtail all publicity and to move the celebration to October in order to reduce its size and the proportion of nonlocal people who participate. A crowd of 70,000–80,000 people tends to swamp a small town of 41,000. The result of this growth has been an inevitable tendency toward making the fiesta elite. Certain parties, breakfasts, and balls must of necessity become exclusive owing either to high admission fees or to selective invitations.

That the fiesta is a civic and civil celebration, in additon to a religious and ethnic one, can easily be discerned from the flags lining the central plaza; they include one from every state, along with several American flags. That the fiesta is a religious celebration is obvious from the paintings of saints which decorate the plaza. The favorite saints of the region are on display: Santiago (Saint James), San Ysidro (Saint Isidore), San Rafael, San Miguel (Saint Michael), San Cristobal (Saint Christopher), San Pedro (Saint Peter), Nuestra Señora de la Soledad (Our Lady of Solitude), Santa Barbara, and Nuestra Señora Refugio de Pecadores (Our Lady of Refuge).

In comparison with the early summer processions the fiesta is a more public, less thoroughly sacred event. A few Santa Feans insist that the fiesta is no less a sacred time than that of the processions. However, no one ever questions whether the processions are religious in nature, but many raise the question about the fiesta. In any case, one can certainly say there are overtly religious events in the fiesta, and I doubt whether any single characterization of the fiesta as a whole can be accurate.

Visits to La Conquistadora Chapel in St. Francis Cathedral increased during fiesta, jumping from roughly twelve per hour during the year to eighty-five per hour during the fiesta. Typically only fifteen simply entered to look around as a tourist might. All others made some religious gesture: prayed, knelt, meditated, genuflected, made the sign of the cross, made offerings, burned candles. So the fiesta is an occasion for some to perform religious homage to La Conquistadora. But numbers alone do not tell the whole story. The mayor expressed the attitudes of a great many others when to the question "How important is the fiesta to Santa Fe?" he replied, "If the fiesta were removed, Santa Fe would lose a great deal; Santa Fe would have lost its soul." The fiesta is not religious for every participant, but for those who view it as a religious event, it is to Santa Fe what the soul is to the body, namely, the animate substance and source of life. If the fiesta is Santa Fe's soul, as many residents maintain, then we know no small amount about the city when we understand the fiesta.

In 1963 the Catholic church withdrew its support from the fiesta, because of secularizing and commercializing trends. However, with the help of members of the Caballeros de Vargas and the Fiesta Council, it now exerts continuous influence to make the fiesta more explicitly religious, so fiesta religiosity still shows some signs of having been imposed from the top. This shows up in the form of official phrases like "restoring the religious" and "Fiesta Theme Is Religious Tribute." My interviews suggest that the attempt to restore historical awareness has been more successful than the attempt to impose general religious awareness. A good many Santa Feans agree in principle with statements like this one: "Religious observances are an integral part of the affair, but quite often the memory of a just concluded church service or procession gets lost in the bubbling foam of enough beer to float a small fleet of destroyers. . . . Thousands of things are lost, stolen, stored, remembered, forgotten, obliterated and consumed during Fiesta" (New Mexican, August 28, 1968, p. 9).

Sometimes purist views are expressed at fiesta time, but the view that the fiesta should be purely religious, purely civic, or purely ethnic is not shared by most. Most see no conflict between worshiping and drinking a moderate amount of beer or between archbishops and fiesta queens. An interesting but somewhat atypical view was expressed in 1963 after the church's withdrawal:

The real reason, of course, for the withdrawal of the Church from the Fiesta is that after all, it is really very difficult for educated people to take the archbishop seriously upon solemn occasions when one has seen him during Fiesta in his sacred robes and at the sacred altar crowning beauty queens with the same straight face he uses to celebrate the Easter Mass. Neither can one believe that he is the most discerning judge of what is fit for a man when we see him blessing Zozobra while Mr. Cartier [who played the role of Fire Spirit; see p. 208] writhes in a most heathen fashion. As for the propriety of his marching to the cross of the martyrs behind a blaring brass band with its vanguard of prancing, twirling majorettes, I shall leave that to the judgment of those who witnessed this year's procession to the cross. . . . Religious men belong in the cathedrals—not behind majorettes. Carnivals belong in the plaza—not in the cathedral. [*New Mexican*, October 11, 1963, pp. 4, 14]

This biting criticism expresses a view which periodically resurfaces to take issue with the less dualistic, more pluralistic, view. Often the either/or attitude typified by this excerpt follows Protestant or Anglo lines, while the more assimilationist view of the fiesta as a combination or blending tends to follow Hispanic and Catholic lines. Of course, there are exceptions to this generalization, but my discussions with participants suggest that most people are not bothered by what appear to outsiders to be strange juxtapositions.

In the view of the people La Conquistadora inspired the actions of De Vargas and thereby became patroness of the entire fiesta, but explicit mention of her or reference to the fiesta as "La Fiesta de la Conquistadora" is of recent origin and not very widespread. La Conquistadora per se is almost never mentioned by informants when asked about the religious elements of the fiesta. Usually De Vargas is mentioned first, and then La Conquistadora. Of course, the two are not entirely separated, but different emphases are clear. The early summer novena-processions are "purer" in several senses. Their dominant symbol is "Maria Purissima," or "Maria Santissima." They are more purely religious, more purely Catholic, and more purely local in participation. They are not "polluted" with tourists, beer, and street fights.

One indigenous summary of the multiplicity of goals which characterizes the fiesta is contained in a memorandum from the president of the Caballeros de Vargas to the president of the Fiesta Council:

(1) . . . To render Almighty God grateful thanksgiving for the Reconquests of 1692 and 1693. . . .
(2) [To promote the] gaiety and neighborliness of a true community celebration.
(3) [To promote] inherent pride in Santa Fe's dramatic past.
(4) To pass on . . . such a venerable tradition to future generations. [April 6, 1965]

Most Santa Feans would concur with this summary, but the power to actuate these goals, to determine their specific content, and to determine their relative emphases rests with certain organizations and depends on specific lines of power.

Kenelm Burridge argues that religion's fundamental concern is the systematic ordering of power (1969:5). The fiesta rituals confirm Burridge's generalization. Power is employed in stabilizing and maintaining value systems, ideologies, and symbol systems. Occasionally, it is used to change or redefine them. Power is employed to effect transformation—spiritual, social, and economic. Even the Mass, which is not normally considered a ritualizing of power, is a mode of gaining access to hierarchically mediated "power unto salvation." So, by "power" I do not necessarily mean force or coercion. Instead, I mean the ability either to maintain or to transform something in the face of inertia, resistance, or pressure. So understood, power has many forms: economic, political, rhetorical, inspirational, dramatic, symbolic. Power is the ability, in whatever form, either to move or to resist movement. Power is what energizes structures and systems so that they become movements and processes.

The fiesta is understood locally as a celebration of the cooperative and constructive use of power, but, as we shall see, the coercive use of power is frequently necessary to produce a fiesta, and conflict is sometimes the result of one. A consideration of powerful symbols is not necessarily a study of power symbols; symbols in the Mass are not power symbols in the political sense. Fiesta symbols, however, are; they are symbols operating to resolve certain conflicts. In the fiesta not only are power-plays involved in organizing and administering the celebration but power itself is symbolized. To anticipate some of the conclusions of later chapters: the fiesta queen symbolizes civic, cooperative power, while the statue of La Conquistadora symbolizes the power of conversion, and the De Vargas figure, the power of conquest. The very selection of these as the fundamental symbols of public ritual in Santa Fe suggests that the exercise of a considerable amount of power is necessary to perpetuate the defining of "civic" in specifically Hispano-Catholic terms.

Organizing the Fiesta

Any study of the symbolism of power must take into account the modes of organizing, transmitting, and administering power. The structure of authority, both official and unofficial, becomes evident in investigating the primary groups which generate the public symbols of the fiesta: the Santa Fe Fiesta Council, the City Council, the Caballeros de Vargas, the Confraternity of La Conquistadora, the Franciscan Order, De Vargas and his staff, and the queen and her court.

The Santa Fe Fiesta Council, a nonprofit organization, oversees the entire fiesta. Its 1973 roster lists seventy-seven members, all volunteers. It has two kinds of membership, regular and representative. The regular memberships are open to any interested citizen, who must be screened by a membership committee, but the number of regular members is limited to sixty. Chartered civic organizations are allowed one representative member each, and there is no limit to this kind of membership. Of the seventy-seven members listed in the roster, twenty-one are representatives of organizations.[1] The Fiesta Council coordinates the efforts of more civic organizations than any other institution. It is the center of a web of civic power. And since approximately two thirds of the council membership is Spanish-surnamed, one expects its *civitas* to be distinctly channeled through *ethnos*.

The Fiesta Council specifies three objectives: (1) to preserve the unity and harmony of those whose interest is to "promote, manage and perpetuate" the fiesta, (2) to "preserve inviolate" "in spirit and letter" the fiesta as described in the Fiesta Proclamation of 1712, and (3) to enlist the cooperation of "local citizenry. The Catholic church, the Ministerial Alliance, the local businessmen and the City Officials" in creating a successful fiesta.

Although the council officially solicits the involvement of other religious groups via the Ministerial Alliance, only the Catholic church has an official representative on the council. He is primarily responsible for the Masses, coronation of the queen, knighting of De Vargas, and candlelight procession— in short, the religious activities of the fiesta. He is also ex officio chairman of the Religious Activities Committee. The fiesta is advertised as an ecumenical event, but the only evi-

[1] In 1973 they were as follows: G.I. Forum, Sunrise Optimist Club, Pilot International, the Catholic church, G.I. Forum Auxiliary, Women's Division of the Chamber of Commerce, La Sociedad Folklorica, BPOE Does Drove No. 57, Active 20–30 Club, College of Santa Fe Alumni, La Union Protectiva, Old Santa Fe Association, VFW Post 2951, Downtown Kiwanis, Zonta International, Fraternal Order of Eagles, Spanish Colonial Dancers, BPOE Lodge No. 460, COPAS, La Sociedad Colonial Española, Caballeros de Vargas.

dences of religious ecumenism is the participation of a Protestant hand-bell choir before the sermon given at the Cross of the Martyrs and the Gideons' use of the plaza platform on one occasion.

The Catholic church has a special status on the council. Because its representative does not have to go through the normal orientation procedures, a special section of the constitution of the Fiesta Council describes the uniqueness of the church's mode of representation: "Inasmuch as the Catholic Church has from the very inception of the Fiesta been an integral part thereof, the Archbishop of Santa Fe is hereby empowered to appoint a representative who will, upon such appointment and without further action on the part of the Fiesta Council, become a full-fledged member of the Fiesta Council" (Article III, section 4).

The 1973 council was divided into twenty-six standing committees in addition to some ad hoc committees. Many of these committees, as well as the council itself, work almost year round preparing for the four-day fiesta event.

The structural bones of any organization are revealed most vividly during struggles over power and jurisdiction. Such a struggle occurred over a period of several years but was particularly intense during 1964–1966. Although part of the struggle was a function of personality conflicts, not of concern to the present study, the issues were largely ones of principle, power, and jurisdiction. The basic questions in the controversy were, "What is the nature of the fiesta?" and "Who should determine the answer to this question?" Before I say more about the course of the conflict, I perhaps should indicate just how much was at stake.

The role of the Fiesta Council is one of considerable influence and therefore of power. Although its 1973 budget was only around $36,000, the fiesta itself generated well over $2.6 million in income for the businesses of Santa Fe during the four days of the fiesta of 1971. This figure is undoubtedly conservative, since it is based primarily on a College of Santa Fe study, which focuses on bank deposits and does not include less formal economic transactions. Unofficial estimates of the tourist attendance run from 70,000 to 80,000 persons. Of the $36,000 budget of 1973 less than $3,500 came from contributions of merchants who are benefiting from the $2.6 million income. The council raises the rest of the money by charging for selected entertainment events during the fiesta itself.

The powers of the council and its president, though not directly legislative, are not to be underestimated because they are indirect. The presidency of the council is a particularly visible position, thus good preparation for a move into the political arena of city and state government.

The jurisdiction controversy over Fiesta Council powers came to a head in the form of a conflict between the Caballeros de Vargas and the now defunct Fiesta Corporation. The Caballeros had been organized in 1957 to develop the historical, religious, and cultural heritage of the fiesta. Specifically, the Caballeros wanted control of the De Vargas Entrada pageant. They wanted to return the fiesta "to the people whose civil-religious festivities it rightfully represents" (*New Mexico*, March 31, 1965). They wanted to choose the man who portrayed De Vargas, to put on the pageant, and to answer directly to the City Council rather than to a private fiesta corporation. Permission to do so was repeatedly denied them by an incumbent chief of police, who was the long-time head of the corporation.

In City Council meetings and in the public media there were repeated confrontations between Caballeros and Fiesta Corporation personnel; the Caballeros even organized a debate committee to present its views. Eventually, the Catholic church became involved in the controversy, and in 1964 it formally withdrew support from the fiesta, citing as its reason excessive commercialism and referring to the fiesta as a "privately owned and operated carnival" (*New Mexican*, April 9, 1964, p. 1). Thus the church and Caballeros were aligned against the Fiesta Corporation, with the City Council in the middle attempting to resolve the crisis. The church's withdrawal was a crucial political move, for even though the fiesta did go on without the church's participation, most Santa Feans felt that the fiesta was not really the fiesta without the approval and participation of the church.

The forces advocating more widespread, popular control of the fiesta won. In 1966 the Fiesta Council through a city ordinance (1966–12) came under the jurisdiction of the City Council. The Roman Catholic church rejoined the fiesta. Membership in the Fiesta Council was made open to the public, and control resided ultimately with a president and board of directors. The selection of the figure who would play De Vargas in the pageant remained with the Fiesta Council, though the pageant came under the jurisdiction of the Caballeros de Vargas.

Presently, the City Council has supervisory control over the Fiesta Council in the following ways: (1) Before it can solicit funds from the general citizenry, the Fiesta Council must have the permission of the Fiesta Committee of the City Council. (2) The Fiesta Council must provide evidence of a satisfactory organizational structure consisting of by-laws, constitution, board of directors, and so forth. (3) The Fiesta Council must petition yearly for use of such public facilities as streets, plaza, and ballpark. (4) The Fiesta Council must submit a yearly report and audit. (5) The Fiesta Council is required to keep its membership open to the public. Although the Fiesta Council is not merely a subcommittee of the City Council, and although in recent years there has been little need for pressure on the Fiesta Council, there now exist ways in which the public or its elected officials can exercise some control over the fiesta itself.

The Caballeros de Vargas

The Fiesta Council is in theory publicly based and has a quasi-civil standing, whereas the Caballeros de Vargas is situated in the liminal zone between religious, ethnic, and civic spheres. It has no legal, governmental links, but it performs the crucial brokerage duty of linking the church to both civic and ethnic groups. Both it and the Fiesta Council are strongly Hispanic in membership, but the Caballero emphasis is on *ethnos*, while that of the Fiesta Council is *civitas*.

The 1973 membership roster of the Caballeros shows 117 members, less than 10 per cent of whom have non-Spanish surnames and all of whom are male. Its official objectives are: (1) to perpetuate the memory of De Vargas (e.g., by performing the Entrada pageant), (2) to honor La Conquistadora (e.g., by serving as her official escorts), (3) to promote "the Hispanic-Christian Culture of Santa Fe and the Southwest in general," (e.g., by performing "Los Reyes Magos" each Christmas), (4) to maintain close relations among those who have participated in the Entrada pageant (e.g., by serving as a club), and (5) to undertake selected philanthropic projects (e.g., by building a monument to De Vargas).

Extremely important is the overlap of the organizations in which Caballeros are involved. One gains entry to the Caballeros de Vargas by playing a role in the Entrada pageant, and to become a Caballero is automatically to become a member of the Confraternity of Conquistadora. Even though one must apply to become a Caballero after participating in the Entrada, and although there is a formal initiation rite into the organization, many informants speak of their participation in the pageant as an initiation. Functionally, this seems to be an accurate description. The official initiation, which occurs in the cathedral and is performed by its Franciscan rector, who is also ex officio *padre-capellan* (chaplain) of the Caballeros, is pro forma. And the application procedure which follows the pageant screens out only a minute percentage of applicants.

Later I will consider the Entrada pageant as drama, but for my immediate purposes its initiatory function is important. By performing in the pageant, the De Vargas figure and the rest of the staff-cast are initiated into the Caballeros. The time between the election of the De Vargas figure in May and the official initiation in October is one in which a supervising committee appointed by the Fiesta Council and usually chaired by a Caballero on the council tries to identify what one member calls "Caballero thinking." The committee and other Caballeros watch De Vargas and his staff during social functions and in the Entrada itself to decide who should be recommended for membership in the Caballeros. There are no specifically stated criteria, except participation in the Entrada, but covert ones are quite effective. No small part of the initiation is learning what the covert criteria are and living up to them. Among those mentioned by older members are "being just a regular guy," knowing how to refrain from swearing in public, knowing how to handle one's liquor, being a "hustler" who takes the initiative, showing cooperation and group responsibility, and having pride in who one is.

Owing to tension created by organizational overlap, service in one of the Entrada roles calls for considerable diplomacy. Some members of both the Fiesta Council and the Caballeros regard the Caballeros as merely an extension of the Fiesta Council. Others vigorously contest this. The result is sometimes a set of inconsistent orders coming to De Vargas and his staff from Caballero officers, on the one hand, and Fiesta Council officials, on the other. This conflict-inducing situation is a microcosm of the conflicting "orders" that frequently characterize symbols of *ethnos* and of *civitas*. The De Vargas figure is elected by the Fiesta Council and supervised by one of its committees, but his activities are a trial leading to initiation in the Caballeros. Navigating between council and Caballeros demands considerable ingenuity and is a true test of cooperativeness and integrity. The controversy of 1964–1966 has obviously not resolved every tension between Fiesta Council and Caballeros de Vargas, between *civitas* and *ethnos*.

Although no precise figures are available, there is a rough consensus about the numbers of men who become active members of the Caballeros after the Entrada. Of a typical group of twenty-six, two are underage and can apply only when they become twenty-one. Around twenty fill out applications for membership, and fourteen attend meetings sometime during the first year. Ultimately, however, only three or four remain active members, because job transfers and lack of time gradually drain away the others. And some of the Entrada participants are either burned out by the intensity of the summer's activities or let down by the change of pace from Entrada participation to the normal routine of club participation which follows.

One Caballero remarks that twenty-six people start off knowing almost nothing and fifty-two (the men and their wives) conclude the summer knowing a greate deal about their tradition and their city. My interviews suggest that a few learn significantly from the experience. The others participate either because they want to have a good time or because they want to help out a friend. But it is true that many learn something and develop some feeling for their heritage.

No women's auxiliary exists in connection with the Caballeros. The wives attend many of the social functions with their husbands, but among some members a strong secret male society ethos exists. To quote one typical remark, "We don't want two staffs [one of men and one of their wives]; we want one." Among some Caballeros a noticeable tendency to joke and complain about wifely intrusions is obvious. Yet, as described to me, the wife's function is important inasmuch as she performs the crucial function of "keeping the guy sober." Any initiation into culture and religion received by the wives is mediated through their husbands.

The organizational overlap which structures the initiation period could create potential problems. Theoretically, the general public of Santa Fe could determine indirectly who will enter the membership of both the Caballeros and the Confraternity of La Conquistadora by exerting power through this channel: (1) the general citizenry can become members of the Fiesta Council; (2) the Fiesta Council selects De Vargas; (3) De Vargas selects at least half of his own staff; [2] (4) staff members, who constitute the pageant cast, become Caballeros with an almost automatic frequency; (5) Caballeros are ex officio members of the Confraternity of La Conquistadora.

An open channel, through which the general public could pour members of its own choosing into a religious confraternity would be little problem for that organization, because membership is open to all who pay dues anyway. But such an open channel would be a problem for the Caballeros. They are an exclusive organization, in the opinions of both some of the members and outsiders. One member compares the Caballeros' esprit de corps to that of the U.S. Marines. Another declares, "You are in the Caballeros because it's part of you; it's part of your heritage." And another remarks, "When somebody asks me what civic organizations I am a member of I say, 'None, I am a Caballero de Vargas.' " This informant goes on to say that the organization is elite in the sense that not just anyone can join; he has to be in the Entrada first. This member's claim that his is an elite organization should not be confused with the elitism which arises

[2] In 1973 he selected all but three of the twenty-six, though the constitution of the Caballeros allows the general membership to choose the last twelve positions of a hierarchically listed twenty-six.

from an ideological arrogance that insists on contrasting itself with "the people" or "the masses." In fact, the Caballeros are characterized by a noticeable strain of populism, as is illustrated by their fight to return the fiesta to the people.

Still, the question remains, "Is there an open membership channel from the general citizenry to the Caballeros de Vargas?" Empirical investigation quickly demands a negative answer to the question. The membership is largely Hispanic and Catholic, so the question is how this selective screening is effected, given the organizational overlap sketched above.

First, there is a great deal of self-selection and self-elimination. Not everyone, nor every group, wants to commit time and energy, and thus gain power, in the Fiesta Council. The Fiesta Council may be a representative cross-section of the city on some levels, for example, occupation or sex, but not on others, for example, age and ethnic identity.

Second, the Fiesta Council imposes prerequisites on those who compete for the title of De Vargas. They include age, cultural origin, residence, linguistic ability (bilingual), and appearance. Numerous informants insist that the man has to have "the right look" or he will not be elected. He must fit the De Vargas image and communicate his spirit. There is no requirement that the other members of De Vargas' staff be Hispanic; the De Vargas figure may choose whom he will. But since he typically chooses other contestants and his friends or relatives, this selection again serves as an informal but effective screen.

An additional screen exists. The Fiesta Council appoints a liason committee to work with De Vargas and his staff. The committee screens De Vargas' selections, and their criteria reflect some specific values. One of the primary screening questions is, "Can you take orders from De Vargas?" The question obviously selects for cooperation, but it goes even further. Some of the older Caballeros advise the De Vargas figure, "You are the general; you are are in command." Some expect the role of commander-in-chief to obtain off, as well as on, the pageant set. Yet the commanding role does not hold in the face of already initiated Caballeros, and it is dropped immediately after the initiation. Hence, one must understand both the hierarchy of command and equality of comradeship and know which situations demand which quality.

Another of the screening questions concerns police and prison records. Adolescent troubles like fights, public drunkenness, and petty theft are usually ignored, but contestants with major or recent criminal activities that might mar the image of the fiesta and Caballeros are eliminated. Another question concerns one's commitment to handle his liquor in public. If one adds to these considerations the self-elimination and occasional committee elimination of applicants between the time of the Entrada and the official initiation, it becomes obvious that new members of the Caballeros and hence the confraternity are a highly select group.

Just as the organizations overlap to some extent, memberships in the groups overlap. In addition to the formal ties which hold together the Fiesta Council, the Caballeros de Vargas, and the Confraternity of La Conquistadora, a significant number of people are members of both the Caballeros and Fiesta Council, and sometimes even the City Council. The power of the Caballeros on either the Fiesta or City Councils is by virtue of influence, not numbers. Typically, high-ranking members in one organization eventually become high-ranking members in one of the others.

The document enfranchising the Caballeros as *cofrádes* states that "the current President General of the Caballeros de Vargas shall act as '*Mayordomo segundo*' " (vice-president) of the Confraternity of La Conquistadora. This particular clause, however, is not generally known among Caballeros. The mayor in 1973 was president of the Caballeros during the jurisdiction controversy and was a Fiesta Council president. The mayor's father was *mayordomo* of the confraternity. His brother was charter president of the Caballeros, was a Fiesta Council president, and wrote the music for the official fiesta song. The second president of the Caballeros was in 1973 a member of the City Council. In 1973 three men were honored for their having held the presidencies of both the Fiesta Council and the Caballeros de Vargas. It is also worth mentioning that in 1973 a U.S. senator was a Caballero. These facts are only illustrations of the symbiotic relationship between four organizations—one civic (the Fiesta Council), one religious (the Confraternity), one civil (the City Council), and one ethno-civic-religious (the Caballeros). The lines of power which link these into a system largely determine the systemic lines between the symbols we will consider later.

Caballero Ritual

The Caballeros de Vargas hold much of their civic and political strength through their ability to foster what one document calls "the spirit of militant Christianity and proud patriotism." In keeping with the gentlemanly traditions of Spanish knighthood, as implied in the term "caballero" (knight, gentleman), they have attempted to devise a structure which generates Hispanic-Christian culture (*ethnos, ecclesia*) while at the same time pursuing civic virtues such as reliability, honesty, sobriety, and social service.

Though they are for the most part quite unrelated to the more rurally based Penitentes, the Caballeros have in common with the Penitentes a concern for two kinds of rites, initiatory and funerary. The Caballeros have a special ritualistic form for each occasion. Excerpts from these two rites suggest their views of life and death:

My friends and fellow Americans, it is my duty to inform you that in joining the Caballeros you may at all times practice complete freedom of inclination. An obligation of Fidelity, however, is required, but this obligation in no way binds you to anything contrary to your civil or religious duties. This obligation only demands that you remain faithful to the Constitution and By-Laws of the Caballeros de Vargas, that you will obey them and observe them and that you will never do anything that will be a discredit or bring dishonor to the organization or any of its members. [Initiation Ceremonies]

. . . The incident of death is no more mysterious and not more uncommon than the incident of birth. We were born to die, and we die that we may live. This is the whole philosophy of human existence. . . . The birth of man does not greatly impress us; but when death invades our ranks, we are greatly appalled. It is not life that bids us pause, but loss of it. There is a sacred dread of death inwoven with the whole fabric of life. . . .

In this simple and reverent memory it is not my purpose to deliver a personal eulogy of our friend and brother, who no longer answers when his name is called. He was an American citizen, responsive to every duty of citizenship and brotherhood, within the limitations of the power with which he was endowed. . . . It devolves upon us to cherish his good deeds, to forget his imperfections and to inscribe his name upon the tablets of love and memory. [Ritual for Visiting the Dead]

In both rituals the member is bound to the ethic of the gentlemanly brotherhood and to patriotic obligations of citizenship. Although individualism is recognized and "freedom of inclination" allowed, the latitude has bounds which are defined by patriotism and the corporate honor and reputation of the organization. The wording of the initiatory oath echos the U.S. Presidential Oath, to "preserve, protect, defend, and enforce the Constitution and By-Laws of the Caballeros de Vargas." For historical and ideological reasons the organization speaks of itself as keeping alive the traditions of "Spain in America," thus emphasizing a Spanish-American link over a Mexican-American link. A letter from the president of the

Caballeros in 1965 called attention to the Americanness of
the group by asserting that no other organization has as
much "old-fashioned 'American Know How' with regards to
the Fiesta Entrada than we do!"

Symbolically, the size of the Caballeros does not diminish,
when a member dies. In the confraternity and the Caballeros, the dead remain a part of the corporate whole through
memory and Mass. The Caballero constitution specifies that
the organization will pay for a Low Mass "for the repose of
the soul of said Caballero." Also a rosary is to be said, and
the annual De Vargas Mass during the fiesta is "for the intentions of all the deceased and living members of the Caballeros." Sometimes Caballeros also drape their colors, red and
gold, over a casket and place a helmet or sword on it. Simi-
larly, the Masses during the early summer processions are
for the deceased and living members of the *cofradía*.

By their symbols and rituals the Caballeros are linked pa-
triotically to the United States, religiously to the Catholic
and sainted dead, culturally to Spain, and civically to Santa
Fe and the Southwest. The Caballeros de Vargas is quite
proud that the descendants of De Vargas, through the Spanish Heraldic Office, have awarded the De Vargas coat of
arms to the organization. The Caballeros find some of their
own values reflected in the symbols of the De Vargas family's coat of arms. Above it is a crown signifying loyalty to
the king; this finds its counterpart in Caballero patriotism.
One quarter-panel of the shield is not genealogically
grounded but religiously inspired. The upper left quarter,
consisting of three silver waves on a blue field, is the symbol
of San Ysidro's miracle of the spring. San Ysidro was a
sharecropper, and later a saint, once employed by the De
Vargas family. This saint, the patron of Madrid, is one of
the most popular in New Mexico, especially in rural areas,
since he is also the patron of farming. The Caballeros take
the willingness of the aristocratic De Vargas family to conde-

scend to a lowly peasant like San Ysidro to be a paradigm of their own knightly ethic of assisting the populace. If there is something of the elite in the courtly and military ethos of the Caballeros, they think that true royalty can walk with the poor without losing dignity. This is the reason for the frequent pairing of "pride" and "humility" in Caballero rhetoric.

The performance of the Entrada pageant is a service to the City of Santa Fe. But it is also a mode of transmitting the heroic image of the knight who does not consider the poor beneath his dignity. Participation in the pageant is but the beginning of an ongoing initiation into the values and virtues of a symbolic knighthood dedicated to Christian Hispanicism with its attendant emphasis upon dignity, pride, and humility before God. Therefore, the Caballeros can only mistakenly be confused with other civic or service organizations, because their service is specific both in terms of religion and culture. The Caballeros pursue Christian Hispanicism (*ecclesia-ethnos*) through *civitas*, while the Fiesta Council pursues *civitas* through *ethnos*.

The Confraternity of La Conquistadora

Related to the Caballeros de Vargas, but characterized by an ethos of *ecclesia*, is La Cofradía de Nuestra Señora del Rosario, La Conquistadora (The Confraternity of Our Lady of the Rosary, La Conquistadora). The confraternity died out in the mid-eighteenth century owing to the many physical hardships facing settlers in New Mexico at that time. It was revived in the 1770s and lasted until 1846, when it again lapsed under the impact of American occupation. Archbishop Edwin V. Byrne re-established the organization in 1956, and it has been growing slowly but steadily ever since. The goals and structures are much simpler than those of the Caballeros and need little exposition here. The confraternity makes this basic pledge: "We hereby pledge ourselves, by our devotion, enthusiasm, and contributions, to keep this selfsame image of La Conquistadora in the state it richly deserves, to make it better known and loved among our people throughout this evergrowing region, and to spread its fame far and wide beyond the borders of her ancient Kingdom" (The Constitution, Section I, Article 1).

The confraternity encourages devotion and physically maintains the statue and the Rosario and La Conquistadora chapels; it also conducts the annual summer novena-processions.[3] Its mailing list contains approximately six hundred names, and the membership fee is five dollars, but this is waived for devotees who cannot afford it. The confraternity produces a few pictures of the statue, a songbook, and a religious medal but does not advertise or propagandize as extensively as many devotional groups do. Unlike the Caballeros, the confraternity is open to both males and females and is in no way an elite organization, nor is its membership as thoroughly urban oriented. The members come from all over the state but are, as one might expect, concentrated in the Santa Fe area. Though Caballeros are automatic members of the confraternity, few actively participate. Confraternity members say that traditionally the intention of Saturday Masses is the glorification of La Conquistadora, though this intention is not now carefully observed.

The Franciscan Order

Another religious organization, closer still to the official center of the church, is the Franciscan Order. Early histories of New Mexico are largely by Franciscans. They always followed the conquistadors and sometimes also preceded them to pacify the Indians. Generally, the Franciscans were closer

[3] For a comparative discussion of the functions of confraternities and godparenthood in Spain and the Americas, see George M. Foster, "Cofradía and Compadrazgo in Spain and Spanish America," *Southwestern Journal of Anthropology*, 9 (Spring 1953), 1–28.

to both Hispanic and Indian peoples than governing or ecclesiastical officials were. A contemporary pamphlet on display
in the cathedral encourages young men to choose the Order
of St. Francis. It appeals to the populist ideology of the Franciscans by referring to Francis as "everybody's saint." Devotees of La Conquistadora have a high regard for the Franciscans and regard them as devout, although informants do
recall one or two members of the order they have not cared
for. The Franciscans have a mystique in the eyes of many
Santa Fe Catholics which the hierarchy does not have. Occasionally people refer to the Franciscan padres as "the real
spirit of the cathedral," and they tend to regard the Franciscans as essentially unchanged from the days of De Vargas,
whereas the archbishops are seen as fluctuating radically between good and bad. This general high regard for the Franciscans is institutionalized by having the Franciscan rector of
the cathedral serve as chaplain of the Caballeros and by having a Franciscan preach the sermons during the novena-
processions and fiesta, with the exception of the Solemn Pontifical Fiesta Mass. Other orders such as Dominicans, Christian Brothers, Sisters of the Blessed Sacrament, Carmelites,
Loretto Sisters, and Sisters of Charity are represented in
Santa Fe, but, because of their historical role in the city,
Franciscans hold a special place in the eyes of most devotees.
Saint Francis is both patron of the Archdiocese of Sante Fe
and patron of the City of Sante Fe. The city's full, but unofficial, name is "La Villa Real de Santa Fé, de San Francisco
de Asís."

One of the most frequently mentioned highlights of the fiesta is the candlelight procession to the Cross of the Martyrs,
which commemorates the death of twenty-one Franciscan
padres during the Pueblo revolt of 1680. In part, the Franciscan image has grown because of the large numbers who have
been martyred in New Mexico—fifty-one men between 1542
and 1731 (Meyer 1926:40).

The people regard the Franciscans as defenders and interpreters of folk piety and are fond of contrasting them to the "foreign" French clergy, who "did not really understand us." Generally, the Franciscans are seen as indigenous whether or not they are in fact. Their coat of arms is prominently displayed in both La Conquistadora and Rosario chapels; it is a frequent motif in the reredos of rural New Mexican churches. Also, the lay Third Order of St. Francis is usually prominent in processions. And the Poor Claires, the female Franciscan order, is intensely devoted to La Conquistadora, despite its being cloistered almost two hundred miles away in Roswell, New Mexico.

The importance of the Franciscan image is illustrated by the value placed on playing the roles of Franciscans during the pageant and fiesta: three young men play the roles of Franciscans. Furthermore, in the children's parade some children imitate these young men. So at a given time there may be in Santa Fe actual Franciscans, young men playing the Entrada roles of Franciscans, and children imitating the young men, that is, imitating the imitations.

The De Vargas Figure and His Staff

Strictly speaking, De Vargas and his staff are not separate from either the Fiesta Council or the Caballeros. They are chosen by the council and constitute an initiatory group aimed at entrance into the Caballeros. Nevertheless, during the period of the fiesta, the role they perform is semi-independent and distinct. I will consider the social dimension of that role here and the dramatic dimension of it in the following chapter.

As Arnold Van Gennep (1960) and Victor Turner (1969) have amply demonstrated, initiatory groups are liminal, suspended, as it were, between structures of the society. In our case De Vargas and his staff are suspended, particularly during the four days of the fiesta, between being stage actors, on

Figure 3. The De Vargas figure (*left*), his staff, and the archbishop (*center*)

the one hand, and being members of an ethno-civic-religious organization, on the other. They must oscillate continually between their social and their dramatic roles. They are symbols of ethnic power, but their power is not fully actualized, nor is it restricted to the Entrada set.

The staff consists of twenty-six members, each of whom has a role in the Entrada: De Vargas, two captains, a lieutenant (*alferez*), a standard-bearer, the mayor, three town councilmen, the town secretary, the Franciscan superior, a Franciscan padre, a Franciscan preacher, two Indian governors (*caciques*), a black drummer, two trumpeters, a sergeant major, and seven soldiers. (See Figure 3.) Each role represents a named historical personage who accompanied De Vargas in 1692. These may later choose to be inducted into the Caballeros de Vargas.

The De Vargas figure epitomizes the ethnic values toward

which the fiesta aims. In Santa Fe, whose patron is Saint Francis, the patron's day celebration is purely ecclesiastical, not public. The city remembers De Vargas with a fiesta, thus he has some, though not all, of the functions of a saint. Some former De Vargas figures describe their role as "the experience of a lifetime." They say, "You feel a bit like a movie star. People come up to you during and after the fiesta calling you 'General De Vargas' or saying 'Oh! I remember you.' "

De Vargas' role during the fiesta extends considerably beyond the bounds for which it was originally created, the Entrada. The De Vargas figure portrays his character during the entire fiesta, and on occasions preceding and following it. As I have already mentioned, some even expect him to "command" the members of his staff as if he were a general outside the Entrada set.

De Vargas is chosen early in mid-spring though the Entrada is not until the fall. Meanwhile, he functions as a publicity agent and goodwill ambassador for the city at various social occasions such as luncheons and grand openings. De Vargas is selected by competition; the judges are members of the Fiesta Council. Each candidate must have a sponsoring group and must meet certain qualifications; he must be: (1) interested in the role, (2) of Spanish descent, (3) at least twenty-one years old, (4) a resident of Santa Fe County for at least a year, (5) bilingual. These are the formally stated qualifications, but the judging actually imposes three further criteria: (6) appearance, (7) poise, and (8) personality.

Usually the man who portrays De Vargas is married, though this is not a requirement. Typically, the men who play the role are already up-and-coming in the civic and business community. Thus, it is not a role for adolescents, and participation in any of the roles is an initiation into civic responsibility and business life of the community.

Each candidate makes a short speech usually three to five minutes long in both Spanish and English; he addresses himself to the purpose of the fiesta and tells why he would like to play the part. Then the De Vargas figure is selected according to the above criteria, particularly as they bear on his speech, and the winner is declared a few days later at the Baile de Mayo (May Dance), an event which the Fiesta Council routinely turns over to the Caballeros de Vargas for supervision.

The speakers recite some portion of the history of the reconquest and make reference to La Conquistadora. Since obtaining help on the speeches is considered fair, they often seek the counsel of devotees and hence usually reflect traditional views of De Vargas and the reconquest. Occasionally, the men do a limited amount of historical reading to prepare for the competition. An excerpt from the winning 1973 speech suggests that the role of De Vargas and the history he represents is more than stage play:

What can we learn from this Magnificent man? Every year his memory is revived as a reminder that we have an obligation. An obligation to our Culture. An obligation to our History. An obligation to our Heritage. And most importantly an obligation to our Language. What a shame if within a few years we will have bearded men and beautiful young ladies in this contest, who will be unable to speak, write or read Spanish. Let us remember "That the man who speaks two languages, is worth two men." [4]

The capitalization of nouns in this speech indicates what the winner of the contest considers important. History, culture, heritage, and language have a certain weight. They are not mere facts, but obligations. The excerpt notes that fluency in Spanish and English is not necessarily an accomplished fact. Though it was no noticeable problem in 1973, some of the candidates have not been proficient in the two languages. One informant even cited the language requirement as a reason for a decrease in the number of can-

[4] Cited in *Official Program of the 1973 Fiesta de Santa Fe*, p. 8.

didates for fiesta queen, a role that also demands bilingual competence. One important function of the contest is to press those whose knowledge of Spanish or English is weak to strengthen their command of the languages. Usually, I was told, the problem is a decreasing ability to speak Spanish, though this trend is being stemmed somewhat by efforts at bilingual education in the public schools. So the role of De Vargas is a symbol of what ought to be achieved by aspiring male Hispanos; it is a heroic model. De Vargas is a symbol of *ethnos* offered as if it were appropriate to define *civitas*. Hence, a local junior high school is named after him and calls its yearbook *The Conqueror*, and a local elementary school has even performed its own "little Entrada" and had bilingual competition for the part of De Vargas.

A certain aristocratic and military air is created about De Vargas wherever he goes. He is usually introduced by his proper name and then by his full fiesta name: "El Capitan General y Gobernador, Don Diego de Vargas, Zapata-Luján, Ponce de León, el Marques de la Nava de Brazinas." Then follow a flourish of trumpets and a triple viva, originating with one of his staff members: "Viva El General don Diego de Vargas! Viva la Reina del Fiesta! Viva la Fiesta!" During Masses, De Vargas is given the largest chair or the only one with arms on it. He receives communion first and sits in one of the front rows of the church. This illustrates the strength of the hierarchical, military imagery, because the church officially disapproves of reserved seats for private persons and of other devices which suggest inequality among communicants.[5]

Typically, the staff marches with De Vargas in the lead and sits with him at the center. His prominent position is compromised only in the presence of the fiesta queen; then she receives the most central or most elaborate chair. The

[5] See, for example, "General Instruction," *The Roman Missal,* article 273; cf. article 271.

relative prominence of De Vargas' and the queen's roles has been the subject of recent concern, especially on the part of religious and fiesta officials. In many ways the queen has come to overshadow De Vargas, so the past few years have witnessed a concerted effort to "restore De Vargas to his rightful place of honor."

That De Vargas' role is not restricted to the pageant set in effect makes the historical reconqueror dramatically present throughout the fiesta, although the man who plays the role does not stay in character the entire time. Only at selected times are his actions appropriate to the general of 1692, particularly at entrances and exits on stages and in parades. For example, at dances he and his staff enter in military formation, but after the formal entrance the man who plays De Vargas becomes himself. Of course, neither he nor the queen is supposed to leave the respective roles so far behind that they forget the dignity of their namesakes, hence the controls on drinking. One former De Vargas comments that one can never be the same after playing the role. Inevitably, some of the dignity and self-confidence sticks, he remembers. Outside the context of the Entrada, the De Vargas figure is never able completely to abandon his role, lest he violate the expectations of those around him. Off the set he does not act as if 1973 were 1692. Instead he acts out the character abstractly; he does not merely imitate, he translates. He consciously or unconsciously must abstract the virtues of the historical De Vargas and embody them in the present. In the Entrada he is De Vargas in 1692, but on other fiesta occasions he is De Vargas translated into 1973. The latter role presupposes an ability to interpret and embody virtues beyond their historical specificity, thus making them visible and present for all to emulate.

In 1973 the fiesta began with the De Vargas Mass, followed by the fiesta proclamation. Since the Mass occurs at 6:30 A.M., the attendance is small. Starting the fiesta with a

Mass is supposed to mark the event as essentially religious. The Mass is entirely in Spanish and is conducted by the archbishop's representative to the Fiesta Council. The sermon extolled La Conquistadora as a symbol of the interpenetration of religion, history, and culture in Hispanic New Mexico and emphasized that the participants did not live in some other place (Spain or Mexico), or in some other time (1692), but here and now. At the conclusion of the Mass the reason for its being labeled the "De Vargas Mass" becomes clear. De Vargas, on behalf of the people, kneels and prays the official prayer of La Conquistadora. Significantly, the man who plays De Vargas symbolizes not only the general but the Spanish people as well. Or perhaps more accurately, he symbolizes De Vargas who in turn epitomizes Spanish culture in New Mexico. This is the only fiesta occasion on which De Vargas and his staff do not make a formal, thus hierarchically ordered entry—an effective way of muting his military connotations and emphasizing his role as symbol of the masses who bow humbly in the presence of Our Lady.

A second occasion of particular importance in understanding the De Vargas symbol is the knighting ceremony. This ceremony is of recent origin, 1972, and it originated as a way of simultaneously making the fiesta more religious and restoring De Vargas to primary status over the queen. It is much more publicly attended than the De Vargas Mass. The actual knighting and coronation, thus, are in English. The knighting-coronation is embedded in a chanted Latin vespers. Both De Vargas and the queen are given blessed robes, but De Vargas is knighted with a sword, whereas the queen is crowned. All four objects—the two robes, the crown, and the sword—are blessed and incensed before being bestowed on the recipients. The officiating priest referred to the mantles as "symbols of dignity to be worn to the glory of the Lord."

These rites are not civic formalities, since they are performed by a priest or archbishop "in the name of the Father, the Son and the Holy Spirit." By performing these acts, the church formally and ritually sanctions the roles. Strictly speaking, these rites do not invest the two people with offices; they bless the symbols of those offices, namely, capes, sword, and crown.

The De Vargas whose sword is blessed is one for whom the sword is not so much a means of achieving power as it is a symbol that he already has power. He has power sufficient to enable him to show grace and dignity in bringing about the submission of forces which jeopardize an Hispanically defined civic tranquility. Religion does not destroy the sword, but it does temper its use. De Vargas is a symbol of Hispanic power without the overt use of violence. He is not a symbolic model of pacifism, but he is one who is imaginative and devout in the way he employs power (the sword). No one expects the De Vargas figure to use his sword, either in the Entrada or out of it. When the church blesses the sword, it is not blessing something it thinks will be carried into actual battle (though, of course, the church on occasion has done this). Rather, the church blesses a symbol of restrained, perhaps even sublimated, power which has civic and ethnic rather than military consequences.

The historical De Vargas was *mayordomo* of La Conquistadora's confraternity; he was also governor. The De Vargas figure, accordingly, wears both a pectoral cross and a sword. If cross and sword were once the symbols of Christian crusaders, they are now symbols of civic virtue and the power of respectability. The man playing De Vargas is not required to be either pious or capable of military engagement. And I suggest that his piety is as metaphoric now as his militarism is. But if the popular view is that the man who plays De Vargas is not "really" a soldier, the people are not usually aware that he is not necessarily "really" pious either. The men who play the role would no more think of shouting in ordinary life, "Praise be the Blessed Sacrament," than they would think of leading a Spanish army—both of which the historical De Vargas did. I am not impugning or denying the devotion of some of the men who play De Vargas. I am simply saying that their devotion may be the result either of Christian piety or of appropriately filling the role of De Vargas during a fiesta.

One De Vargas figure candidly stated that he was not particularly religious, nor, he said, had his Caballero advisers made any particular effort to discuss the religious dimensions of the roles of him and his staff. Participating in a fiesta role is not a religious initiation but an ethnic-civic one. Nevertheless, when one De Vargas confessed that he and many of his staff forgot to take communion and did not know many of the prayers during one of the first Masses, they vowed to take communion and learn the prayers before they portrayed their Spanish forefathers in the next religious rite. If piety is not a prerequisite, it is in some cases a result. Fiesta and church officials assume that members of the staff and court are sufficiently religious to participate without embarrassment. A more accurate assumption would be that participants have sufficient respect for religion and public opinion that they will learn religiosity in the course of the fiesta, if not for God, then (in the words of one staff member) because, "I would feel that I had let down the old people." The motivation to compete for a staff or court position, according to several candidates, is closely connected to the desires and opinions of relatives and friends. But it is not unusual for what begins as respect for the tradition and the elders to end with "a most humbling and moving experience," to quote one participant.

Franciscan and Indian Figures

So far I have commented only on De Vargas without discussing the rest of his staff. The general public usually can

identify only some of the twenty-six roles. Typically, they
mention De Vargas, Indians, Franciscans, and soldiers. A
few further distinguish those playing seventeenth-century
councilmen from soldiers and mention the captains and *al-
férez* (second lieutenant and standard-bearer). Apparently in
times past the public recognized the *tamborero* (drummer),
because historically he was a black man and the role has been
filled on occasion by a black Caballero.

At one time local Franciscans played themselves in the Entrada, but most fiesta-goers today do not remember this. Except Franciscan figures, few staff members are asked whether
they are really who they portray. Ambivalence on the part of
spectators is evoked by the roles of these three men. Both
role players and spectators express considerable respect and
reverence toward Franciscans. Yet at several formal entries
the *padre presidente* (presiding father) turned to bless the
crowd with a sign of the cross and was met with surprised
laughter. Those playing the roles of Indian governors occasionally greeted an audience with a "how" sign but without
similar audience reaction.

Not fully understanding the audience reaction, I asked
those playing Franciscan parts if they could interpret it. One
suggested that the people laughed to express appreciation at
being blessed. He considered the blessing to be the injection
of a serious, religious note into the fiesta. Another Franciscan
figure, who seemed better to perceive the contradiction of the
situation, suggested that the people laughed because they
knew "we are not really priests." But neither of these responses adequately explains the occurrence of surprised
laughter—the first, because it mistakes laughter for appreciation, and the second, because it cannot account for the absence of laughter in the presence of all the other staff (Indian
figures and soldier figures) who are not what they portray.

It is not entirely illogical for the public to wonder whether
real Franciscans are playing the roles, since Franciscans are

still present and influential in Santa Fe. No one, of course, wonders if the other members of the staff are really *conquistadores*. And those playing the roles of Indians deviate sufficiently in costume and image that it is clear to most, except perhaps children, that they are not Indians. Yet the costuming and looks of the conquistadors are authentic enough and the image of De Vargas important enough that the crowds consistently *choose* to view the conquistadors *as if* they are real, though they know quite well they are not. The matter of dramatic suspension of disbelief is ambivalent in the case of the Franciscans: are they or aren't they? Of course, some local spectators know they are not.

Before the Franciscans appear, blessing the crowd with flamboyant signs of the cross, the crowd has already suspended disbelief and is reveling in the color and splendor of the military and civil figures of the staff who have already entered. The crowd is serious about the pomp and splendor taking place before them; they are seriously imaginative. But when the padres enter, some of whom have previously been delivering mock blessings to people on their knees outside the arena of attention, they overplay their roles as they enter the arena. Were they to make signs of the cross in the Entrada, they would evoke no laughter whatever; the laughter we are now considering occurs only during the semidramatic entrances to entertainment events. The people who laugh at their signs of the cross would never laugh at a Franciscan. Suddenly they are jolted out of their serious suspension of disbelief. The obvious overplaying of the role reminds the crowd that *all* of what they are witnessing is only role playing. On one occasion the laughter was so surprised that it broke into applause as the padres made their sign of the cross. The crowd responded as if a burden had been lifted. Instead of adding to the heavy pomposity of the quasi-drama, the padres unwittingly reminded the people that even such occasions as these are dramatic ones and thus composed of very human men playing roles. The padres remind the people that there is a difference between the roles and the men who play the roles.

This does not mean the padres are being irreverent, but rather that they make both themselves and the spectators aware that they cannot reach the goals crystallized by the roles. The crowd breaks into laughter as it slips on the incongruity between person and role.

In a sense, the padres play the role of court jesters. They represent Catholic humor and Catholic iconoclasm; both elements are scarcely visible on most fiesta occasions. The padres, of course, could play their roles in other ways, and undoubtedly in the past they have. As court jesters, they tell the spectators the truth in the midst of humor. The truth: this is role playing. A typical comment heard during a dance is this, "Even the padres are dancing." And the reply, "Yes, they are full of the dickens!" The incongruity of the sacredness of the role and the humor of having the role filled by ordinary men jolts the spectators into reflection. The incongruity provides a relief from the heaviness of the pompous, royal patterns which suffuse grand entries and exits.

The roles of sacred or priestly figures are particularly suited to jesting at the power laden. The history of religions is replete with instances of divine-demonic alliances, and it illustrates the proximity of the sacred and the whimsical. By allowing themselves to be seen as "full of the dickens," the padres profoundly express a humility which stands as a complement to the serious pride of the other characters.

By drawing public laughter to themselves, the Franciscan figures temper a proud occasion with humility and relieve a great many people of the burden of pretentiousness. Hispanic New Mexicans speak often and positively of both pride and humility. They refer to "typical Spanish pride" alongside "typical Spanish humility." The word "pride" has two different meanings; otherwise, pursuing both virtues would be an obvious contradiction. Pride can simply be vanity, but when Hispanos speak of pride, they usually mean a certain dignity and lack of self-pity even in relatively poor circumstances. Pride does not mean the inability to laugh at oneself as is implied in the phrase "the sin of pride." Rather it means the opposite—the ability to laugh at oneself at the very moment of power. Hence, De Vargas' symbolic kneeling in prayer at the opening Mass and the comic blessing of crowds by the Franciscans mean essentially the same thing: humility at the moment of pride's apex.

Public reaction to the roles of Indian figures on De Vargas' staff is quite different. One comment, typical in content though more strongly stated than most, is, "Bunch of fakes! Why don't they get real ones?" No one seems bothered, only curious, that the Franciscans are not real, and most *choose* to regard the military and civic roles of the staff as if they were real. Implicit in this comment is a demand that Indians be played by Indians, a view expressed by actual Indians, Hispanos, and Anglos alike. Why demand a "real" Indian and not a "real" Franciscan?

Both Indians and non-Indians seem subliminally aware that relations between them are strongly colored by stereotyped images. By implication a "fake" Indian is either a non-Indian playing the part of an Indian or else an Indian seen through a screen of stereotypes. The demand to see a "real" Indian is in one sense a self-contradictory demand, hence the ambivalence and frustration of both those making the demand and those having to live with the demand. The demand means, on the one hand, "I want to see someone who looks and acts like my image," and, on the other hand, "I want to see someone who is himself and does not allow himself to be defined by a spectator's expectation." The circle is particularly vicious, because it is largely unconscious and thus all the more pervasive.

The public reacts differently to the three groupings of

roles of actors: Spanish military and civil authorities, Franciscans, Indians. The relation between person and role is viewed differently in all three cases. For the four days of the fiesta the men playing De Vargas and staff are imaginatively identical with their roles. Because of a radical but willing suspension of disbelief on the part of the people, De Vargas is "with us." In contrast, the men playing Indians are never believed. Not only are they disaffiliated from their roles, they are fakes. And structurally mediating between these two positions are the Franciscan figures, who are easily confused with their roles but who readily overplay them and thus remind the public of the difference between individual and role. In the next chapter we will view these roles as they become part of a dramatic process. But roles condense values, so I wish to discuss these before turning to public drama.

Fiesta Rhetoric

Values can be communicated via images, dramatic performances, ritualistic enactments, or simply stated in abstract language. Very often in fiesta rhetoric these values are interpreted or described quite overtly, for example, "De Vargas is a symbol of dignity." A rhetorical analysis of the language of interviews and public speeches during the fiesta provides a list of civic virtues. All of the terms are indigenous, and they are listed roughly in order of descending frequency: pride, dignity, humility, honor, dramatic, cooperation, work, solemn, spirit, color, flavor, blending, respect, simplicity, devotion, peace, coexistence, and festivity.

These values become virtues as they are focused in symbolic personages like De Vargas, the fiesta queen, Our Lady of the Conquest, or occasionally the other figures of court and staff. The medium of their concretization is far from irrelevant. Peace means one thing when focused, for example, through La Conquistadora, and another when focused through De Vargas, and still another when focused through the Franciscans.

The frequency of some of the terms is a function of the fiesta itself. I suspect that words like "flavor," "festivity," and "spirit" are not quite as important before and after fiesta. But words like "dramatic," "dignity," and "pride" were prominent in interviews both before and after fiesta, even in conversations not directly concerned with the celebration. These terms point to goals rather than descriptions; they are an abstract cross-section of what participants want to generate and sustain by having a fiesta.

An important facet of rhetoric is its use of abstraction. Typical statements like the following are important precisely because of their vagueness: "The queen is a symbol of Spanish pride"; "Sprinkling flowers signifies devotion"; "He did a lot of work"; "Let's get the spirit of fiesta!" That the kind of pride, the object of devotion, the results of the work, and the motivation for spirit are generally left unspecified creates a noncontroversial atmosphere in which every hearer can hardly help affirming this "rhetoric of the obvious." The response is, "Of course, we believe in dignity, pride, and drama." In short, rhetorical abstraction maximizes agreement by refraining from specificity. The list of rhetorical terms above would by no means appear the same if it were done in another region or in Anglo- or Indian-defined celebrations. Only if we began to specify whose dignity, under what conditions, and with what results, would the listening audience begin to factionalize. De Vargas acts out Hispanic-Christian dignity; fiesta rhetoric speaks simply of dignity in general. The former defines certain kinds of dignity as out of bounds, while the latter is all-inclusive. Rhetoric allows people to agree with one another while reserving to themselves the right to interpret, act out, and thus make specific. Civic rhetoric allows individuals and groups otherwise separated to feel some sense of unity, even at the very moment when their diversity is being acted out in pageants, rituals, and parades. Such unity is of extreme importance, but rhetorical unity should not be confused with, say, religious, ethnic, or ideological unity.

Rhetoric is not mere rhetoric any more than symbols are mere symbols. I have no doubt that some Santa Feans exercise both economic and physical power to maintain the "honor," "flavor," and "simplicity" of their fiesta. When informants refer to the fiesta as a religious event, they mean, among other things, that they would maximize their resources of power to protect, propagate, and preserve what it stands for. Already I have tried to show how power was maximized in the struggle for jurisdiction over the Entrada pageant.

The language of the *civitas* is rhetorical. The language of *ethnos* is assertive. The language of *ecclesia* is petitionary and exclamatory. And the language of *civilitas* is imperative. A question of immense importance in Santa Fe is who has the symbols and the power to determine the ethnic and religious tenor of the transition from rhetoric to imperative. Since our concern is with a ritual cycle in which Hispano-Catholicism determines the transition, an example of a shift from rhetoric to imperative will help. I have not done what Robert A. Hahn calls an "ethnography of sincerity" (1973), but the following example at least shows that fiesta rhetoric is sincere insofar as its chief values are defended outside the context of the celebration itself.

The Theft of La Conquistadora

The fiesta is said to be "in honor of" La Conquistadora, yet only a replica of her appears in the Entrada, and she is scarcely mentioned during the fiesta. However, if one infers from her relative unobtrusiveness that she is not sincerely valued by the people, he is grossly mistaken. On March 19, 1973, the statue was stolen. For two years the theft of sacred objects from Roman Catholic churches and Penitente *moradas* (meetinghouses) in New Mexico had resulted in the loss of nearly a hundred valuable objects. The events which followed the theft of La Conquistadora surpassed all the others in public interest, media coverage, and the exercise of civil power. All available detectives, as well as the Santa Fe County Sheriff's Department, the New Mexico State Police, and the Santa Fe Metro Squad, entered the search. The mayor of Santa Fe declared, "I will do anything in my power to see that La Conquistadora is found" (*New Mexican*, March 19, 1973, p. 1). By the next day the Santa Fe Fiesta Council was offering a $500 reward for her return and was soliciting funds to increase the amount of the reward. A Santa Fe detective and a New Mexico state policeman, both of whom had previously recovered stolen *santos* (sacred objects), were placed in charge of the case. As if pleading for the safe return of a kidnapped person, a local Franciscan priest declared that the theft was a "sacrilege against centuries and centuries of persons who have venerated her," and appealed to the thief to "examine his conscience" and "realize the indignity of the act" (*New Mexican*, March 21, 1973, p. 1). Because he considered the theft an affront to the entire Southwest, Catholic and non-Catholic alike, he offered his plea in the name of all the people.

La Conquistadora's devotees still comment on the shock they felt. They simply could not imagine the theft of this statue. By the third day after the theft, the Caballeros had turned their shock to economic power; they added another five hundred dollars to the reward money. The editorial page of the same day had an editor romanticizing about the "flawless wooden statue" and citing the governor himself as referring to La Conquistadora as the patron saint of all New Mexico. By March 25 the public was reading a newspaper account of the history of La Conquistadora and an explanation of her link to the fiesta, supposedly "a strictly religious celebration" (p. 4). The outrage continued to build, as a priest compared the statue's loss to New Mexico with the loss of the Statue of Liberty to the United States. For him this value obtained despite the numerous carving faults in the statue: "So whoever stole it only has a piece of junk—it's so mutilated. It's only value is its history" (*New Mexican*, March 27, 1973, p. 1).

The twenty-fifth of March was declared a day of mourning by the mayor, and bells were to toll in all churches as every citizen was asked to offer "a small prayer" for the safe return of La Conquistadora. People began to say, "Something will happen to the thieves, you'll see"; "No New Mexican, nor any Catholic, could have done it"; and "Churches used to be respected."

Money and phone calls continued to pour in, and even a search-and-rescue team normally limited to searching for humans joined the search for the statue. People continued to pray in the La Conquistadora Chapel. A few stories began to develop. In one, La Conquistadora, at whose feet are sometimes placed lost articles, was said to have gone off in search of the lost *santos* which had been stolen in the state. In a second story La Conquistadora left on March 19 to be with her husband Saint Joseph on his feast day. And in a third story La Conquistadora went to get "old dumb San Miguel," who had been stolen from San Miguel Chapel and could not find his way back. The fact that these stories had virtually died by the end of the summer of 1973, however, illustrates the resistance of La Conquistadora to myth and miracle traditions.

A special meeting of the Confraternity of La Conquistadora was called, and on March 27 the *mayordomo* sent a letter to all *confrádes*, noting the deep shock and grief of members and mourning, "The empty niche on the altar is lifeless without her sacred presence!" It goes on to announce that $1,500 had been raised for the reward. The confraternity showed its faith was not directly or totally dependent upon the presence of a wooden statue by announcing an "old-fashioned mission in honor of Our Lady." Not since 1771, at the time of a Comanche "scourge," the letter declares, has there been a rededication of the "Kingdom of New Mexico" to La Conquistadora; therefore there was to be one in June of 1973. The confraternity thus made clear its intention to intensify, rather than slacken, devotion in the face of the theft.

The statue was recovered on April 15, along with several other sacred objects after a widespread search, which led to both coasts. The demand for $150,000 ransom was thwarted and two boys were arrested, though only one name was released, because one was a juvenile; the other was only a few days beyond the age which would have classified him as a juvenile.[6]

April 15, the day on which the recovery was known to the public, also witnessed the arrival of a former prisoner of war from the Vietnam War. He was presented with a symbol of providence, an *ojo de Dios* (eye of God). He was greeted by another former prisoner of war (who was to declare himself a candidate for governor only a few months later) with these words, "La Conquistadora is home, the snows are gone, and you have returned to us. This is truly an enchanted state." In view of the return of a soldier and La Conquistadora at the same time, the mayor noted, "This must certainly be a most memorable day in the history of Santa Fe" (*New Mexican,*

[6] Since the only name which was released was Anglo (because he was no longer a juvenile) some Hispano informants assumed that both were Anglo and expressed considerable relief that "they were not one of us." If they were "one of us," the implication was, they not only would have violated religion for the sake of greed but would have violated their own culture as well. However, the second name was, in fact, Spanish, and some local people who knew this mistakenly identified this second boy as the son of a prominent government official.

April 15, 1973, p. 1). The recovery and subsequent celebration were so important that coverage of the Watergate scandal, so prominent at the time, was relegated to the bottom of page one of the local newspaper.

The police played an important role not only in recovering the statue but in the return celebration itself. The police force was an instrument of the moral, political, and economic powers of the city and state which consolidated to recover a religious symbol. During the investigation the police themselves became symbols of the combined strength of *ecclesia* and *civilitas*. Functionally, their role coincided with that of De Vargas and the Caballeros as defenders of the faith and guards of La Conquistadora's honor. The police carried the statue in the return procession.

The celebration was a solemn mariachi Mass to which the confraternity invited the chief of police, district attorney, mayor, city manager, and city councilmen. The two police officers who had led the investigation marched in the procession under the honorary designations "Padrinos de la Fiesta." The term *"padrino"* is not lightly used in New Mexico; it means both "godfather" and "patron." A kinship term is used symbolically to link a religious celebration to civil authority. One reporter reflected on the "kidnaping": "La Conquistadora has earned the right to be a completely public figure" (*Viva*, April 29, 1973, p. 8).

An excerpt from the prayer which welcomed La Conquistadora home clearly shows the link between civil and religious gratitude:

From the day you were stolen, deep in our hearts we believed strongly that you would return. And, from the very first, our trust in the efficacy and investigative work of our Police never faltered. From the Most Holy Triune God obtain for Our Police, both State and City, and all the other agencies and officers of the courts, whatever graces only God can bestow in your name and honor. We will never forget their sincere interest in finding you, in returning you safely, and now they've returned you symbolically in today's ceremonies of Thanksgiving. [from a typescript of the ceremony]

The prayer is a striking conflation of rhetoric, imperative, petition, and exclamation; prayer and address are one. La Conquistadora's return was considered so significant that some compared it to her return from exile in 1692–1693, and her theft to the "sacrilege of 1680." The Franciscan who delivered the sermon called attention to the partnership of religious and civil power: "We are honored to have these men [policemen] as Our Lady's *armed* [my italics] escorts of La Conquistadora" (*New Mexican*, April 30, 1973, p. 1).

In addition to honoring the police with titles and positions in the procession, the confraternity minutes (June 7, 1973) record the gift of Fray Angélico Chávez' book (1948) to the two supervising officers and thirty La Conquistadora medals to the Santa Fe police, the latter at the suggestion of the chief of police himself.

Informants now refer to the boys who committed the crime as "crazy." Devotees think the boys should have known what kind of power lies behind the tiny, symbolic statue. Some of those I interviewed said they wanted no revenge, but they felt the boys should be given maximum sentences "for their own good." Newspaper accounts described the sentencing as stiff, yet devotees were still extremely irritated by what they consider too light sentencing. A longer sentence would serve to protect the boys' lives, I was told. Some informants felt insulted when they thought they saw one of the boys at the fiesta several months later.

Purity and Power

Symbols not only condense meaning, they also condense value and power, which can be expressed in formidable force if the occasion calls for it. The set of values-virtues I listed earlier are terms which do not describe La Conquistadora so much as they describe the expected behavior of a citizen. They are devotee values offered as appropriate for civic emulation. Stealing La Conquistadora did not hurt the people economically or physically; it insulted their dignity and pride. It was a symbolic blow. To violate La Conquistadora is to deny everything important to the defenders and devotees of Our Lady, and since they view her as patroness of all New Mexico, all citizens, not just devotees, are expected to behave with civility, to exhibit the civic virtues.

The term "virtue" itself etymologically suggests both power (*virtus*) and manliness (*vir*). De Vargas is a symbolic model of "manly" power which becomes effective whenever there is an affront to the meaning condensed into the symbol of La Conquistadora. Inescapably, the public life of Santa Fe is wedded to two symbols, De Vargas and La Conquistadora. Their meanings are different but integrally related. Because of her symbolic purity, La Conquistadora is above the dirty business of administering power and enforcing laws and values. But De Vargas is not. Even he, however, because of her influence, finds a way of employing power without stooping to overt violence. Devotees imply a scale of power and purity in which the movement from symbols of *ecclesia* through those of *civitas* to those of *civilitas* implies decreasing purity. I chart the scale as follows:

Symbolic Entities	*Types of Power*
God, La Conquistadora, Christ	Pure spiritual power
Church, Confraternity	Spiritual power plus the power of dignity and influence
Caballeros, De Vargas figure, Fiesta Council	Power of influence and civic pressure
City council, mayor	Civil power
Police, military	Legitimate force
Thieves, agitators	Violence

The ranking on the chart is not based on my judgment about the amount of actual power possessed by each entity. Instead, it lists symbols of power, each of which has a different mode of exercising power. As one moves down the scale, power becomes increasingly regarded as subject to question, criticism, and restraint. In moments of anger people speak of power on the lower levels as "dirty" or "corrupt." The chart does not reflect the views of Santa Feans on the *actual* purity or corruption of the entities mentioned, but rather indicates the *kinds* of entities most likely to become either pure or corrupt.

Informants tend to identify real power with the extremes but operate most often in the middle range. The language of the extremes tends toward exclamation, while that of the upper-middle moves toward rhetorical abstraction and the lower-middle toward imperative. Power becomes increasingly coercive, literal, and visible as one moves down the scale, although the lower categories frequently appeal to the upper categories for legitimation. Hence, for example, the legitimate force of the police becomes all the more legitimate when it exercises power in relation to La Conquistadora's purity. And even though the historical De Vargas belongs in the fourth and fifth categories, the De Vargas figure has been "purified of his power" in the course of pageantry and civic courtesy. Categories can be invoked together systemically, and entities can shift categories. Increasing purity on the scale brings with it a removal from day-to-day conflict and the consequent pollution which accompanies it.

Hispano-Catholics seem to identify the legitimate use of power with civic, civil, and familial symbols. Power is legitimized to the extent that it has descended down some hierarchically organized structure. Violence falls beyond the limits of legitimacy regardless of its cause. What separates violence from legitimate coercion is not the extent of destructiveness or the use of weapons but the mode of legitimation. As I shall show shortly, De Vargas' countersymbol is identified precisely on this basis.

Santa Feans who eagerly discuss the theft and return of La Conquistadora are reluctant to speak of the trial and sentencing, not because the use of legal power to imprison is wrong but because the display and discussion of power, like the display of wealth and money, is "just something you should not do." This kind of reluctance was also evident when I posed questions about the "disturbances" of the 1970 fiesta, the scene of police tear gas. What makes De Vargas such a potent symbol of power is his having the authority, not only of king, but of God and La Conquistadora, along with the power of his army; he had the power of coercion but did not display it flauntingly. He is the heroic ideal who has clear access to gun and sword but wins with petition and rhetoric instead. A military figure thus successfully becomes a hero of city-consciousness.

Tijerina as Countersymbol

I have tried to show specifically what mode of power employment is symbolized by the De Vargas figure and what organizational structures actualize the meanings and values condensed in the symbol. Because informants frequently opposed the name Reies Lopez Tijerina (though seldom in public rhetoric) to that of Don Diego de Vargas, I shall discuss Tijerina as a countersymbol.[7] Both Tijerina and De Vargas are ethnic symbols, but the disagreement between them crystallizes the question how ethnicity is related to the *civitas*. I no more identify the Tijerina image with Tijerina than I identify the De Vargas figure with De Vargas. Obviously, connections exist in both cases, but this is a study in symbols not primarily in history and autobiography. I am trying to

[7] For a discussion of the countersymbolic relations between heroic and villanous images see Klapp 1962.

interpret certain symbols as they relate systemically to other symbols, and one way symbols can be related is by their mutual opposition.

Tijerina is a Chicano land-grant activist who regards himself and is regarded by others as a symbol of the Indo-Hispano (his term) ethos, much as De Vargas is a symbol of the Spanish-American (Hispano) ethos. The two obviously share the Spanish language in common, otherwise I would consider them simply as symbols from different systems rather than countersymbols. A nationally televised program treated Tijerina under the title "The Most Hated Man in New Mexico." Hispano informants sometimes comment that they are sympathetic with the issue of land-grant reform but "dislike everything he stands for." Tijerina's support is concentrated largely north and south of Santa Fe rather than in Santa Fe County itself; in fact, Tijerina has considerable opposition in Santa Fe.

A mimeographed handbill, the date of which I was unable to determine, was circulated at fiesta a few years ago in Santa Fe. It expresses the conflict between the ethos of De Vargas and Tijerina:

fiesta—siesta

While the Fiesta de Santa Fe goes full blast—dancing, singing, plays, eating and drinking, Reies Lopez Tijerina is imprisoned only a few blocks away in the Santa Fe city jail: A political prisoner of the same Federal Government that 123 years ago in this same city bought out through a secret agent the original "vendido" Mexican general Armijo with thousands of gold pieces. For these pieces of gold Armijo turned over the city—and the entire Southwest—to the Anglos without a fight even though he had superior forces under his command.

Tijerina, who refuses to sell out regardless of the price—or of the penalty—fights on for La Raza: for Spanish history, culture, language and the Treaty of Guadalupe-Hidalgo and the Mercedes; for an end to discrimination in employment against the Indo-Hispano, for an education system that is something more than Anglo brainwashing that prepares Indo-Hispano children for the prison, the battlefield and the janitor's broom, and for a system of justice that is not just an arm of the modern, Washington-nourished Santa Fe Ring that rules New Mexico.

Alianza Federal
¡Viva Tijerina!

The events that led to Tijerina's imprisonment, subsequent release, and finally founding of the Brotherhood Awareness Conferences are complex. Since much has been written about Tijerina, I shall attempt only to sketch these events, paying particular attention to the religious and symbolic elements involved.

Dreams, both the waking and sleeping kind, seem to be important to Tijerina. He often tells how his mother urged him when he was hurt to remember what he saw in heaven. As a boy of four he saw a vision of Jesus. His pious mother would comfort him by reminding him of this vision, one of his earliest dreams. When asked if his dreams are still important, Tijerina remarks that they are probably not as important as they once were. But then he tells of a dream he had in prison, and the emotional intensity of its impact is clear on his face. Like the early one, this one is simple but powerful. Tijerina dreamed that he was where Jacob had pitched his tents. Jacob was not there, but Tijerina knew that was the spot, because all the utensils Jacob had used were still there. Then someone started kicking two green mushrooms growing on the spot. Tijerina shouts as he tells how his anger flared in the dream and he shouted, "Don't you know that is where Jacob was!" Because a friend later told him there are two mountains in Israel whose names in Hebrew mean "mushroom," he is sure that he can be of aid in helping the Middle East crisis. As added confirmation, Tijerina tells that his mother is of Sephardic Jewish extraction and her name, "Lopez," was originally "Lope," but the "z" was added during the inquisition to make an originally Jewish name sound Spanish.

Reies was the child of Texas migrant workers, and his is a story of vision, protest, and conflict in the quest of social justice. In 1946, Tijerina was attending a Bible school in Isleta, Texas, training to be an evangelist in the Assembly of God Church. His apocalypticism in both religion and social relations stems undoubtedly from his pentecostal background. He married a fellow student, and was suspended from the school after only a short stay there. Later, he says, the school offered him a diploma, but he refused because of this initial injustice.

Shortly afterward he began to feel the urge to "overcome everything" and went to hide out in a cave in California, where he learned that denominations made no difference. The account recorded by Richard Gardner is a vivid one:

So I told my wife that I was going to seek the light, a better opening, and I built this place all by myself, this cave in El Monte, California, up on top of a hill all covered with brush. I lined it with cotton I pulled out of an old car seat, and I had to crawl like a snake to get in there. I had in mind that it had to be so that I couldn't turn back, that I wouldn't get out of there unless I could find something better, and if I died, I wanted it to be where they wouldn't find me. [1970:39]

In the late 1940's, Tijerina tried to live up to the image he had of the prophets, particularly Moses and Paul. In my discussions with him in 1973, he still was making repeated allusions to biblical characters and events, particularly those of the Old Testament.

After some time of preaching as an evangelist and pastoring a church, Tijerina established in Arizona a community known as Valle de la Paz, a communal experiment to build a society akin to the Kingdom of God. The failure of this endeavor, due largely to harassment by the local community,

drove Tijerina into New Mexico, where he became interested in the land-grant question; he became a Roman Catholic in 1961 "for obvious political reasons," he unabashedly
explains. The move, like most of the crucial decisions in his
life, was marked by both a crisis and a dream. Again, Gardner's version is the fullest:

I left my warm bed into the cold weather because I wanted to
pray, you know, in the open. I felt very sick about all the trouble
in Arizona, and I wanted to ask God to show me the future of my
life. I fell asleep, and I saw frozen horses and this old kingdom
with old walls, you know, and these tall pines. The horses started
melting and coming to life, and three angels came in my dream to
my house to help me, and my wife got angry and she left me. And
she did too, later, in Albuquerque.

Later he was able to offer an interpretation of the dream:

I thought about all that I had found out, and I decided that this
was what I had hoped it was, this was my life's work, like a mission. And then was when I understood that dream that I had in
California. Those tall pines, they were in New Mexico. And the
old kingdom, well, I found out that New Mexico used to be a kingdom. The three angels were the angels of the law coming to tell me
what I should do and how I should do it. And the frozen horses,
they were the land grants, the *mercedes*, and when I found the true
and perfect titles of the grants and common lands that belonged to
the *pueblos*, and the president confiscated them, just like that, I
realized they were not dead. They could be brought back to life. I
tell you that when I realized that, it was one of the biggest moments of my life. [1970:47, 84]

The land-grant question involves claims of Hispanic ownership to New Mexican lands which were given by the Spanish crown to settlers and subsequently guaranteed by both
the Mexican and American governments, but have since been
appropriated by others. Although some privately owned
lands are involved, Tijerina maintains that he is concerned

only with the return of public land to the descendants of its
rightful owners and does not want to get tangled in fighting
for the return of private land which was purchased in good
faith by individuals. The public land of which he speaks consists largely of national forests (about one eighth of the state),
many of which were originally held in common by villages
for grazing purposes. New Mexico has a history of violence
and corruption related to the issue. Out of land-related quar-
rels arose the notorious Sante Fe Ring and the Lincoln
County Wars, which catapulted Billy the Kid to notoriety.
When Tijerina begins to speak of regaining these large areas
of land, many laugh, remarking that he is crazy and absurdly
unrealistic. When he begins to talk about common land,
others have all the excuse they need to disregard him as a
communist.

Tijerina's study and library is filled with land maps and
law books, which he handles with ease and enthusiasm as he
discusses the question. Awarded with the land, which was
given to the Spaniards and their descendants, was the dignity
of the title *Hidalgo*—a "son of something," a somebody, a nobleman. Land and dignity are linked.

The years 1966–1969 were the peaks of Tijerina's confrontation with the power of the legal, economic, and ecclesiastical establishments. In 1966 he and his followers symbolically occupied Echo Amphitheater in the Santa Fe National
Forest, claiming it under the Treaty of Guadalupe Hidalgo
and naming the new "independent free city state" the Pueblo
de San Joaquin del Rio de Chama. A prominent state historian and archivist made the usual charge of "outside influence," but Tijerina had by this time achieved national publicity with his four national conventions of the Alianza
Federal de Mercedes (Federal Land Grant Alliance), so he
was not so easily discounted. Meanwhile, he was interpreting
his actions in terms of Moses' leading his children out of slav-
ery and Joshua's distribution of the land to the people.

Under the *Recompilation of the Laws of the Kingdoms of the Indies*, which had been reaffirmed by Philip II of Spain in 1570, and which was a basic source of Spanish colonial policy, Tijerina again tried to enact a communal vision based on the land. The publicity cast Tijerina alongside César Chávez, who in the same year had carried Our Lady of Guadalupe to Sacramento, also as a form of symbolic protest.

Other similar events followed, but the one still remembered vividly and recounted by New Mexicans was the so-called raid on the courthouse of Tierra Amarilla in 1967. A gun battle broke out when followers of Tijerina sought to place a district attorney under citizen's arrest. During the trial which followed, the jailer, a key witness, was found murdered. Those who were looking for a reason used this to blame Tijerina himself, although he was not convicted of the murder. Some blamed Tijerina, some blamed his followers, some blamed the political and economic powers of the state. The search which followed the incident was billed as a hunt for a communist; thus it had many of the trappings to fit the imagery. The National Guard, which had also been called up to pursue Pancho Villa in 1916, rolled out M-42 tanks bearing 40 mm. cannons under the command of General John Pershing Jolly. His men carried 20,000 rounds of ammunition with another 20,000 on the way (Nabokov 1970: 108–109). Participating in the search were 350 National Guardsmen, 250 state policemen, and 35 mounted patrol.

Tijerina was acquitted in 1968 of most of the charges stemming from the Tierra Amarilla incident, but other charges followed, and Tijerina was hustled in and out of prisons. Nevertheless, he had time to make demands on two ecclesiastical groups in New Mexico, the Episcopalian and Presbyterian churches, both of which were subsequently split with raging controversies over the issue. The controversies surfaced at their national meetings in 1969. Although Tijerina now regards himself less and less a religious leader, he still feels that the churches ought to be morally obliged to recognize the justice of his demands.

The United Presbyterian church, owner of Ghost Ranch near Abiquiu, New Mexico, finally responded by instructing its Board of Christian Education to negotiate the release and development of a specific area of the ranch to "a group of local Spanish American leaders"; to assist them in obtaining water rights; to support investigation of land-grant claims; to offer Ghost Ranch Center for conferences on self-determination; and to request Congress to investigate in the context of public hearings land claims stemming from the Treaty of Guadalupe Hidalgo (*Minutes of the General Assembly*, 1969, p. 680). Ghost Ranch is composed of land amassed originally from tax foreclosure sales and land grants.

The Episcopal church responded with a grant of $40,000 from its General Convention Special Program Staff (*Southwest Churchman*, December 1969, p. 4). Since the money came from a national body, and since the Episcopal bishop of the New Mexico diocese (Rio Grande Diocese) had almost unanimous local support in opposing the grant, the church entered into a struggle over the powers of national ecclesiastical bodies versus those of the diocese. Someone referred to the fight as a "religious states' rights controversy." Eventually, the controversy resulted in requests for the resignation of the president of the Council of Bishops, who had been sympathetic to Tijerina's demands. By 1973 the Episcopalians had withdrawn aid to Tijerina. The director of the aid program remarked, "There is little difference between church and state. When the state starts cutting back on community action programs, the church follows suit." [8]

Tijerina was last released from prison in July 1971. He has disaffiliated himself from his former organization, the Alianza, though not his goal of land reform. Now he heads a

[8] Leon Modeste cited in the *New Mexican*, Nov. 2, 1973, p. 2.

new organization called the Institute for the Research and Study of Justice, which claims "world harmony as its purpose and justice as its creed." The two most frequent phrases on Tijerina's lips as he speaks of his new vision are "brotherhood awareness" and "cosmic consciousness."

He insists that his Brotherhood Awareness Conferences, which have been attended by New Mexico governors, clergymen, and presidents of the chambers of commerce, are balancing ethnic awareness with brotherhood awareness (*ethnos* with *civitas*). He wants to make men aware of the kinship of all men regardless of ethnic or economic status. He envisions a new movement which transcends the limits of a single church, nation, or race. And New Mexico, he thinks, is a center of spiritual forces. New Mexico, he says, "is a little Israel." "It is the Middle East of the Western hemisphere." It is the home of the Indo-Hispano, a race now come of age, and from which brotherhood and justice can emanate to the whole cosmos.

Tijerina argues that his support is now much more widespread; one of his conferences was supported with a gubernatorial proclamation. Furthermore, he asserts, the Hopi Indians have become interested in brotherhood awareness. Hence, he thinks the groundwork is laid for an internationalizing and interracializing of the quest for justice and harmony.

Three emblems which Tijerina thinks embody his dream are a large mural, a rock, and a birth certificate. The birth certificate consists of an excerpt taken from the *Laws of the Indies* (Law 2, title 1, book 6), which is dated October 19, 1514. At this time the Spanish crown gave legal recognition to the legitimacy of the "Indo-Hispano." This is the birthday of a new race, Tijerina exclaims. The mural is a highly symbolic depiction of the young, world-conscious Indo-Hispano, who is shown to be the offspring of Spaniard and Indian. The earth and sun are at his sides; the world hangs around his neck as a pendant. And the large rock, which is inscribed with the names of leaders attending a Brotherhood Awareness Conference, is, according to Tijerina, a kind of treaty. It is a sign of brotherhood which is signed by Indians, Hispanos, and Anglos as a testimony to their desire for world harmony. A particularly prominent inscription by Vernon Bellacourt of the American Indian Movement reads, "May Sacred Mother Earth endure her suffering."

To Tijerina the land is still an important symbol of ethnic awareness despite his more cosmic vision. And though he disclaims the role of religious leader and is by his own admission only a nominal Catholic, his language and symbols are still strongly religious. He has become an ardent critic of institutional religion as "one of the worst enemies of justice." As for him, he says, he will keep his relationship with God on a direct, personal basis. He will transcend the boundaries imposed by men and try to view the world cosmically, "as if heaven and earth will pass away."

From De Vargas to Tijerina

Despite the contrasts between Spanish-American and Indo-Hispano ideology, symbolized by De Vargas and Tijerina respectively, they hold much in common, otherwise the conflict would not be so painfully deep. Adherents of both ideologies appeal to a Spanish heritage and struggle over common issues of land, genealogy, and justice, and both speak fondly of the Penitentes of New Mexico as repositories of cultural wisdom and resistance against Anglo intrusions on land and culture. Both attempts to symbolize their relations with the Indians, one in a pageant, the other in a mural, birth certificate, and rock.

Tijerina is a contemporary; De Vargas is an historical personage with a ritualistic counterpart in a contemporary celebration. Obviously, a contemporary is more likely to be criticized. Even though many Santa Feans know that De Vargas had children by a woman other than his wife and that he was imprisoned and later exonerated, the imprisonment of Tijerina for two years is considered enough to discredit him. Whereas Tijerina has many times challenged the legitimacy of civil authority, De Vargas is an instrument of king and religious hierarchy, the epitome of civil and religious authority. The present De Vargas is never absolutely identified with the historical De Vargas, so even gross errors on the part of a De Vargas figure would not discredit the heroic De Vargas image.

Tijerina recounts the consternation created among civic and civil authorities when a review of Richard N. Ellis' *New Mexico Past and Present: A Historical Reader* (1971) used the phrase "from Coronado to Tijerina" rather than "from Coronado to Montoya" (an incumbent U.S. senator). La Conquistadora devotees associate Tijerina with the pollution of violence, whereas Coronado, in their eyes, can claim at least the purity which accompanies royally authorized conquest. And because of the bloodless reconquest, the De Vargas image commands even more purity in the exercise of power.

Pushed to their caricatured limits, De Vargas is a symbol of royal, crusading imperialism while Tijerina is a symbol of militant, grass-roots revolution. De Vargas conquers and reconquers land from the Indians; Tijerina wrests land from the Anglos. De Vargas brings the power of king and church to bear on Pueblos occupying Santa Fe; Tijerina brings the power of symbolic seizure and occupation by the poor to Rio Arriba County. And in the popular view of the symbols, both back up their demands with the power of arms, whether they actually use them or not. Yet Tijerina is viewed in Santa Fe as a villain, while De Vargas is viewed as a hero. De Vargas claims the authorization of the king while Tijerina claims the *Laws of the Indies*. Both feel it important to elaborate moral, legal, and religious grounds for their activities. De Vargas appeals to his banner of Our Lady, makes frequent use of rosaries and crosses, and incessantly shouts praises to the Blessed Sacrament. Tijerina appeals to dreams, visions, and basic human nature, that is, brotherhood aware- ness.

So how can two figures who share this much in common be at such variance in the minds of Santa Feans? I do not locate the difference primarily in their means; the difference is not between violence and nonviolence, because neither is a pacifist symbol. De Vargas has his bloodless reconquest and Tijerina his Brotherhood Awareness Conferences. De Vargas has the bloody reconquest of 1693 and Tijerina has Tierra Amarilla. So the difference, I think, is that they have dif- ferent modes of legitimizing what they do. One appeals to the hierarchy; the other appeals to dreams.

The Catholic royal metaphors surrounding La Conquis- tadora are inherently hierarchical. In contrast is Tijerina's appeal to unmediated, direct contact with the sacred and moral grounds of justice. Despite his joining the Roman Catholic church, Tijerina's charismatic style and mode of thinking are still basically grounded in the inspirationist ideol- ogy of pentecostalism. Tijerina does not go through chan- nels, either religiously or socially, but goes directly to the source of highest authority. Structurally, his appeal to direct inspiration from God parallels his threat several years ago to take his case to the United Nations or the International Tri- bunal at The Hague in the Netherlands. He is a radical in the etymological sense of the word: he insists on going to the "root" of absolute power. He avoids carrying his case step- by-step through the hierarchy and appeals instead to abso- lutes like justice, God, and cosmic consciousness.

De Vargas too appeals to God and other absolutes but does so mediately, not directly. William Christian Jr.'s obser- vation about life in a contemporary Spanish valley can apply to De Vargas. Christian shows that mediation between top and bottom is the typical pattern: the people go through Mary, the saints, and the souls in purgatory to reach their fathers, and villages go through patrons to reach the bureaucracy of the Franco government (1972: 173–177).

In New Mexico the formal proposal for marriage sometimes is still mediated through a respected elder or godfather of the bridegroom. Legitimation by indirection and mediation is still the rule in many areas of Hispano-Catholic life. Therefore, De Vargas' use of La Conquistadora, civil authorities, and the priests as intermediaries between himself and God is considered a sign of devout humility, while Tijerina's direct claim to religious and moral authority is considered illegitimate and arrogant. His use of power is regarded as impure.

In the views of La Conquistadora's devotees, descending and ascending through the hierarchical ranks is just as important genealogically as it is religiously. De Vargas' importance is as much a result of his genealogical claims as it is of his religious ones; both depend on a legitimacy of descent. Devotees deny a similar legitimacy to Tijerina by speaking of him as a Mexican national and outsider, despite his having been born in Fall City, Texas.

The very terms "Spanish-American" (a common but somewhat dated term in Santa Fe) and "Indo-Hispano" indicate how the respective ideologies wish to portray their lines of descent. Tijerina emphasizes that the Indo-Hispano is a new breed, originating in the sixteenth century and only recently come of age. The Spanish-Americans insist that, although they have intermarried with Indians, their line is very old, going back traceably to the *conquistadores* and beyond into medieval Spain. Therefore genealogical descent and apostolic succession are structurally opposed to new breeds and direct revelation. Spanish-Americans speak of Tijerina as if he sprang from nowhere and claimed everything. We can summarize the difference between the two symbolic heroes as the difference between militaristic and militant images of power. The former confirms man's pride and dignity by his power to condescend from authority to humility, and the latter confirms his pride and dignity by his power to rise up from humble circumstances to the seats of authority.

CHAPTER 4

Public Drama

Fellow Countrymen: At last the moment has arrived when our country requires of her children a decision without limit, a sacrifice without reserve, under circumstances which claim all for our salvation.

The eagle that made us equal under our national standard, making of us one family, calls upon you today, in the name of the supreme government and under the Chief of the Department, to defend the strongest and most sacred of all causes.

Today that sacred independence, the fruit of so many and costly sacrifices, is threatened, for if we are not capable of maintaining the integrity of our territory, it will all soon be the prey of the avarice and enterprise of our neighbors from the north, and nothing will remain but a sad recollection of our political existence.

Mexican Governor Manuel Armijo, Santa Fe,
August 8, 1846 (Twitchell 1967: 23–24)

Pageantry is public drama of the *civitas,* and the ideological heart of the Santa Fe Fiesta is the De Vargas Entrada, a reenactment of the events of 1692. The Entrada is a pageant, a public spectacle, in which the relations between various symbols are enacted in a dramatic process; they "move" along a plot line. The plot is calculated to parallel the movement of Spanish history, which many Santa Fe Hispanos speak of as "dramatic."

The Tradition of Drama in New Mexico

Public drama should be distinguished from more rurally based folk drama, on the one hand, and more professionally oriented artistic drama produced by local theater groups, on the other. Public drama has some distinct characteristics. First, it is historically preoccupied. Second, it is akin to the morality play insofar as it is didactic, theological, and ideological; it aims to communicate and strengthen a specific set of values. Only secondarily does it aim at producing a work of art. Third, the ethos of public drama is spectacular and thus more akin to Hollywood in its staging than to either folk or artistic drama. And in Santa Fe most public drama is explicitly Catholic in its attempt to link religiosity with both ethnicity and civicality.

Pageantry and folk drama are quite old traditions in New Mexico. The oldest and probably the most fully developed folk drama tradition in the United States is to be found in northern New Mexico. C. E. Castaneda has dispelled the commonly held belief that the earliest play in North America was written in Williamsburg in 1718. In his article "The First American Play" (1936), he argues that the first play written by a European in America was in 1619 in what was then known as New Spain. The play was "Coloquio de la Nueva Conversion Bautismo de los Cuatro Reyes de Tlaxacala en la Nueva España."

The Entrada is produced by persons strongly influenced by the folk tradition of religious drama among Spanish descendants in the Southwest. The origins of some of these dramas can be traced to medieval Spain, and the repertoire contains the following plays or variations of them: "Los Pastores," "Los Moros y Christianos," "Los Reyes Magos," "El Niño Perdido," "Adán y Eva," "Las Posadas," "Los Comanches," "La Aparicion de Nuestra Señora de Guadalupe," "Cain y Abel," "Coloquio de San José," "Los Matachines," and "La Aurora del Nuevo Día."

The Entrada pageant is considerably later than these plays but is sustained by the same cultural matrix modified somewhat by the commercial, urban, and artistic environment of Santa Fe. Many of the folk plays are still being produced in northern New Mexico and southern Colorado. I have studied scripts for most of them and have seen "The Moors and the Christians" and "The Commanches," the two most akin to the Entrada in theme.

The earlier plays are Spanish morality plays, often depicting the devil and events concerned with the birth and childhood of Christ. Consequently, many of them are performed during the Christmas season. Some of them, known as *autos sacramentales* (one-act religious plays), were developed for use on the feast day of Corpus Christi. Others were performed and written for the evangelizing and teaching of Indians. "Los Matachines," a nonverbal dance-drama, is still performed frequently by Pueblo Indians. It is the mimed story of Malinche, who was given by Montezuma to Cortés; her part is played by a little girl symbolizing purity, while the role of evil is played by El Toro (the bull).

Inasmuch as the Entrada is about military conflict and religion, it is thematically closest to "The Moors and the Christians," a play Spanish in origin and popular among Spanish soldiers. De Vaca and others performed it in 1536 in Mexico to commemorate the Feast of Santiago; it was also performed in 1598 to celebrate the colonizing of New Mexico by Oñate. So the tradition of military pageants, along with *autos* and *coloquios*, (dramatic dialogues), is quite old among the Spanish and their New World descendants. It was, perhaps, no accident that a revival of the fiesta in 1919 was scheduled to coincide with the return home of World War I veterans (Marie 1948: 128).

In 1944 the fiesta included one of the traditional folk dramas, "Los Pastores," along with the fiesta pageant. According to Sister Joseph Marie (1948:130), the script for the De Vargas pageant was bilingual, with most of the text in Spanish. She claims that it was composed by Fray Angélico Chávez and Will Shuster and rearranged for the 1944 production by Fray Theodosius Meyer.

The present Entrada script is almost entirely in English. Few copies of it exist, and these are carefully guarded by the Caballeros, who lend them to the performer-initiates each year. I was able to study two versions: "Scenario and Scheme—The Reconquest of Santa Fe by General Diego De Vargas" (1958) and the considerably longer "Fiesta Entrada

Script" (1967). I also talked at length with the authors of these two most recent versions. The 1967 script contains twenty-three pages of text and stage directions in comparison to the six pages of the 1958 version. The later version is much more prone to long speeches, along with moralistic and dramatic elaboration. A major change is the addition of a lengthy flashback scene in the 1967 version, in which Naranjo and Popé, two Pueblo revolutionaries, tell of the events leading to the revolt of 1680. The primary author of the revisions explains that the additions were the result of new research discoveries, notably Chávez' article on Pohe-Yemo (1967), and the desire "to let the Indians tell their side of the story." A slightly modified version of the 1967 script was followed in the performance of 1973.

The revisions, additions, and omissions which take place between the two scripts are informative. I categorize the principles dictating the revisions resulting in the 1967 script as follows: practical revisions aimed at easier, more efficient production; historical revisions designed to make the pageant more accurate; dramatic revisions intended to strengthen the emotional power of the play; didactic revisions, usually in the form of additions, which point out the morals and lessons of events; and ideological revisions, representing changed beliefs and values, most of which are concerned with the related issues of violence, war, peace, and Hispano-Indian relations.

An Entrada Performance

In comparing these two scripts, I will also draw from the performance of 1973 and De Vargas' "Journal" of 1692, a primary historical source. The Entrada pageant takes place on Sunday afternoon on the hill overlooking Fort Marcy Ballpark. Usually, a huge banner, bearing the Spanish coat of arms, flies over the set. The audience sits or stands in the ballpark, looking up a hill toward the pageant set. The set was constructed in 1967 of plywood panels and scaffolding and consists of three major pieces: an entry gate to the city, a replica of the Governor's Palace and a replica of the old *parroquia* (parish) church (later to become the cathedral). Most of the action occurs between the gate on stage right and the Governor's Palace in the center. The nearby hills are used to extend the set when De Vargas' army marches to reclaim the city.

After a welcoming and introduction of dignitaries, the narrator invites the audience to participate in the "dramatic" reconquest "in the brilliant light of your own individual imaginations." The adjuration "to forget the present," found in the 1958 script, was omitted in the 1967 script and in 1973. As De Vargas approaches slowly, far in the background, the narrator refers to him variously as "immortal," "intrepid," "heroic," "virile," "handsome," "unafraid," "courageous," "manly," and "devout." Meanwhile, he directs the audience's attention to the top of the Governor's Palace, as dreamy music and a cloud of dry ice smoke announce the appearance of two Indian "ghosts from the past."

The actors mime the parts as readers behind the set recite the lines over loudspeakers. A third of the pageant in 1973 was taken up by the two initial speeches of the ghosts of the Pueblo revolutionaries, Popé and Naranjo, who do not appear in the 1958 script. Many in the audience continue to talk or otherwise express boredom, because of the didacticism of the opening speeches. The pageant begins to hold their attention with the arrival of De Vargas and his staff.

The two soliloquies are read in stilted cadences, supposed to imitate an Indian's way of speaking English. The voices—crude and strong to accompany the sweeping, powerful gestures—are gruff and villainous, as in a morality play. They are highly "Indianized" by the elimination of articles and demonstratives and the changing of past tense verbs to

present tense verbs. The bodies of both men are stripped to
the waist and covered with dark brown body paint.

Popé's soliloquy describes his own actions and feelings
about the revolt. He expresses many anachronistic judgments
about himself as he delivers his speech, for example, "I am
the great leader Popé . . . a great warrior." He exonerates
the Franciscans as "friends" who "were not ambitious men
who wanted slaves," and who had "even learned, carefully,
our different dialects" and had "built new and large places of
worship." The speech argues that the revolt was not the
result of racial hatred between Hispanos and Indians but was
an aberration to be blamed on a few malcontent Indians and
a few "lousy, greedy" Spanish governors. Popé the revolutionary is made to refer to the Franciscans as "those new
amigos [who] were even poorer than we were." The "poor"
missionaries and "ordinary settlers" wanted peace; only the
greedy and ambitious governors wanted to get rich by op-
pressing Indians. Popé's speech concludes with his telling
how he used a knotted yucca rope to count off the days until
the revolt.

Then Naranjo, the second Indian "ghost," appears from
the past. Naranjo, whose voice is considerably more stereotyped, also expresses judgments properly belonging to others
on himself. For instance, he tells how "I master-mind [sic]
the cruel and bloody Indian revolt." Naranjo describes himself as yellow eyed, tall, and black, "in comparison with the
average small and not too tawny Pueblo Indian." He tells
how he tricked the Pueblo Indians into thinking he was a
representative of Pohe-yemo, the youthful sun god. Thereby
he claims to have used them to avenge himself on the Spaniards, who would not let his faher be a conquistador because
he was a black slave in Mexico. As a black Spanish Indian,
Naranjo explains that he chose Popé as a figurehead for the
revolt which he himself masterminded from behind the

scenes. He portrays both himself and Popé as "rebels" and "firebrands" who play on the fears of witchcraft among Pueblo people. The sole purpose for the revolt, according to Naranjo, is "my wild dream of sweet revenge!" Naranjo even cites the Franciscan judgment that the revolt must have been the work of "the very Devil himself" "so evil were the effects and so destructive the force used."

The didactic and rhetorical tenor of the pageant can best be illustrated by a few excerpts from the Naranjo soliloquy:

> To the majority of the Pueblo Indians, I represented someone very important: I was none other than "the lieutenant of Pohe-yemu [sic]." But perhaps the title "lieutenant" is not the best translation; a better one would be "the Representative of Pohe-yemu," "the person taking the place of," or "the one assuming the person of. . . ."
> And who was this Pohe-yemu, who was feared greatly . . .? These Indians were afraid of offending the god "who made the sun shine," and I, as the "Representative of Pohe-yemu," I could not but succeed, could I ???!!!

After Naranjo tells the audience he is going to his "rightful place" in the past, and following an interlude of Indian music, the narrator pronounces moral judgment on Popé's leadership and begins a dramatized description of the approaching "tall, dark and slender Spaniard, with long straight black hair and dark eyes, [who] is mounted on a spirited stallion."

The 1958 script begins only now with this introduction by the narrator. The 1967 script spices up descriptions of De Vargas by multiplying adjectives and by inserting an account of De Vargas' genealogical heritage. He is described as a man of "noble dignity" whose only fear is "the Lord God!" De Vargas and his army are now rapidly approaching the city from a distant hill as music from "El Cid" plays over the loudspeakers. Spectators begin to come alive and are heard expressing admiration with exclamations like, "Ooh, isn't that dramatic!" The narrator declares, "It is now September 14, 1692." And De Vargas is coming to reconquer the land in the name of "both Majesties: God and King." An Indian scream indicates that the Pueblos have spotted De Vargas coming over the hill.

The narrator announces the inevitability of a battle as the Indians begin a war dance to the beat of tom-toms and De Vargas' army approaches the city gate. Rhetorically, the narrator asks whether there will be peace or bloodshed, as Chief Domingo comes out to talk with De Vargas.

At this point in the 1967 script there is an excursus solely for the information of the actors. It adjures them to remember "the historical truth":

. . . De Vargas' ideas on a peaceful reconquest were too far-fetched in the Spaniards' minds, in both the soldiers' and the padres' minds as well; De Vargas was risking a great failure. . . . De Vargas was playing into the hands of fate; this is the place where De Vargas' ideas of a peaceful reconquest are fully baptized, and where his tremendous confidence that La Conquistadora would remember the "vow made at El Paso" kept him going, calmly no doubt, but with interior nervousness, naturally! This is the exact time when his motto was put to the test: "What man will not risk his life to gain eternal glory!"

Stage directions urge the actors to enact this part with "dramatic flare" to convince the audience that De Vargas' peaceful reconquest was a dream become reality only because of his "confidence and guts."

In the 1958 script the narrator simply describes what transpires between De Vargas and Chief Domingo, but in the 1967 version long conversations about peace between the two sides are made part of the dialogue. De Vargas pleads with Domingo to convince the other Indians occupying Santa Fe to surrender and accept his offer of forgiveness and pardon from Charles II. He wants peace but threatens to attack if the Indians do not yield the city and the pueblos and submit again to Christianity and Spanish rule. De Vargas has not given up the Spanish goal of conquest of the Indians; he simply wants to achieve that goal without the loss of life.

The 1973 performance shows modification of the 1967 script's version of Domingo's speeches. As in the other Indian speeches they are "Indianized" by the omission of adjectives and demonstratives. In addition a simpler vocabulary has been developed for Chief Domingo so that, in the words of one Entrada participant, "he won't sound like a college graduate." For example, "thoughts" is substituted for "intentions" and "hard" is substituted for "difficult."

Domingo too asserts that he prefers peace, not war, and he returns to the city to try to persuade the still angry Indians, after De Vargas shows him two power-laden symbols—a rosary and a banner with the Virgin Mary on one side and the Spanish coat of arms on the other.

The angry Indians, played in 1973 by Hispano children, reject Domingo's counsel. When he reports this rejection to De Vargas, the General decides to convince the Indians of his peaceful intentions by removing his helmet, sword, and armor. De Vargas, who has until now been on his horse talking down to Domingo below him, dismounts amid the protests of his soldiers and padres. The statue of La Conquistadora, which was carried in by the Franciscans, is nearby. De Vargas prepares to enter the villa of Santa Fe by leading his soldiers in a triple verbal salute to the Blessed Sacrament, "Alabado sea el Santisimo Sacramento del Altar!" and a single shout of praise to La Conquistadora, "Honrada sea siempre Nuestra Señora La Conquistadora!" De Vargas enters "with the strength that comes from sincere confidence and faith in God," having declared earlier that no one ever gains an illustrious name without risk. The Indians immediately submit; they are caught by surprise at this heroic deed. A Spanish general has removed his armor and advances unarmed! The Indians erect the cross which has been lying in front of the Governor's Palace since the 1680 revolution.

Then occurs the formal taking-possession rite. De Vargas restores the civil administration to the City Council amid the hoisting of the royal banner and shouts in Spanish of "Long live our lord, King Charles II." He returns custody of the church to the Franciscans and declares the pardon of those Indians who will submit to both God and "His Catholic Majesty." Then follows a crucial and controversial speech:

> Pueblo Indians of New Mexico: Our Lord and King, Don Carlos Segundo, your lawful King and mine, having overlooked the apostasy with which you have repudiated the Christian religion; your sacreligious conduct in the butchery of the Franciscan Padres; the desecration of the temples, the breaking of the sacred images, and the contamination and burning of the sacred ornaments and vessels; the cruel killing of the settlers . . . sparing neither the women nor the children; your barbarous methods in the ruthless burning and destruction of the haciendas and missions buildings, and the consequences which followed such actions. Nevertheless, I have been sent here by His Majesty the King, with full pardon for all of you! The only condition being: that you return to the Christian Religion, and Holy Mother Church will receive you back as a Good Mother! You are to beg humble forgiveness of Almighty God, with penance and tears of sincere repentance; and you are to swear anew: allegiance to His Catholic Majesty, as your Lawful King!

Those performing the 1973 pageant felt that the wording of this speech was too strong and consequently changed "apostasy" to "repudiation" and "butchery" to "killing." This speech of "forgiveness" is supposed to mark the beginning of harmonious intercultural relations, but as a matter of fact, it still provokes criticism and controversy.

The Indians accept the rule of the king, acknowledge the Christian religion, and surrender legal possession of their pueblos. And the pageant concludes with the padres' chanting of the Te Deum Laudamus in Latin and De Vargas' wishing aloud that "for all time a special season of Fiesta should commemorate this day." He declares his hope that the people will never forget the intercession of La Conquistadora.

Interpreting the Entrada

The De Vargas pageant is not, of course, an objective presentation of historical data. As the work of admirers of De Vargas and devotees of La Conquistadora, it shows marks of commitment and dramatization. The sources of the 1967 script and the 1973 performance are oral tradition, previous scripts, the "Journal" of De Vargas, the Chávez article on Pohe-yemo (1967), and J. Manuel Espinosa's *Crusaders of the Rio Grande* (1942). A comparison of the pageant to less dramatic, more historical, sources can give us some idea what admiration and devotion have interpretivley added. The pageant deviates in several important respects from the "Journal," which, although it has its own special point of view, is most basic historically. Several Caballeros say they think the Entrada is now as historically accurate and fair as it can ever be, so a look at the "Journal" gives us some perspective on this view.

The "Journal" (Espinosa 1940) shows quite clearly that there were two *entradas*—the bloodless one of 1692 and the subsequent violent one of 1693. De Vargas planned the first one as an exploratory entry to reduce the Indians and reclaim the territory. The second one was to be a colonization effort. After the first one he traveled on behalf of the king to the various pueblos formalizing his claims on them. When De Vargas and his forces returned in 1693 with the colonists from San Lorenzo (near El Paso), the city was still occupied by the Tano Indians; the obedience of the Indians in 1692 had been only partial. After waiting, pleading and negotiating, De Vargas attacked Santa Fe to destroy the resistance of the Indians. Eighty-one Indians died, seventy of them in executions after the battle. One Spaniard died in battle; twenty-two others died of exposure to the harsh weather. Around four hundred of those Indians who surrendered were given to soldiers for ten years of involuntary servitude.

The authors of both the 1958 and 1967 scripts are aware of what happened historically. Yet the 1958 script makes only confused allusions to 1693, and the 1967 script makes no allusion to it at all. The pageant obviously focuses on 1692 alone in order to emphasize the historical grounds for harmonious Hispano-Indian relations. In fact, the moral of the pageant is that the contemporary "tricultural coexistence" is a direct result of De Vargas' peaceful and imaginative tactics. The pageant implies that De Vargas knew exactly what his deeds promised for future generations.

Another deviation of the pageant from the campaign journal is the displaying of La Conquistadora. The "Journal" describes De Vargas' displaying his rosary and banner of Our Lady of Remedies, but never La Conquistadora. So the pageant draws on oral tradition in having La Conquistadora present (though only in replica). The De Vargas of the "Journal" was quite fond of rosaries and used them as gifts and as emblems to show that Indians had accepted Christian-Spanish rule. As he traveled to the various pueblos, he handed out rosaries to Indian leaders and friends. Sometimes he even gave them to those he wished to have passage of safe conduct through Spanish lines (cf. Espinosa 1940:123, 127–130). He commanded the Indians who surrendered the city of Santa Fe to wear crosses around their necks as signs of submission, so the Indians did not submit to La Conquistadora as such.

Devotees occasionally speak of La Conquistadora's role as miraculous; more often they refer to it as "providential." But a somewhat different tradition is now developing among some Pueblos. One Pueblo informant argues that there was nothing unusual about the reconquest at all. "What was miraculous, daring or providential," he observes, "about De Vargas' coming to Santa Fe when he had been invited here by Indians to help resist Popé, who had become a tyrant after the revolt? Not only was he invited back, he was accompanied on his return by Indian messengers who had been sent from the pueblos." Whatever the historical facts are—and I do not wish to enter the historical debate—the fact is that there are at least two or more traditional stories.

A small booklet entitled, *Did Vargas Win His Battle with a Banner?* contends that the use of images to obtain ceremonies of obedience or reduction was quite common in the Southwest. Sister Mary Philibert insists that the General's actions were "an imitation of the Franciscans who accompanied him, for they were accustomed to use the crucifix and the rosary they wore to gain the confidence of the Indians" (n.d.:7). To have entered Santa Fe, she argues, would have been a senseless risk without the accompaniment of a sacred image; furthermore, it would have been contrary to the usual Franciscan practice.

Sister Philibert's research and arguments raise questions only about the uniqueness of De Vargas' tactics. They do not account for the easy and bloodless victory. However one accounts for it, the event has been considered extraordinary for over 260 years. One might suspect that the De Vargas legend of popular tradition would continue regardless of the course of historical research, but such a contention ignores the importance of historical studies to Santa Feans. It is quite true that the legend is somewhat independent of the best historical reconstructions; tradition lags behind historical scholarship. Yet between historical scholarship and popular tradition stands the Entrada pageant, which is performed annually during the fiesta and is the primary agent for keeping the story alive. And the Caballeros de Vargas, who produce the drama, have shown that they are interested not only in the popular traditions, but in scholarly, historical studies.

So legend is not likely to divorce itself from history in Santa Fe, as sometimes is the case in predominately oral societies. The Caballeros view their pageant as having an objectivity that many Indians and some Anglos vigorously deny. I have tried to show that the play is devotedly Catholic and normatively Hispanic rather than neutrally objective.

Whatever the facts about the bloodless reconquest, the victory is traditionally held to have set De Vargas' vow in motion. At its most elaborate, the tradition describes this vow as De Vargas' promise to build La Conquistadora a chapel, to start the novena-processions in her honor, and to initiate a fiesta in commemoration of the reconquest of 1692. Historically though, the content of the vow is not so clear. That De Vargas vowed to build a chapel for La Conquistadora is clear enough from the primary sources, though the chapel which fulfills that vow is La Conquistadora Chapel, not Rosario Chapel, as popular tradition sometimes maintains. The fiesta began not with a vow of De Vargas but with a city council decree in 1712. The decree could possibly have been made with the De Vargas vow in mind, but I can find no evidence to support this. As to De Vargas' vow regarding the novena-processions, no evidence can be found. Father Chávez' conclusion on the matter is, "But how or when the present so-called 'de Vargas Procession' began is impossible to say" (1948:49); the best conjecture seems to be that the novena-processions began in the nineteenth century. It is not possible historically to determine why the processions are held the Sunday after Corpus Christi.

The vow traditions are closely linked to the tradition of La Conquistadora's providential intervention. "Journal" entries closest to the event itself speak of the banner of the Virgin as a "testimony of the truth," but a later entry, concluded on September 21, interprets the role of Mary in such a way that it might be partially responsible for the belief in a semi-miraculous intervention of La Conquistadora:

I despaired of their reduction, nevertheless I continued to tolerate their excesses, looking toward the greater service of both Majesties, and finally their rebelliousness was successfully vanquished. For although they remained incredulous and obstinate and unconvinced by my efficacious arguments, which, imbued with the spirit of a fervent breast and with Catholic zeal, I repeated to them, finally the aim was achieved, the aurora and guiding star of my thoughts, and the protector, in short, of our holy faith, attributing to remove the shadows from their blindness; for who could have been always assisting us, other than most holy Mary of the Remedies, who was the protector of the said enterprise and the one who guided my steps in the victory over so many devils? She delivered us once and for all from danger, regaining for us the joy in the happiness which was achieved upon seeing the said natives come out submissively from their stronghold to their plaza to render obedience to me and also to her blessed Majesty, the former of which I received. [Espinosa 1940:114]

Another point at which the pageant differs from the "Journal" is on the matter of De Vargas' entering the villa unprotected. Whereas the Entrada depicts the padres and soldiers as trying to discourage De Vargas from going in unarmed, De Vargas says in his "Journal" that he restrained two friars from so entering (Espinosa 1940:84, 86, 92). After the padres have asked twice for permission to enter, De Vargas finally allows them to proceed as a dozen Indians come out peacefully. Meanwhile, according to his own account, De Vargas remains outside, embracing those Indians who have surrendered. Contrary to the Entrada and the tradition on which it depends, De Vargas does not walk in first nor does he enter without protection. However, his doing so in the pageant obviously makes it more dramatic.

As to De Vargas' having removed all of his armor as a sign of good faith, this tradition is only partially supported by the "Journal." De Vargas says in his "Journal" that he complied with a request of the Indians to remove his morion so they could see him, but this act is not a strategy dreamed up by an idealistic general. Rather, it is a response to an Indian desire to be sure the Spaniards are not Apaches or Pecos Indians disguised as Spaniards. The tradition that he removed all his armor as a sign of peaceful intentions could have originated from a later occurrence. On the feast day of the Holy Cross, a day after the entry, De Vargas says he appeared dressed "in gala" though he was advised to attend the absolution rites occurring on that day fully armed. Because it is a dramatic production, the pageant concludes as if all hostilities ended with the chanting of the Te Deum Laudamus. Actually, this and the absolution of the Indians occurs on September 14, when De Vargas is still taking precautions against the "treacherous Indians" (Espinosa 1940:94).

The "Journal" also shows that the surrender of the Indians was not altogether due to De Vargas' personality or faith. He tells how he cut off the water supply to the city. To be sure, his patience and pleading are exceptional; he constantly insists that he does not want bloodshed but a return to the true faith. Nevertheless, he backs up his faith in the Virgin and his desire for peace by letting the Indians know that "I would consume and destroy them in fire and blood without quarter" (Espinosa 1940:87). What occurred may have been bloodless, but it was still a conquest.

In the pageant the Indians express their fear of certain Spaniards, whom they name, but in the "Journal" another fear is expressed:

They answered that they believed that what the governor and the fathers said was true, but that they also knew that they would be ordered to rebuild the churches and the houses of the Spaniards, that they would have to work hard, and that they would be whipped if they did not do as they were told, as had been done by the Spaniards formerly. [Espinosa 1940:83]

In both pageant and "Journal" De Vargas assures them they will not have to tolerate certain named Spaniards, but nothing is said in the pageant about their fear of being whipped into building churches. The pageant does not link the oppression of Indians to the church, it depicts the Indians as feeling positively about the church, especially the Franciscans, but a contemporary Pueblo anthropologist and historian (Dozier 1970:48–49) argues that it was a general practice to circulate the missionaries among pueblos to prevent too close ties between friars and Indians. Some considered such ties harmful to the missionary cause. This practice, along with whipping Indians for "idolatry" or for lack of zeal in church-building, tended to break down communication and the learning of native languages by missionaries. This obviously is a viewpoint different from the one presented by the pageant.

De Vargas' courage and piety are not groundless creations of folk tradition, however. The historical De Vargas moved his cannons into place after giving the Indians one hour to accept his offer. Many Indians—who had left a dance at Santa Clara Pueblo—began to appear and surround De Vargas. De Vargas sent out emissaries to keep them at a distance, but the numbers were large, and De Vargas found himself in an even more precarious position than is shown in the pageant. A battle could have sandwiched De Vargas' forces between the surrounding Indians and those in the city itself, but De Vargas convinced the leader of the surrounding Indians, Domingo, a Tewa, to enter the villa and plead the Spanish case, a deed of considerable diplomatic ability. De Vargas depicts himself in the "Journal" as one whose faith and devotion to the king are integrally related. He insists upon full submission to God and king; he never accepts only political surrender. In the "Journal" the soldiers and De Vargas himself serve as godfathers for the baptism of Indian children who were born during the exile of the Spanish. De Vargas consistently has the priests baptize and give absolution to those considered apostate. This is a ritualized way of recovering souls back from the devil, who stole them away during the rebellion (Espinosa 1940:82). By October 16, 1692, 969 children had been baptized; by the end of the expedition the number was 2,214 (Espinosa 1942:110). These acts, along with his repeated exclamation, "Praise be to the Blessed Sacrament" as both battle cry and greeting, suggest the pervasiveness of his crusading religiosity.

These few comparisons of the "Journal" and pageant illustrate how a figure from the past can become a contemporary symbol by interpretive selection and dramatic modification. Though the Caballeros de Vargas have consulted primary sources, they are not attempting to write histories so much as strengthen values and provide heroic images with the power to determine feelings and behavior. The De Vargas figure is a repository, a condensation, of the virtues which define in part what it means to be a modern, Hispano Santa Fean. Such Santa Feans could have selected Coronado or Oñate, or they could have selected the De Vargas of 1693, but they selected the De Vargas of 1692 instead. He is the prism through which Hispanic *ethnos* views *civitas* and *ecclesia*.

This De Vargas is a highly idealized heroic image. In fact, the seriousness of the image stands in considerable contrast to similar images in folk dramas like "Los Moros y Christianos," for example. In this play the drunkenness of one character provides comic relief in the midst of a serious battle. In contrast, the Entrada pageant places all of its emphasis on the dignity, competence, and piety of the central figure, so in this respect De Vargas resembles a modern movie hero more than a figure from New Mexican folk drama. The pageant has no humorous elements. One informant accounts for this extreme seriousness by telling how Santa Feans used to jeer and make fun of De Vargas and the Entrada. Hence, he and others set out to create an image with dignity. And now, he remarks, any jesting about De Vargas would result in "serious trouble" from the Caballeros de Vargas and perhaps even from the Hispanic community generally.

Dramatizing Hispano-Indian Relations

The Entrada pageant dramatically symbolizes the relations between Pueblos and Hispanos. Informants find questions about ethnic conflict painful so they are reticent on the subject. Some even deny that the fiesta and Entrada say anything about interethnic relations and view these performances as merely historical or imaginative. However, some Hispanos admit that the question of Indian participation in the fiesta is problematic and emotionally explosive.

At one time the roles of Indians in the pageant were played by Indians. Sometimes even a governor of a nearby pueblo played the role of Domingo (Marie 1948:131), but in 1973 all Indian parts were played by Hispanos, most of whom were children of the Caballeros de Vargas. The Caballeros whom I interviewed insist that they have done everything possible to attract Pueblo participation in the fiesta and Entrada. They say they have written to the Pueblos inviting their participation and even offered to pay for food and lodging as well as a fee, but the Indians simply do not show up, or else show up intoxicated. Fact and stereotype are distressingly tangled in such responses.

Intercultural endeavors during recent fiestas are the arenas of conflict and stereotyping. For example, during rehearsals for the 1973 Entrada, the De Vargas staff and some Indian baseball players, who were practicing nearby, almost came to blows over the pageant; the "peaceful reconquest" came very close to lapsing into a street brawl. Overt blows were avoided, but the tense moment is an example of what lies packed away in stereotypical and heroic symbols.

Hispano informants say the Caballeros have modified and

remodified the Entrada so that it will not be offensive to "our Indian brothers." After all, many of them insist, few, if any, of us are "bluebloods." Some Hispanos are emphatic on the issue: "Anyone who claims he is pure Spanish just does not know what he's talking about!" One hears this kind of response frequently, even from people who are intensely concerned about tracing their genealogies to the original Spanish conquistadors. The rhetoric of complete harmony and mutual appreciation, however, stands in contrast to symbols of conflict.

The intention of fiesta officials is to include Pueblos on an equal basis and to transcend ethnocentrism. Their intentions may be unimpeachable, but intentions are not identical with consequences. One Pueblo Indian, who identifies himself as a "realistic militant of sorts," states flatly that a few years ago the Fiesta Council was racist, although he considers the present council to be genuinely interested in Indian participation. However, that really does not make any difference to us, he concludes. The fiesta still does not celebrate anything which Pueblos could be enthusiastic about celebrating. Consequently, participation is steadily getting worse, and one prominent Pueblo leader declares that "a silent, unannounced, but effective boycott" of the fiesta has been growing among his people.

Caballeros account for their casting children in the roles of Indians by pointing to the lack of Pueblo interest and to their own lack of active adult members who could fill the roles. A few Caballeros think that the 1973 casting was unfortunate; others blame the Indians themselves. During the fiesta's American Indian Day, a Pueblo master of ceremonies sarcastically alluded to the tendency of his people to "get lost like children." Whatever the reasons for casting children as Indians, the pageant unfortunately played into the hands of an old stereotype, the "childlike primitive."

In 1966 an angry letter to the editor from a couple at San

Juan Pueblo criticized the "arrogant charge of apostasy and the blatant demand to repent as dramatized in the Entrada script" (*New Mexican*, September 15, 1966). The letter refers to the Entrada as the "most insulting of melodramas." Revisions of the script followed in 1967, but the charge of apostasy and demand for repentance are still present. So are Indian criticisms.

The 1967 script specifically tries in its opening scene to avoid making all Pueblo Indians appear rebellious and warlike. It lays ultimate blame on Naranjo, a man of mixed Spanish, Indian, and Negro descent, and upon a few Spanish governors. The blame is individualized and restricted to a part-Pueblo who used Popé, who in turn used the other Pueblos. Naranjo even refers to "these" Indians, as if he were not one of them.

Still, there is no way to change the basic fact that the Entrada celebrates an Indian defeat and a Spanish victory, even by blaming a few atypical Indians. The Entrada provides no Indian heroes. The Indian "ghosts" are made to return to "their rightful place in the past." They are not re-presented, as De Vargas is, so the Entrada presents only one scantily developed Indian figure, namely Domingo, who might serve as a contemporary Pueblo heroic symbol. But dramatically developing the figure of Domingo would have its complications too, since De Vargas says of him, "I recognized in him a conquerable heart and good will" (Espinosa 1940:88). Some Indians view such figures as "apples" (red on the outside, white on the inside).

Some have suggested that the Entrada's message is not the defeat of Indians. The 1972 fiesta program declares, "Realizing that the reconquest was not over one another but over violence and that the victor was peace and goodwill to man, this bloodless re-entry is the entrada which is celebrated during Fiesta" (*New Mexican*, August 20, 1972, p. 5). A concerted effort is being made to reinterpret the reconquest. If such statements ever go beyond stating the goal of the fiesta to describing the actual symbols and structure of the fiesta (and the Entrada in particular), Pueblo participation will become more probable.

Fiesta symbols sometimes covertly transmit messages Pueblo people find degrading and insulting. For example, considerable research and expense is involved in producing authentic costumes for the Spanish characters, but the costumes of the two Pueblo characters on De Vargas' staff are inauthentic. They wear headdresses of Plains Indian style, and they wear velveteen shirts and concho belts in Navaho style. Sometimes they even wear blue jeans and boots. At the time of the reconquest the Pueblos and Navahos were enemies, so in effect De Vargas' two *caciques* are clothed in enemies' clothing. In Santa Fe this oversight is not the result of mere ignorance about the differences between Pueblos and other Indian peoples, because during the controversy about the word "savage" engraved on the monument located in the Santa Fe plaza, many people defended leaving the monument intact on the grounds that "savage" refers to Navahos and Apaches, not Pueblos. That Navahos and Pueblos were at war during the time of the reconquest is quite well known.

Another example of fiesta Indian imagery is the dress of Popé and Naranjo during the pageant. Both are covered with body paint to darken their bare skins. If this were simply because Naranjo was supposed to have been black, only Naranjo would be covered with brown paint. Only a symbolic interpretation of skin colors can explain the actors' having to darken their skins at all. Skin colors are supposed to coincide with ethnic groups. Anglos in New Mexico frequently regard themselves as white men, but Hispanos of Spanish-American ideology insist that Spaniards were fair— "perhaps even whiter than you are." But in New Mexico, after generations of intermarriage, skin color alone is no longer an indicator of ethnic identity for any of the three major groups. The assumption that as a biological fact Indians are red, Hispanos are white or brown (depending on one's ideology) and Anglos are white is a poor one. The color distinction is largely symbolic even though it once may have had a firmer genetic basis. Therefore, when Hispanos feel that they must darken their skins to play the parts of Indians, they are symbolically dissociating themselves from the Indian side of their heritage. Yet, as I have already noted, few Hispanos verbally deny their Indian genetic heritage. Fiesta symbols and fiesta rhetoric sometimes convey conflicting messages which make it difficult for a Pueblo to participate.

The sum of the Entrada's symbolic message about intercultural relations, then, is one of intense ambivalence. On the one hand, a brotherly attitude is expressed toward Indians. On the other hand, there are subtle assertions of superiority, such as a father might have over a son, and there are indirect suggestions of cultural competition rather than cultural cooperation—one might call it "ethnic sibling rivalry."

So far we have only an unbalanced picture of the symbolic mode of handling intercultural relations in the public ritual of Santa Fe. The role of Anglos in this tricultural situation is not yet clear. Therefore, I want to turn to another pageant, performed in 1960, Siglos de Santa Fe (Centuries of Santa Fe).

Santa Fe as Drama

While the Entrada has a distant kinship to the early folk dramas of New Mexico, it has a closer kinship to other historical pageants, of which Santa Feans seem particularly enamored. Two of these were the Siglos de Santa Fe, performed in June 1960 to commemorate the 350th anniversary of the founding of Santa Fe, and the Entrada of Coronado, performed in 1940, the cuartocentennial of Coronado's *entrada* (exploratory "entrance"). I was able to interview some participants in the Siglos celebration, but few people remember the Coronado pageant, so I had to use Thomas Wood Stevens' account (1940). A large banner from the Coronado cuartocentennial still hangs on the plaza during the annual fiesta, but most participants either do not notice it or do not know what it is. The dramatic patterns and symbols of the Siglos, the Coronado pageant, and the Entrada overlap. In fact, the author of the 1958 Entrada script was instrumental in the production of the Siglos pageant; he says that he began with the Entrada script as a basis.[1]

The Siglos celebration was ten days long, from June 17 to June 26. It was the occasion of historical reminiscences, the printing of pictures of old Santa Fe, and a general displaying of the three cultural heritages. Typical of Santa Fe's historical-dramatic ethos is the following description of a time-capsule ceremony:

This climaxes the gathering and assembling of Santa Fe 350th Anniversary Momentoes, all of which are placed in a permanent container which will be buried in a public place and marked for opening fifty years from now, in 2010. Items selected for this container will include names of all the 350th Anniversary Committees, members of the Spectacle Cast, Anniversary Editions of the New Mexican, pictures of celebration events, histories of civic organizations, churches, schools and business organizations, Anniversary souvenirs and similar historical curios. Metro Goldwyn Mayer, producers of the award winning "Ben Hur," will make available films of the epic to be buried along with other historical items.[2]

---

[1] The following official credits are printed in the program booklet for the celebration: "Staged and directed by George S. Elias; Annabel Looker, assistant to Mr. Elias; Based on an outline by Ruth Alexander; Jack Looker, director of the celebration; 'A John B. Rogers Spectacular Presentation.' "

[2] This particular film is included because Lew Wallace, a former New Mexico governor, was author of the novel *Ben-Hur*. Preceding this time-capsule burial, twenty-six volumes of the novel in as many different foreign languages had been presented to the Museum of New Mexico.

The celebration, like most celebrations and fiestas in New Mexico, had its own queen and coronation. One day was dedicated to "moral rearmament." The same day was the occasion of an annual Corpus Christi procession led by the archbishop. The final day, designated "Prayers for the Future," was the occasion of the solemn papal coronation of La Conquistadora discussed in the first chapter. Other days were specially designated for ladies, Indians, and the armed forces. Armed Forces Day was particularly elaborate, involving an atomic energy display by the Los Alamos Scientific Laboratories, a Navy flying team, a SAC bomber fly-by, parachuting by paratroopers from North Carolina, and a Marine fighter corps team from a Pacific carrier. The celebration precipitated a general display of the military, religious, civic, and cultural power of the city.

The general chairman of the celebration, also one-time mayor of the city, explained the purpose of the celebration. His speech crystallizes the civic veneration of history and the extolling of dignity characteristic of public rhetoric in Santa Fe:

In exactly the same spirit of pride and reverence that we commemorate other important events in our history we want to call to mind the great events that happened here in our own Southwest. . . . We want to pay tribute and venerate the memory of the founders and settlers of this western part of our country. . . .
. . . We are not unmindful of the material benefits that our community may derive by reason of this Celebration. We can attract favorable state and nation-wide publicity through which Santa Fe may become better known. We have endeavored to create an impressive and enduring image of what Santa Fe really is. . . .
Lastly and very important is the fact that since all elements of our population are actively and enthusiastically participating in making this the most memorable event in our history, it can be reasonably expected that more harmonious relations, better understanding and greater cooperation will be the result of this effort.

. . . Let it be said that dignity, courtesy and respect were the out-
standing characteristic of each and every one of us as we paid tribute to the memory of the "caballeros" of 350 years ago. [*Siglos de
Santa Fe Program*]

This short statement of purpose is a veritable catalogue of
civic virtues: dignity, courtesy, respect, cooperation, harmony, pride, reverence, material benefits, and a good image.
Furthermore, religious terminology is rhetorically employed
to heighten the sanctity of the civic virtues; the attitude is
one of reverence and veneration.

The performance of the pageant lasted approximately an
hour and a half. It consisted of an overture, a prologue, and
twenty-four scenes and was divided chronologically into five
eras: Indian, Spanish, Mexican, "Gringo," and American.
Basically, the scenes were historical in nature, though some
fictional characters and scenes were introduced; they spanned
the time between pre-1610 to 1945.

The narrator, "Fray Sebastian," is dressed as a Franciscan
and is described as "rotund," wearing a "radiant smile," and
having "pixish" eyes. This choice represents an apparent recognition of the role of Franciscans in chronicling much of
New Mexico's history. A Franciscan is an apt symbol of continuity, as a narrator must be. Fray Sebastian describes
Santa Fe as one of the earliest "cradles of Christianity" in
America and as "the epitome of the American legend." Although he acclaims the "harmonious blending" of cultures in
Santa Fe, he tellingly omits laudatory adjectives for "Anglo"
and substitutes a derisive term: "of the proud Indian, the
pioneering Spaniards, the peaceful Mexicano, and the
Gringo." He then proceeds with a quick recitation of historical dates important to Santa Fe, beginning with 1610 and
culminating in the "1950's! *The Tourist Invasion.*" Curiously,
1693, the date of the bloody reconquest, not 1692, the date
of the peaceful reconquest, is included.

Scenes from the Indian period show Indians dancing a ceremonial which the narrator views as "rich in the tradition and steep[ed] in the superstition of the Red Man."

As Oñate arrives, the narrator tells the audience that Spain outranks its [English] rivals on the Atlantic Coast in terms of military, political, and ecclesiastical consequence; he displays a common Southwestern irritation with the cultural arrogance of "Easterners." Since Oñate says he has come to convert the Indians, a Franciscan finally lures the Indians out of hiding by playing music on a flute and later pantomiming the Lord's Prayer because of the language barrier. The padre cows a protesting medicine man with a cross.

When Don Pedro de Peralta founds the city of Santa Fe and builds the *palacio* (palace) as a "symbol of Spanish greatness," he chooses the name Santa Fe ("Holy Faith") in commemoration of the Spanish city of the same name, which was founded by Ferdinand and Isabella as they directed the final conquest of the Moors. Thus, the Peralta figure implies a comparison between the conquest of the Moors and the conquest of New Mexico. Both, after all, involve a crusade to enable the "holy faith" to triumph in the midst of "infidels."

Later, a figure portraying Father Benavides illustrates the church-state conflict of early New Mexico as he protests that the Indians working to build churches are not being paid; the conflict is slight as staged, since the governor immediately accedes to Benavides' wishes.

Next follows an abbreviated version of the Pueblo revolt of 1680 and a "ballet of fire" to symbolize the burning of buildings and churches, as a woman saves the statue of La Conquistadora and flees. As the pageant moves to the reconquest of De Vargas, much of the language comes directly from the 1958 Entrada script. De Vargas' El Paso vow is transposed to Santa Fe itself, and a woman playing the role of La Conquistadora appears on stage to assure De Vargas and provide strength for his mission, thus her dramatic role here is con-

siderably stronger than it is in the Entrada. Like the 1958
Entrada script, the Siglos script confuses, or at best, con-
flates the 1692 and 1693 *entradas*.

After the reconquest, a long episode in the pageant, the
play depicts the incursions of the French and the establishment of the Santa Fe Trail. Discussions onstage begin to
pose the question whether the growing presence of Gringos
or the Mexican Revolution is the biggest problem; the pageant merely declares that the Mexican Revolution has occurred without attempting to enact it.

After a quick succession of scenes depicting the City
Council's choice of Saint Francis as the city's patron in 1823,
the complaints of an underpaid schoolteacher, and a "Dance
of Seducation" [sic] of Governor Armijo by Doña Tules, the
"Gringo problem" comes to the fore. Mexican provincial governor Armijo objects thus to what an American is telling
him:

Granted what you say is true, [that is, that resistance will cause the
loss of property] what of my people—? Already you Americanos
have taken over our economic life. How long before you attack our
institutions and our customs—Are we just to exchange masters—
this time for one who speaks a foreign tongue? Are we to suffer like
our relatives in Texas? . . . We don't seem to have much of a
choice, do we?

Armijo's speech echoes the grounds of contemporary Anglo-
Hispano conflict as much as it does the beginning of Mexican-American conflict.

At this point, indicating the depth of feeling which marks
the Anglo invasion, the first and longest Spanish speech in
the pageant occurs. Earlier the narrator had asked Oñate if
he would mind speaking English; Oñate and the other characters comply. But the following speech shifts into Spanish:

The Americanos will march upon New Mexico. We cannot be reinforced in time. We can fight one suicide battle and die, or we can

run—or . . . we can make a deal and as amigos we can hold on to our lands, flocks, and trade. I have not committed you. Each will have to search his own heart: Those who stay will have to become Americans; those who wish may return to Mexico, secure in what you believe. It is up to you.[3]

The only other Spanish speech printed in the script also occurs at a sensitive point, as the mother of a pretty Hispano girl tells her to come away from the roving eyes of an Anglo soldier who has accompanied General Kearny in his claiming of New Mexico. The question in both cases is the same: "How shall Hispanos become and remain Americans without losing their culture?"

The speech above seems to be addressed specifically and intimately to the Hispanic members of the audience; the first few words of the Spanish speech are not translated even in the script. They are, *"Hermanos de sangre"* (blood brothers). This indicates the contemporary intensity and relevance of the speech beyond the bounds of the pageant itself. If one compares the relations between Hispanos and Indians with those between Hispanos and Anglos as they are presented in the play, there are some obvious differences. The Hispanos have conquered the Indians, and in the Santa Fe of the play they exercise a benevolent, paternal superiority. They seek a kind of "pax hispanica." On the other hand, the Hispanos of the play must make a difficult choice between accommodation and flight, and accommodation threatens the integrity of culture, language, and custom. The difficulty of having to make such choices is still present in New Mexico as is evident from the fact that the pageants are largely in English.

Novena-processions, fiestas, and pageants represent an

[3] "Hermanos de sangre. Los Americanos vendran a Nuevo Mexico. De Mexico es imposible obtener ayuda en tiempo. Podemos batir asta la muerte o podemos avisari altacon o podemos tratar con ellos can los Gringos, y asi asegurar nuestros terrenos y poseciones. Y no me he comprometido a nada. Cada uno tendra que hace su propia decision."

Hispanic attempt to mitigate the choice so alternatives are not so absolute. They are symbolic ways of "being American" and retaining Hispanic identity. The desire to accommodate with dignity and without capitulation accounts for the tremendous amount of energy and money spent on producing public ritual and drama. Of course, Anglos and Indians have to make similar accommodations, but the rituals and symbols we are considering here belong primarily to Hispanos.

But let us not lose the narrative thread of the Siglos pageant. As the American flag is raised over Santa Fe, a proclamation is read which commits the United States to respect the religion and church property of largely Catholic New Mexico. Religion, then, becomes the most important single social institution through which Hispanic New Mexico can retain its cultural ties with Spain. A short scene follows, depicting the French-born, first bishop of Santa Fe, Bishop Jean Baptiste Lamy. Strangely enough, it depicts him in glowing terms which ignore his strong criticism of native *santero* art and the Penitentes, two strongholds of Hispanic-Christian culture.

A short vignette depicts a "fighting mad" Texan [4] of the Confederacy who is verbally put down by a Union soldier, as the narrator reminds the audience that the New Mexico Territory contributed more men per capita to the Union army than any other state or territory in the union. Then follows an excerpt from Abraham Lincoln's Gettysburg Address.

The concluding part of the pageant, "The American," begins with a rapid-fire sequence of scenes: Lucien Maxwell,

---

[4] *"Tejano"* (Texan) is frequently a pejorative for any Anglo who is considered pushy, wealthy, or prejudiced toward Hispanos. This concept, in part, accounts for the juxtaposition of pageant roles designated in the script as "Union Soldier" and "Texan" rather than "Union Soldier" and "Confederate soldier."

founder of the First National Bank of Santa Fe; Lew Wallace, governor and author of *Ben-Hur;* the railroad; covered wagons; hoedowns; arriving Anglos; Billy the Kid; Geronimo; mining booms; the social entertainment provided by Governor Prince and wife; cancan dancers; "culture" fads (such as food, fashions, opera); the Spanish-American War; New Mexico statehood; Pancho Villa; World War I; the arrival of artists and writers in the 1920's; the Depression; World War II.

All of these scenes are mere short flashes until World War II is depicted. Santa Feans are still proud of the participation of their "boys" in the Bataan Death March. Some informants simply digress into this story when asked how they might feel about using an image of La Conquistadora in a modern military engagement. The pageant slows down to depict anguish over the "boys at Bataan," and Fray Sebastian, the narrator, takes time to comfort a girl whose fiancé has been killed in the war by saying, "Now, Viola, you mustn't waver in your faith—there will come a time when Edward will return to you if it is God's will." G.I.'s onstage wish for the good enchiladas back home as the pageant and the war both end with a staged, pyrotechnic explosion of the atomic bomb, developed at nearby Los Alamos. The epilogue is simply "the long heralded moment" of the arrival of the queen of the Siglos celebration escorted by four *conquistadores.* She concludes the pageant by urging her audience to become "ambassadors for Santa Fe" and by announcing the national anthem.

Drama and Conflict

The Siglos celebration and pageant help us understand the public ritual of Santa Fe in a way not provided by the Entrada and La Conquistadora rituals alone. Because it dramatically chronicles the whole of Santa Fe's history, it provides a view of the symbols which mark Hispanic encounters with

Anglo culture, whereas the De Vargas pageant focuses solely on Hispano-Indian interaction. I have already tried to point out that the encounters differ. Symbolically, the Siglos Indian appears as a dancer and convert in the early part of the play; he does not appear at all in the latter part. The Hispano appears as priest, conqueror, soldier, and chronicler-supervisor (the narrator). The Anglo is symbolized as Texan, soldier, artist, and invader-tourist; he does not appear in the early part of the play. The Hispano is the basic source of continuity of both the plot and structural framework of the pageant. History in the pageant does not begin until Hispanos begin to record it, and until Fray Sebastian, as symbol of this historical consciousness, begins to recount it. Indians are present in the beginning, Anglos in the end, but Hispanos in beginning, middle, and end.

If one considers only the history (that is, written accounts of the past), not the culture, of Santa Fe, it is clear that the play is accurate in this respect. Although Indian cultures precede both Hispano and Anglo, historical records as such began with Spaniards, and, as far as I can tell, the most historically minded Santa Feans are probably Hispanos. I mean to suggest not that there are no important historical studies being done by Anglos and Indians but that Hispanos stake their prime claims in the area of history while the other two cultures, as they are represented in Santa Fe at least, stake their primary interests elsewhere. Religion, along with the drama, folklore, and art which draw upon it, is crucial for maintaining the Hispanic-Christian culture, and its primary way of understanding religion is historical. One finds this confirmed over and over again in interviews and discussions. Questions about the meaning of some practice are answered, not with a mythical story or an account of the function of some act, as is often the case in other religio-cultural traditions, but with a historical recitation. Futhermore, history is viewed metaphorically as a drama, and, of course, when history is translated into pageant, it literally becomes drama. Drama is not merely something one performs, it is something one lives as a history. This, I take it, is the meaning of informants' unceasing references to their city as "historic and dramatic Santa Fe."

In Santa Fe, as in the Siglos pageant, Hispanos occupy a mediating position. In more than one sense, Hispanos are "between" Anglos and Indians; they are the hinges on which the door of the city swings. Chronologically, they come between the Indian and Anglo presences in New Mexico. They are between in another important respect: they have intermarried and intermingled with both other cultures in a way not typical of either Anglos or Indians. Anglo-Indian intermarriage is rare in contrast to Hispano-Indian and Hispano-Anglo intermarriage. Religiously, Hispanos again appear in the interstices. Their Catholicism links them to Indians in a way the Protestantism of most Anglos in New Mexico does not; Pueblo Indians are likely to be Catholics. The same pattern holds true linguistically; Indians spoke Spanish long before they spoke English. What little synchronous cultural continuity there is among the three cultures is projected as diachronic, historical continuity in the Siglos pageant, and the source of that continuity is largely Hispanic, hence the importance of Hispanically related symbols to the public life of Santa Fe.

Language itself is usually a good barometer of what is happening culturally in Santa Fe. All of the public dramas discussed here are largely in English; Spanish appears in crucial spots and the Pueblo languages do not appear at all. In the Catholic Mass Spanish tends to appear in the most intensely sacred parts. In Siglos de Santa Fe it appears in episodes that are still painful, emotionally loaded, and likely to become issues of cultural conflict. I take this use of Spanish to mean that although Anglos dominate Santa Fe in terms of economic "size" and "weight," Hispanic culture dominates the structural joints of the city; Hispanic symbols tend to be coextensive with civic symbols. Superficially viewed, Anglo commercial and political values are on top, but below the surface, one finds Hispanic symbols marking most of the hinges between *civitas, ethnos, ecclesia,* and *civilitas.*

Anglo and Hispano cultures have to accommodate themselves to one another. Hispano culture was and is strong enough to elicit cultural compromise from the Anglos. In the midst of mutual accommodation, each culture asserts its superiority, but what keeps the conflict from becoming as overt as it is in some other areas of the state is that the claims to superiority are on different levels. Each can be "superior" in its own way and in its own relatively distinct sphere—hence, coexistence.

Overt mention of social conflict and cultural competition is almost absent during the public, ritualistic occasions we have been discussing. The religious occasions look for cultural reconciliation and harmony symbolically in Christ and eschatologically in the Kingdom of God. Therefore, it is left to public drama to handle symbolically and indirectly the facts of cultural change and ethnic conflict. This practice has a distinct advantage. If one begins to enact the conflict-dominance theme in an historical pageant, a conflictive situation can be avoided with two disclaimers, both of which are offered by informants. On the one hand, an informant can say, "Oh that's in the past, not today." On the other hand, he can say, "Oh that's just a play; it's not real." Public drama can make assertions about touchy situations without actually precipitating them, because any particular issue can be banished either to the past or to the never-never land of the imagination. Hence, it is not unusual for participants stoutly to defend the importance of the Entrada but later suggest that it is "only" historical or "only" a play.

However, I would maintain that *every* symbol in a ritual or drama expresses some presently held value or belief, even when it does so in the guise of saying something about the past. Whereas a historian might have asked how accurately the pageants portray the past, I have tried to show that the symbols of these pageants are able to invest figures of the past with contemporary meaning. That this is an interpretive procedure not altogether foreign to Santa Feans is evident from the rhetoric of the pageants, which typically calls for peace, coexistence, and harmony after having dramatized the conquests and cultural intrusions of the past.

The Development of the Fiesta

Having now considered two pageants, one of them occasional (Siglos) and the other annual (Entrada), I want to offer a historical perspective on the fiestas. Informants have a great deal to say about the fiestas of the old days, for instance, that they were less Anglo dominated, more religious, more thoroughly local, and less elitist. In an attempt to know the difference between ritualized complaining and historically considered observation, I studied issues of the *New Mexican*, since its descriptions are usually rather thorough at fiesta time. I selected data at approximately ten-year intervals.

An editorial of September 5, 1919, spoke of "this first staging of the Santa Fe Fiesta" (p. 4), suggesting that it had not been held for quite some time. Actually attempts to revive the fiesta had begun in 1912, but the war kept its celebration to a minimum until 1919, even though in 1913 the city decided to claim the tourist-attracting title, "Oldest City in the United States." Despite advice that St. Augustine, Florida, already claimed the title, some Santa Feans argued that they should not accept "second place" and proceeded to make the claim anyway.

No small impetus to the revival which began in 1919 was the return of American soldiers from World War I. General John J. Pershing was invited to the fiesta but could not attend, so the commander of the U.S. Marines and a Navy rear admiral attended instead. The fiesta started on a patriotic note which has been re-echoed ever since. The fiesta lasted for three days, each with a distinct emphasis: Indian, Spanish and "patriotic."

The Knights of Columbus portrayed Franciscan missionaries, and headlines proclaimed, "Stage Coach Attack by Red Indians to Be Picturesque Start," and "Texas Cowboys to Give Real Wild West Show Here Friday." The De Vargas figure read his proclamation of mercy to the Indians, as "motion picture men" photographed the event for showing all over the country. There was no De Vargas pageant, simply an entrance and proclamation. De Vargas, played by the local sheriff, referred to the Indians as "savages, the enemies of Christianity and civilization." An enthusiastic reporter declared that this was the first time in history that Pueblo ceremonials had been performed outside the pueblo and kiva in all their sacred detail. Santa Clara did the "Matachines," one of the "weird dances of Pueblo Indians." And paralleling the De Vargas entrance was a ceremony in which the American flag was raised and General Kearny's speech read.

The fiesta of 1919 began with a strong cowboy-and-Indian ethos; by 1927 the tone was becoming increasingly tricultural. The fiesta did not get its feet firmly on the ground until 1926–1927, when Edgar L. Hewett of the American School of Research produced a collection of papers for fiesta use (Hewett 1926). These papers laid the groundwork for Santa Fe pageants and were intended to root the drama in the history and culture of Indians, Hispanos, and Anglos from prehistoric times to the time of the annexation by the United States.

The *New Mexican* of September 6, 1927, asserted that this was the third year of a new public drama referred to as the "Pageant of Old Santa Fe." This pageant, apparently originating in 1925, was directed by Thomas Wood Stevens of Chicago. According to Stevens, he drew on the previous works of Ralph E. Twitchell, F. S. Curtis, Jr., and Lansing Bloom. Stevens claimed to have produced over thirty pageants of various kinds. The pageant described in the *New Mexican* was not the modern De Vargas Entrada at all but a dramatization of the history of New Mexico, consisting of twelve episodes, the most dramatic of which was a battle scene between Coronado and the Indians (September 6, 1927, p. 1). The two-and-a-half-hour presentation covered the period from conquest to settlement and concluded with a masque in which the Spirit of the Land called upon the spirits of gold, air, water, and fire to destroy the invading explorers and missionaries (August 20, 1927, p. 2).

The pageant itself was clearly more akin to the 1960 Siglos de Santa Fe than to the present fiesta Entrada. And occurring along with the 1927 pageant was the "Procession of Triumphal Entry of De Vargas, the Conquistador," which was not a pageant so much as an equestrian ride-in accompanied by a planting of the cross and reading of formal pardon to the Indians. The present-day De Vargas Entrada is a combination of the subject matter of the early triumphal entry and the dramatic form of the early pageants. Also included in the 1927 fiesta were productions of "Los Moros Y Christianos," "Our Lady of Guadalupe" and a Billy the Kid melodrama (August 19, 1927, p. 5, and September 3, p. 1). It is obvious that no single dramatic production was viewed as central, as the contemporary De Vargas Entrada is.

Nineteen twenty-seven was the year in which the Chamber of Commerce transferred the administration of the fiesta to an independent corporation in which any individual or business could buy membership and a vote for ten dollars. The change in organization was eminently successful because by September 2, the *New Mexican* announced that membership fees had exceeded the goal of $4,000, which is more than the amount of contributions made in 1973. Daily lists in the newspaper testify that monetary contributions to the administering body of the fiesta were stronger then than now.

Participation too had its rewards. A one-hundred-dollar prize was given for the best costume at the Conquistadors' Ball; nothing was given in 1973. Stores were asked to close so employees could participate, and much time was spent getting ready for the financially rewarding competition among participants. Prizes were given for Indian dances, Indian costumes, Indian musicals, Spanish dances and folk dances, and the cash amount in the Indian categories usually was twice that in any other categories.

At least eight pueblos pledged their participation. Many Indians arrived in groups as large as 150, and publicity for the fiesta, which appeared in all seven Chicago newspapers, used an Indian eagle dancer, not the modern stylized conquistador, as its symbol (August 17, 1927, p. 6). The streets were described as "full of real Indians." Also, one article told how Episcopalian, Methodist, Baptist, and Presbyterian women were making costumes for the fiesta; as of the time of the article, the Catholic women had not yet been heard from.

By the time of the 1937 fiesta a distinctly religious note was becoming evident. The fiesta was being described as a combination of worship and fun. Masses were held, and La Conquistadora was being referred to, though under the erroneous title "Our Lady of Victory" (September 8, 1937, p. 4). Mention was also made of a "La Conquistadora procession," but probably this referred to the replica used in the procession to the Cross of the Martyrs rather than the early summer novena-processions. The reason for not using the real statue was cited as a long-standing prohibition of Archbishop Lamy, who wanted the original statue protected. By 1937 the fiesta was being regarded as a festivity in honor of De Vargas' 1692 reconquest.

In 1947 the Entrada was performed by the Catholic War Veterans (August 30, 1947, p. 1). The cathedral rector criticized the lack of dignity in the coronation dances, while a fiesta sermon declared that "ownership and religion are the only sure antidotes against atheistic communism." This speaker, a bishop, insisted, "An ownerless and landless population suffers from an inferiority complex." Hence, "the Latin-American pioneers of this area" should resist communism lest they become "peons" and "migrants" (September 2, 1947, p. 3). And in 1947, as in 1973, burglers and robbers used the festivities to cover their activities and keep the police busy.

By 1957 the crowning of the fiesta queen was being treated as the principal event, with a traditional kiss expected of the mayor (August 30, 1957, p. 2). The fiesta proclamation was being described as a direct result of a pledge by DeVargas. There also began around 1957 a noticeable trend to look back to fiestas of the past in an effort to discern what should be the true nature of the fiesta. By 1957 people felt that the fiesta was a tradition and that all traditions should have their noble purposes and historical reminiscences.

It is plain that Indian and non-Catholic participation in the fiesta have eroded since its modern inception. This, along with the fact that Anglo names are more frequent in accounts of earlier fiestas, suggests that a process of Hispanicization has occurred between the fiestas of 1927 and 1973. A reporter in 1957 cited Gustave Baumann as describing the early "Twitchell Pageants" of the 1920's as "an Anglo chorus warbling Spanish songs" (August 30, 1957, p. 9).

The fiestas of 1926 and 1927 were of particular importance because they attempted to break down the elitist "walled in" pageants and added free productions so the whole city, not just the wealthy, could participate. This proletarian rebellion led by artists resulted in an open fiesta. Only in the 1920's did Santa Feans begin to attempt systematically to tap the Hispanic heritage and de-Anglicize the fiesta (cf. LaFarge 1959:295, 302). The 1920's and 1930's were decades of intense interest in the Hispanic heritage. These were the years of Anglo "Penitente hunting" and of the establishment of societies for the preservation of Hispanic culture. So, contrary to the contemporary complaint of increasing Anglicization, the development of the fiesta has been toward an Hispanicization of the dramatic aspects of the celebration. To be sure, the contemporary fiestas have included more and more events and involve more and more tourists, but the symbols themselves have become increasingly Hispanic.

Furthermore, the early days of the fiesta were far more secularized than those of contemporary times. Early accounts showed a trend toward competition with other public celebrations in other cities. A writer who thought the fiesta was "our one big advertizing medium" wrote, "We should have the same feeling of sportsmanship about our Fiesta as a college does about its rowing crew or football team" (August 24, 1927, p. 4). One writer compared the Santa Fe "Spanish carnival" to those of California and Florida, only to declare the others "artificial," "in the fashion of the movies" (September 8, 1927, p. 4). The competitive, secular ethos drove Santa Feans to compete with "little Taos" much as one would try to defeat a rival football team. It is a long way from the title "Queen of the Carnival" or "Queen of Pasatiempo" used in 1927 to the 1972 the fiesta queen's referring to herself as a symbol of La Conquistadora. The popular view that the fiesta has become less and less religious and more and more commercial-competitive simply cannot be supported.

In sum, from 1919 to 1973 the following trends are evident: (1) The fiesta pageants have become more culture-specific and their symbols narrower in scope. (2) The queen's importance grew steadily until early in the 1970's. (3) Indian participation has gradually receded until it is now limited to the sale of crafts and occasional dances. (4) Anglo participation has changed from initiating and organizing largely to spectating and buying. (5) Religious events have slowly grown in number. (6) The total number of events comprising the fiesta has gradually increased. (7) Ethnic or ideological conflict has remained the source of most of the dramatic pageantry (for example, cowboy-Indian, conquistador-Indian, Moor-Christian, the world wars, communist-capitalist, Anglo-Hispano). (8) Regardless of the style and scope of the public drama, it has consistently envisioned or proclaimed the end of cultural conflict, even while enacting it.

Fiesta Entertainment

Many fiesta participants categorize the pageants, along with the fashion shows, parades, and musical performances, as simple entertainment. However, those who supervise the fiesta tend to differentiate the Entrada from the other spectator events, and I have chosen to follow their distinction because of the Entrada's etiological function of ritualizing and dramatizing the origin and justification for the whole fiesta complex. Those who participate more than casually do not view the Entrada as mere entertainment, nor do I. However, participants, whatever their level of participation, often regard the events I wish to discuss now as nothing but entertainment. But I see in them a dramalike quality which prevents my omitting consideration of them; one might call them dramatistic, rather than dramatic, enactments. The entertainment events of the fiesta are functionally protodramas or protorituals; they are highly stylized, ceremonious occasions. Therefore they should be viewed as part of the ritual-drama complex of the fiesta.

Pre-fiesta events (see Appendix B) are largely musical entertainment. The function of many of them is to generate "fiesta spirit," and much of the rhetoric used by the masters of ceremonies draws upon the vocabulary of the cheerleading associated with athletic events. Complaints that resemble those heard in public schools about "school spirit" are frequent, and they often make their way into the media in the form of letters to the editor or reminiscing articles on "how it used to be." It is something of a tradition to complain about the loss of fiesta spirit. This complaining is not limited to older participants, though the folk wisdom has it that they are the ones doing the complaining. I found many in their mid-twenties lamenting the passing of the "real" fiestas. In contrast to this lamenting, masters of ceremonies and officials typically declare this the "greatest fiesta ever." Nevertheless, they clearly recognize that spirit must be generated; it does not occur on its own initiative. Audiences are primed and asked for applause until they begin to offer it of their own accord. The most commonly cited enemies of the fiesta are inertia and passivity, and the Fiesta Council, in addition to its role as organizer and administrator, must rally enthusiasm. Rallying is strongest and clearest at the beginning of the fiesta, particularly in entertainment events. To cite one example, in describing the concluding dance of the Fiesta Show of August 28, a mistress of ceremonies noted that each year such-and-such a dance group does one special number as their "gift to the fiesta." The dance, she said, is such that every gesture and movement in it says, "Fiesta Spirit!" The Spanish style dance which followed drew wild applause from the crowd, which pushed up next to the stage area instead of hanging safely back as it had previously, as the dancers threw flowers into the air and released flying pigeons.

In terms of sheer time and money spent, entertainment events clearly rank first among fiesta events. Only two kinds of occurrences are continuous throughout the fiesta—entertainment and commercial (for example, the sale of food, art, jewelry). At virtually any time during the day or night either the central plaza or the carnival grounds at the edge of the city are filled with entertainment. The carnival is now on the edge of town as part of a recent decentralizing effort by the Fiesta Council. In past years conflict arose because of the congestion around the plaza area, much of it occurring between teenagers and carnival workers.

The entertainment consists largely of musical concerts, but also includes style shows, art shows, dances, variety shows, parades, and drawings for prizes. Music and singing are generally Hispanic. Strongest Anglo participation is in parades and fiesta melodrama (not to be confused with the Entrada pageant). Indian presence is visible primarily in dances and the selling of crafts. Indian attendance is obviously the most limited of the three cultures, but it is difficult to assess the relative proportion of Anglos and Hispanos.

Entertainment has two important functions during the fiesta. First, it is the prime source of continuity. It forms a background for the other events, thus giving people something to do between major events. Significantly, the Santa Fe plaza, the symbolic center of the city, is dominated by entertainment and economic activities, while the most overtly ritualistic and dramatic events occur *ad limen*, away from the center.

The second function of the music is to be a continuous reminder of the Hispanic nature of the fiesta. Ethnicity is emphasized repeatedly by the fact that most of the rhythms are mariachi. In addition, much of the narration of these events is in Spanish, though this is not true of other events. That the music is not "mere" entertainment becomes obvious when participants are asked whether they would mind using the songs and rhythms of some other linguistic and ethnic tradition. "The fiesta would no longer be the fiesta," they say. The music is essential, not accidental, to what makes a fiesta.

The majority of speeches during the fiesta are English, but the majority of lyrics are Spanish. There seems to be at once a practical recognition that English communicates more information to more people but that the Spanish language is necessary for the perpetuation of Spanish culture and spirit. English is consistently linked to the transmission of information, while Spanish is linked to the creation of what some participants call "atmosphere," "mood," "tone," and perhaps more frequently, "color." So entertainment, specifically the language and style of music, is crucial in communicating to Hispanos that this is their celebration, even though they share it with others as an offering to the *civitas* and though the English language and Anglo economic power play such a large part in it.

The rhythmic sounds of the fiesta are Latin, and rhythms communicate moods more effectively than discursive, spoken language. Rhythms "move" us. As Anthony Jackson (1968:293–299) points out in his short essay, "Sound and Ritual," highly rhythmic sounds of music have a neurophysiological effect. We feel the power of music even when the words are not understood. The music emanating from the plaza bandstand both literally and symbolically pounds Hispanic rhythms into the heads of fiesta-goers. Some find themselves repeatedly humming tunes and singing Spanish lyrics, even though their Spanish is less than fluent. The cultural impact of the entertainment cannot be overlooked just because it is nonverbal or so obvious. Its very obviousness tends to make participants unaware of its effect, and thus more unconsciously receptive to it.

Entertainment has another important function, a civic-civil one. One can hardly miss the pervasive presence of city officials and fiesta royalty. Symbolic personages are on exhibition. The Exhibicion de Modas is not only an exhibition of fashion but of people who are symbols of the citizenry of Santa Fe. Entertainment is not simply performance by entertainers; it is also the city's viewing itself on exhibition in the form of exemplary roles. That De Vargas, his staff, the queen, and her court are not merely in attendance because they enjoy the performances is evident from their being placed where they can best be seen by audiences, not necessarily where they can best view the entertainment. They serve as living icons of ethnic and civic virtue. Recognition of civic virtue usually occurs during the entertainment events. These are occasions for long lists of introductions, the presentation of certificates and plaques of appreciation, the presentation of gifts, the expression of gratitude—all rituals of commendation aimed at the flow of *ethnos* into *civitas* and vice-versa. Of course, I am not suggesting that people do not enjoy the entertainment, nor that entertainment is but a propaganda device, but I am suggesting that it has a serious function in addition to its obvious function of entertaining.

Fiesta dress ought not be understood simply as decoration or adornment. In the first place, the mourning of the lack of fiesta spirit sometimes takes the form of a complaint that people are not wearing costumes as they used to. Exterior clothing is interpreted by fiestaphiles as indicative of interior spirit. An article by Oliver LaFarge in the *New Mexican* (c. 1959) expresses an attitude often echoed in conversations with fiesta goers:

All sorts of things can be done—provided the crowd is in a mood of participation, not merely waiting for another free show to be put on. What we have these days is a dense mass of people in everyday dress crowded in front of the bandstand, passively absorbing whatever the authorities offer them. What we have now is in no important way different from what can be had in a thousand other places. A little more stress on Mexican music and dancing is all.

Strolling about the Plaza has ceased to be interesting. The crowd can no longer have fun looking at itself. Nothing spontaneous happens. A very important part of what once made Fiesta famous was the way all the people got into it, the rather simple, unprofessional, folk character of so much of what went on.

At the heart of this, I think, is that matter of wearing costumes. People who dress up express a mood, but also, they put themselves into a mood. Costume affects behavior.

To stimulate a renewed interest in fiesta costume the Fiesta Council instituted in 1973 a judging of dress and offered cash prizes in the following categories: (1) Indian, (2) modern, (3) Spanish colonial, (4) territorial, (5) Mexican. The classification broke down during the competition and judging, because not all costumes neatly fit into an appropriate category, and it was clear that these categories would have to be revised for the next year because they failed to account for the cultural assimilation and syncretism embodied in fiesta dress.

The fiesta is a time for the display of turquoise and silver jewelry on both men and women, especially women. The most prestigious piece is the traditional squash blossom necklace, and it is a good example of the problem created by classifications of symbolic dress. The necklace is made of silver and typically is studded with turquoise and occasionally red coral. The beads are stylized squash blossoms; a crescent hangs as the pendant. Some authorities say that the squash blossoms were originally pomegranates, and the crescent, a Muslim crescent moon introduced to the Spaniards by the Moors. Spaniards, however, do not make most of these necklaces; Indians do. They are worn by all three cultural groups. The problem is whether this piece of jewelry is modern, Indian, or Spanish. The difficulty of judging fashion categories is obvious.

What a person wears during the fiesta is not an accurate symbol of his ethnic commitments, though it is a better indication of his regional and civic ones. One of the fashion shows partially overcomes the categorizing dilemma by speaking of "fiesta styles." This manner of designation suggests that the fiesta generates temporary "culture" which is not identical with the ordinary cultures of any of the three major ethnic groups. At least symbolically, fiesta dress transcends the usual ethno-cultural divisions. But, of course, fiesta time is not ordinary time, thus the "temporary culture" it creates is fleeting and incapable of sustaining a city for more than a few days. The fiesta, insofar as it is a culture of *civitas*, is a kind of superculture. It seems to rest on top of the other cultures and comes into play only four days out of the year. This conclusion is based not only upon my observations about styles of clothing, but on a discernible fiesta ethic which is also generated and noticed by participants, especially those who sell wares during this time. Many of them comment that they do things, eat things, say things, and think things during this time that they would never do during the year. For example, overcharging is justified during the fiesta by persons who would consider it unethical at any other time.

But back to the matter of costume. One informant who has participated in the fiesta for many years and who always dresses for the occasion, made a typical response to my questions about the meaning of dress. I reminded him that Oliver LaFarge had remarked that nineteenth-century pioneer poke bonnets were out of place in the fiesta. I asked whether as a Hispano he would prefer to see adherence to seventeenth-century Spanish colonial costuming. He responded, "Well, by that standard even Mexican costumes are out of context too. I see no reason for such a rigid view of fiesta dress. As a boy, I just wore a red sash and white pants. What is important is not the culture or the period represented but simply that the clothing is different. People should just wear any kind of festive attire."

The syncretistic quality of fiesta attire precludes a view of dress as an ethnic symbol. In this respect the dress conveys a symbolic message different from that conveyed by fiesta music or Entrada. If the music proclaims, "This is an *Hispanic* city," the dress proclaims, "This is an Hispanic *city*, and this is fiesta, a time of civic ritual celebration."

Dancing, like music and costume, helps generate a fiesta spirit. The fiesta is an occasion for a flurry of folk dancing, most of which is performative; it is done for spectators. Not all the folk dancing is Spanish or Mexican in style, though most of it is. Performative folk dancing is largely the product

of groups specializing as a hobby in the learning and preservation of folk dances from Eastern Europe, Spain, Mexico,
and rural America. Many of these groups are middle-aged
performers for whom a folk dancing club serves as a combination of civic organization, service club, and recreation
group.

What one might call "polite" dancing occurs primarily during the two balls and during some of the private parties given
over the course of the fiesta. At these events ritualistic elements go beyond the usual polite dance format. At the *Gran
Baile de los Conquistadores* and the De Vargas Ball, as well as a
private dance given by the De Vargas figure for his staff, the
queen, her court, and friends of all of these, there are proces-
sionally ordered ceremonies of entry, sometimes announced
as a "grand entry" or "grand march." These are occasions for
short speeches, exchanges of gifts, and introductions of all
the fiesta royalty; at these dances the De Vargas figure and
queen are paired with their spouse or escort, respectively,
whereas at most other events De Vargas and the queen are
paired.

Ritual gestures of the *civitas*, rites of courtesy, are most
concentrated at polite dances. I have in mind gestures like
shaking hands, slapping on the back, bowing, curtsying,
marching in lines and patterns, tipping the hat, bestowing
and exchanging gifts, opening doors for others, toasting, insisting on paying, applauding, standing in others' presence,
"viva" shouts, escorting, carrying the trains of dresses, ad-
dressing by formal titles, and kissing.

In contrast to these polite dances, pervaded as they are by
civic rituals, are the peoples' dances (bailes de gente) on the
plaza. Whereas the polite dances are held indoors at a local
school gymnasium and are not only orderly but formally ordered (at least at the beginning), the peoples' dances are generally disorderly and occasionally the scenes of violence.
They are attended primarily by teenagers and are marked by

courting and group solidarity rites, some of which are illegal, but they are generally ignored by the police unless violence seems imminent. The styles of behavior at the two kinds of dances are noticeably different. During the polite dances people sit, most of them drinking whiskey. During the peoples' dances people mill around the plaza, many of them drinking beer or smoking marijuana. Both groups play Hispanic music; and although the musical style in the balls sometimes deviates to slower, traditional favorites and the music of the plaza dances deviates into acid rock, both typically return to the same Hispanic rhythms and lyrics.

Indian dances are also performed at the fiesta, on American Indian Day (see Figure 4). They begin with a proclamation by the governor and a reception of the proclamation by representatives from the pueblos. However, in 1973, neither the governor nor an official Pueblo representative appeared. Instead, the governor's wife read a proclamation in the presence of the master of ceremonies, who was an Indian. The proclamation declared that the day was American Indian Day because of the "unique culture" and "contribution to society" of American Indians. The Pueblo master of ceremonies responded, "Every day is American Indian Day. Please tell that to your husband for me." Afterward, the master of ceremonies implied that the absence of Pueblo officials was not accidental, and his own response to the governor's wife foreshadowed what was to follow during the Indian dances.

The crowd for the Indian dances is the largest crowd for any entertainment event occurring at the plaza bandstand. The dances are not the sacred dances of the Pueblos but are designed specifically for performance and competition, and they include fast and slow war dances, a Plains two step, hoop dances, circle dances, a belt dance, a blessing dance, and a shield dance.

Punctuating the intervals between dances were humorously barbed comments, which the largely Anglo audi-

Figure 4. Indian dancers sitting below a painting of a conquistador

ence cheered and enjoyed, even though many of the barbs were aimed at them. The master of ceremonies ridiculed prejudices about Indians while at the same time generating an atmosphere of festivity: "How many of you have seen a *real* Indian?" he asks. Some hands go up, but the master of ceremonies laughs and ignores them. "We are thinking of *not* surrendering." He then plays on the wording of a road sign labeled "falling rocks": "The last time we saw Falling Rocks he was chasing Custer's horse." Next he tells an Indian myth in which men were created by being baked in an oven: the black man is overdone; the white man, underdone. The "wonderfully golden, toasty brown Indian" comes out just right. Next: "I once was a cute little Indian!" Then: "Indians, not *conquistadores*, not Columbus, discovered America." And: "There was a time when Indians really came to the fiesta; I wonder what happened this time." And finally: "You folks have been real nice immigrants today."

Meanwhile, an extremely serious group of Indian dancers were doing what the master of ceremonies later referred to as a "cultural demonstration." Though the dances were not sacred, he insisted in an interview, the dancers were sacrally serious, because they were dancing the living symbols of their culture. Among the dancers was the first Miss North American Indian. Although the dance group was paid, and they made it clear that they were giving spectators the images they wanted to see, the seriousness of their performance was unmistakable even in the context of the master of ceremonies' humor and irony. The problem presented to the Pueblo dancer in a situation such as the fiesta is how he can "represent his Indianness," to use the words of one Pueblo, and do so in a way that is profitable without simply succumbing to images developed by the other two cultures. The Pueblo performance dances, in contrast to the sacred dances, are highly syncretistic, borrowing from other Indian groups and relying on technological devices, and they are more dependent upon their audience than when the audience is the Holy.

"Pagan" and Iconoclastic Drama

To conclude this consideration of public drama we turn to the parades, the melodrama, and the burning of Zozobra, all of which are viewed by informants as the most secular, most iconoclastic, least sacred, of dramatistic occurences during the fiesta.

Both the general parade and the children's parade are occasions for satire and ridicule of current events and values, including, in recent years, national issues such as women's liberation and the Watergate scandal and local ones such as dog leash laws and the use of plastic garbage bags. The general parade has earned the title of "Hysterical-Historical Parade" because of its combination of satirical and historical themes. Recently, however, both kinds of themes seem to be less prominent than they were a few decades ago.

In the mid-1930's a float featured a forty-foot dragon symbolizing Texas, which many thought to be impinging on New Mexico's water rights. Another, labeled "Dr. Quack's Remedies for the Uncultured," protested the suggestion that Santa Fe build a permanent culture center. In 1959 a controversy arose over the satirical elements in the parade. Many still refer to the "disgusting, filthy, and obscene" floats. One float, entitled "The Rape of New Mexico," bore a girl lying on her back with blood on her legs and dress. Phrases on other entries like "A burro kicked New Mexico in the ass-fault" were criticized, as were lampoons aimed at the incumbent governor. Catholic informants still remember with considerable disgust a float that depicted the Archbiship of Santa Fe playing golf. Many felt this in bad taste, even though the archbishop actually did play golf. The result was a controversy over censorship that finally issued in guidelines now administered by the 20–30 Active Club, which runs the general parade. The guidelines specify that no entry derogatory toward the church or any individual representing the church is permitted and also that no "obscene, lewd or immoral" floats are allowed. As a consequence the satire has become somewhat noncontroversial and harmless, although in 1970 a float advertised "The Best Government Money Can Buy," while another pleaded for the return of prisoners of war and those missing in action with a float called "Have a Heart Hanoi."

The desire to minimize conflict was still evident in 1973 as a float advocating a Chicano-sponsored boycott of a na-

tionwide foodstore chain was allowed, but was not announced when it passed the review stand. Incidentally, the
prize-winning children's parade entry of 1968 was called
"Los Fritos Banditos," a reference to a television commercial
strongly opposed by Chicano groups. So the iconoclasm of
the parades should not be viewed as a total freedom to criticize and lampoon. The implicit ideology of the parades supports fiesta values and supports and protects certain images.
One observer seems to have gotten his wish when he commented, "If this thing keeps on going like this every year, it
will sure ruin our fiestas. Let's keep politics out of our Santa
Fe Fiestas. There is a time for everything, but during Fiestas
let us be gay and not mix politics and ruin the atmosphere of
gaiety" (*New Mexican*, c. 1959).

The fiesta melodrama is largely a non-Hispanic affair. In
1973 the play, performed nightly by a local community theater group, was called "The Burgeoning Blight of Biggy's
Brown Bags." A string of scenes melodramatizing the events
of the year, it is issue oriented. The melodrama seems to
have become the arena for jesting social criticism—a role
once played more strongly by the Hysterical-Historical
Parade.

The most typical comment made regarding the 1973 melodrama by both spectators and performers was, "It was a pile
of shit." Some were expressing a value judgment; others
were punning on the fecal themes which provide the source
of continuity for the play. The script, anonymously written
by a local community theater committee, is filled with the
punning, pretentious vocabulary, and alliterations of melodrama. Its goal is openly but good naturedly iconoclastic. It
aims to break what it considers the idolatry of "scared cows"
by caricaturing, exaggerating, and satirizing. As one might
expect, the melodrama is marginal to the symbol system of
the rest of the fiesta (as iconoclasm generally is marginal to
public ritual), although the attendance and revenue from the

production are considerable. I have already commented on the absence of humor in the Entrada as compared to older, rurally supported folk drama. The three fiesta events marked by consistent and concentrated public humor are the melodrama, the children's parade, and the general parade. Humor is given its specific quarters, quite distinct from the historically and religiously oriented events.

The primary themes of the 1973 production of the fiesta melodrama were dog leash laws, garbage bags, and potholes in the streets—the latter two being the source of scatological punning. The melodrama makes explicit reference to the central symbols of the fiesta and links them to scatological themes:

What you see before you [an outhouse over a pothole in the street], my dear, is a functional monument [an allusion to the controversial plaza monument]. Don't be too hasty about moving it away. After all, it's conveniently located near the Plaza and it *is* Fiesta time. All we have to do is put a coin box on the door. Think of the traffic, think of the demand, think of the profit. Think of it, all those people sitting where De Vargas sat. It lives on in a sense of the majesty of history. And if you don't like that idea, I'll just rip this historic hovel apart and fill in your pothole with the debris. Think of the public outrage if the citizens should discover that your ignominious ineptitude has permitted the loss of not one, but two irreplacable historic treasures.

Taking De Vargas as a central symbol of the fiesta, I have already discussed two other symbols with antithetical relations to De Vargas, namely the Franciscan figures and Tijerina. In the Franciscan figures' case the antithesis is momentary, finally resulting in a complementary relationship in which humility supplements dignity. In Tijerina's case the antithesis remains, as De Vargas moves from dignity to humility and Tijerina's "Indo-Hispano" moves from humility, humiliation, and humble circumstances to dignity. The characters of the melodrama also stand in antithetical relation to

De Vargas, but they neither complement nor threaten De Vargas. The reason, I think, is because the melodrama's iconoclasm is thorough and all-pervasive. Instead of breaking idols in order to replace them with another absolute like God or justice, it replaces what it has broken with nothing. The melodrama turns upon itself and destroys itself as both drama and ideology. Consequently, when the play is over, so is the criticism; no one is significantly threatened by the melodrama, because it does not take even itself seriously.

Previous melodramas show a consistent tendency to employ "impure" language, concepts, and characters. Frequent reference is made to scatological and sexual matters, prostitutes, "dirty money," corruption, garbage, and pollution. The association of money, impurity, feces, and corruption is quite common in the history of religion; they serve as symbols of the profane state. The profane is not identical with the demonic. The profane is not so much antisacred as nonsacred; it is simply removed from contact, negative or positive, with the sacred. If devotees of La Conquistadora regard Tijerina as demonic, that is, in active opposition to what they consider sacred), they view the melodrama as profane (that is, irrelevant, in a different sphere, nonthreatening). The distinction I am making between demonic and profane is, perhaps, not a common one, but I find it necessary to distinguish between positively sacred, negatively demonic, and neutrally profane states. One laughs at the villain as long as he is melodramatically profane and thus self-defeating like a clown. But laughter turns to anger when he ceases to trip over himself and rises up in pride. The pride of the mustached villain, the pride of the new Indo-Hispano, and the pride of the Spanish conquistadors are not the same. Which of these is identified with the pride supposed to characterize Lucifer's challenge to God depends on one's social and cultural position. And it is clear that the Anglo iconoclasm represented by the melodrama is not the same as Reformation

iconoclasm, because Santa Fe's iconoclasts are also its icono-
philes, its archetypalists. The iconoclasm of the melodrama
is largely the negative moment in a process by which Anglos,
Protestants, and former Protestants come to terms with
Santa Fe's strongly symbolic ethos. Iconophilia belongs to
the same process which includes iconoclasm. Catholic piety
functions differently. It neither breaks nor loves icons; it uses
and venerates them.

The last event for our consideration, though one of the
first to occur during the fiesta, the burning of Zozobra, is
regarded by many participants as the most awesome event of
the fiesta. I suspect that if the giant, forty-foot effigy named
Zozobra (in English, "Gloom," "Worry") were hallowed by a
religious tradition, it could constitute the pinnacle of the fiesta for many informants. But Zozobra has no tradition outside the fiesta itself, so awe never turns into devotion, and
Zozobra, like the melodrama, remains a profanely removed
phenomenon. It is no threat to Hispanic Catholic religion.

Apparently the idea of burning "gloom" began with a
group of artists in the 1920's. Zozobra is a puppet made of
chicken wire, wood, cloth, and paper. The first one was
designed and burned in the 1920's by a prominent Santa Fe
artist, Will Shuster. Copyright and responsibility for the
event now belong to the Kiwanis Club, which inherited the
project from Shuster. Many fiesta goers regard this ritualistic
burning, rather than the De Vargas Mass, as the beginning
of the fiesta. If the number of people attending is any indication, the burning of Zozobra is the most popular fiesta event.

Zozobra looks a bit different each year, but his basic features communicate terror, destructiveness, and gloom. During World War II he was designed with slanted eyes and
nicknamed "Hirohitlmus." He is hung from a tall pole on a
hill so he can be seen by the thousands who watch his destruction. And his eyes, mouth, and arms are manipulated
by persons hidden behind the hill who control his move-

ments by means of long cords attached to the giant puppet. The immolation itself takes place at night in the midst of an elaborate display of fireworks, explosions, lights, and sounds (see Figure 5).

Long lines of bonfire and torches are lit as the Fire Spirit dressed in red begins his taunting dance at Zozobra's feet. The death of Zozobra, which is eventually induced by the Fire Spirit, who puts a flaming torch to Zozobra's highly flammable gown, is supposed to symbolize the death of gloom and the resurrection of gaiety and happiness sufficient to provide enough fiesta spirit for four days. One writer speaks of the rite as "a pagan ritual with overtones of a religious cult" (*New Mexican*, September 3, 1970, p. C2). Another writer observes, "As Christ died for man's sins, Zozobra dies for man's sadness year in and year out" (*Official 1972 Fiesta Program*, p. 23). Santa Feans, of course, have not overlooked the archetypal possibilities of this "modern mythical battle" between the spirits of gloom and fire. The Spanish term *zozobra* has religious overtones; it connotes moral pollution or guilt and does not merely mean "spoil sport" or "party pooper" as some current suggestions imply.

As the bonfires are lit and darkness comes, "little glooms" come out of Zozobra, dancing in white robes and descending the hill like rats abandoning a ship about to sink. Zozobra's moaning inundates the spectators through giant loudspeakers. The archaic sounds and stilted gestures of the effigy become increasingly animated and human as the Fire Spirit, imitating the dance of flames, leaps and taunts up and down the hill. Children in the audience begin to shriek and cry. Terror is intensified by the human traffic jam which presses spectators tightly against one another. Zozobra's groaning is punctuated by aerial bombs and suspended strings of colored fireworks which fill the air with noise and smoke. Children from about ages ten to fourteen are fascinated and climb over fences to get closer, despite the danger and repeated warn-

Figure 5. Zozobra, "Old Man Gloom"

ings from policemen. It is a heyday for children who are in their monster movie stage. For younger ones it produces tears.

At the peak of excitement Zozobra's groans become increasingly pitiful as if pleading to be spared. The Fire Spirit's dance becomes frenzied, and spectators scream for Zozobra's death. When the torch touches the effigy, it is quickly engulfed in flames and the pitiful groans become screams of panic. As the flames die down and a few sparks and cinders are still falling, the sounds fade out into the silence of death. Then follows a night of celebration, drinking, and mischief which resembles Halloween and the Mardi Gras.

Conversations among adults after the event testify to feelings of primal awe and fear, and some of the less traditionally religious observers even say these are the only authentically religious feelings they have during the whole fiesta. In an article on the retiring Fire Spirit dancer, a local writer even developed a speculative theory on the pyrotechnic origin of religion, insisting that the fascination with, and even worship of, fire is basic to man's religious impulse (*Viva*, August 26, 1973, pp. 6–7). His hypothesis about the origin of religion has no empirical support, but it is perhaps significant that the two events participants seem to consider most moving, the burning of Zozobra and the procession to the Cross of the Martyrs, both occur at night and involve the use of fire.

The procession, on the penultimate day of the fiesta, follows a Mass which commemorates the death of twenty-one Franciscan martyrs. It begins at the cathedral, where participants are given lit candles. Then the procession, which is usually quite long, winds its way to the top of a hill overlooking Santa Fe. At the top of the hill is a large cross beneath which a Franciscan priest delivers a sermon, usually related to the theme of death by martyrdom. The path is lit with bonfires and the cross is illuminated with large spotlights, thus creating a patchwork of strangely shaped shadows and impressive, winding rows of candles and bon-fires.

In both the procession and the burning of Zozobra the normal sounds of everyday life are radically altered. During the Zozobra drama-rite the noises are chaotic and bombastic; during the procession and subsequent sermon an awesome silence dominates. The usual church organ and mariachi-style guitar music are minimized or missing from both, except as preludes. Instead, one hears drums at the Zozobra burning and hand bells at the sermon of the martyrs. Both events occur on the edge of the city removed from the central plaza, and both involve unusual physical heights. Whereas the Zozobra burning is considered pagan, the procession and sermon are considered normatively Christian. Zozobra is an example of latent *ecclesia* and the Procession of the Martyrs of actual *ecclesia*. Both events touch the emotional centers of most participants in a way unmatched by any of the other events. Both are concerned with the theme of death—on the one hand, the death of the martyrs, and on the other hand, the death of gloom. In both rites some form of renewed life comes from the ritualized contemplation or enactment of death.

I heard only a few informants linking the burning of Zozobra with the Procession of the Martyrs. Popular conceptions tend to follow ecclesiastical views in keeping the two conceptually isolated. Yet the structural similarities are striking, and many informants mention both as high points. Some participants insist that Zozobra and the martyrs have absolutely nothing in common, the one being imaginative and "pagan" while the other is historical and Christian. But the literal disbelief in Zozobra as a supernatural entity does not seem to effect the awe his death elicits. To be sure, the martyrs are part of an ongoing, highly developed tradition and system of rituals, while the immolation of Zozobra is not. Zozobra is not likely to develop a cult. Still, feelings which informants identify as religious are evoked by one as well as the other, the crucial difference being that Zozobra has not spawned institutions.

The Feminine Icon

I told him to silence all of them [the Indians], for did they not remember that, when they were Christians, a saint or the Virgin was received with much devotion and on bended knee, not shouting, and that they should fall upon their knees? And through the divine will I succeeded in having them do so.

Don Diego de Vargas, *Journal*,
November 19, 1692 (Espinosa 1942:96)

It is my wish, with those with whom I enter, that they should first and foremost, personally build the Church and holy temple, setting up in it before all else the patron of the said kingdom and villa, who is the one that was saved from the ferocity of the savages, her title being Our Lady of the Conquest. . . . At the same time the said construction will be hastened, so that by our example the conquered will be moved to build gladly their churches in their pueblos.

Don Diego de Vargas to the Viceroy,
January 2, 1693 (Espinosa 1942:116)

Robert Bellah says of the relation between Marian devotion and American religion:

If the cult of Mary does not worship her as God it at least mediates divinity through a feminine image, the image of the mother of God, and so retains a dimension of religious experience that Protestantism has ruthlessly repressed. Indeed, much of traditional Catholic piety is redolent of earth religion. The cult of the saints tends to localize and concretize religious experience, and the emphasis on sacrament tends to give material form to spiritual vision. Yet, due to the special historical vicissitudes of the Catholic Church in America—its largely urban setting, the continual movement of the faithful—there is little connection, outside, perhaps, some of the older Spanish-speaking enclaves in the Southwest, between religious life and the American land. American Catholicism is not of the American earth the way Italian, French, or Spanish Catholicism are of the Italian, French, or Spanish earth.   [1973:224–225]

A study of La Conquistadora can be of particular importance since her domain is within the enclave of which Bellah speaks, but her shrine is in semiurban Santa Fe, which lends to her reign over the land a distinctly public character, as opposed to the naturalistic-folk quality Bellah finds in Marian devotion.

Santa Feans have a proverb which translates, "He who gathers with wolves will learn to howl." We have been investigating what kind of company La Conquistadora keeps as a clue to her meaning. Interpreting La Conquistadora in terms of her context in a symbol system is a necessity, because in contrast to many Marian advocations, she is surrounded by comparatively little theology or indigenous exegesis in the form of myths, miracle traditions, and theologies. Veneration of the icon usually takes the form of either a ritual, a drama, or a historical narrative about her role in the reconquest. This relative silence on the part of devotees requires the interpreter to depend less on what is said about her and more on what is done in relation to her.

La Conquistadora is a statue, an iconic symbol. As such, she is relatively immobile. Her iconic form is not inherently dynamic as a ritualistic or mythic form is. When an icon moves it does so only as part of a larger mythic or ritualistic movement. An icon is a thing in space, while a myth or a ritual is a process in time. Theologically speaking, the Virgin is "above" this icon, this thing of wood. Devotees, under stresses such as the theft of the statue, do recognize that the statue is "only a piece of wood," not the Virgin herself. Whereas a devotee might conceive of continuing devotion without the presence of the icon, he could not conceive of continuing without the stories of the Virgin or the rituals of the church. As symbolic forms, icons seem to have a latent dispensability that myths and rituals do not have. Nevertheless, the statue of La Conquistadora is not usually regarded as a mere piece of wood. Devotees have proven that they will pay dearly to keep it, because "it" is usually "she," and only crises induce interpretive separations between icon and heavenly personage.

God's presence in the word and elements differs from Mary's presence in her wooden statue. The bread is the body; the statue is not Mary in the same way. Iconic symbols, more than other symbolic forms, tend to keep devotees aware of the essentially transparent nature of symbols. Because devotees "see through" an iconic symbol more readily than through mythic or ritualistic symbols, "iconoclasm" usually connotes in the Christian world the destroying of painted or sculpted symbols, rather than narrated or enacted ones.

Icons have served Catholic Christianity in a way they have not served Protestant Christianity. Protestants have been more prone to channel devotion through mythic and, only secondarily, through ritualistic symbols. Both the veneration and the study of icons are quite highly developed in New Mexico. One does not fully understand La Conquistadora until he has understood the importance of sacred images to New Mexico Catholics. Marian devotion would survive the loss of any particular iconic representation of the Virgin, but it would not survive the loss of icons altogether. Icon and Virgin are typically inseparable as form and content—so much so that the Virgin herself sometimes is depicted as acting iconically, that is, statically. Even though the separation of Virgin and statue can be made, it usually is not; La Conquistadora is Our Lady.

The figure is twenty-eight inches high. Since it was probably made in the seventeenth century and not in New Mexico during the so-called Secular Period (1790–1850), it is not a *santo* in the more restricted, regional sense of the word. The term *santo* may refer generally to any sacred object or, more specifically, to sacred objects of a certain style of this period in New Mexico history. The two primary types of New

Mexico *santos* are *retablos* (paintings on flat boards) and *bultos* (statues). La Conquistadora is a *santo* only in the more general sense of the word. Like many Southwestern *bultos*, she is draped by devotees in acts of piety. Fray Angélico Chávez, in his "autobiography" of the statue, has her complain:

The images painted on flat pieces of board [*retablos*] are all most charming. But only a very few of the statues are true works of art; they even foreshadow by more than a century the style of art that is called modern. The vast majority, however, though well meant, and having admirably served their purpose in their day, are monstrosities unfit to represent holy Mary and the saints. . . . The bishops of Durango rightly condemned them, as did the first bishop of Santa Fe and his clergy regard them with strong disfavor.

Now that the collecting of them has become a fad, almost like that of collecting old shaving mugs, and the word *santo* has become an arty byword for old sacred images, many are prone to class me among them. Please, I am not one of them. [1954a:111]

Frequently the word "dramatic" is applied to the icons of New Mexico. Sometimes it is simply a laudatory term indicating how a viewer feels about a *santo*. He is "moved" by it, and movement is dramatic. But at other times the term applies to the distinctly human quality of some of the saints represented by the icons. For example, some *bultos* such as that of San Ysidro Labrador are carried through the fields to help the crops grow, and if results do not ensue, the saint may be set out in the field so he can feel the hot sun. Sometimes a *bulto* is burned and its ashes scattered on a field so the field can absorb its sacred power for fertility purposes (Shalkop 1967:24).

The *santos* as iconic objects have very little formal dramatic quality. Artistically, they do not move or flow. Their drama lies in the stories about them or rituals performed with them. Mills says, " 'Bultos' tend to be isolated figures engaged in no particular action which might interrupt the worshipper with a story of history. . . . The more static 'santos,' " he says, "inhabit a space of their own, a container of spiritual forces which would be hermetic were it not for the opening toward the worshipper" (n.d.:61).

These observations are applicable to La Conquistadora. The "drama of La Conquistadora" frequently mentioned by devotees does not reside in the artistic quality of the icon itself, nor even in her ritual processions, but rather in the myth, drama, and history which account for her presence in New Mexico. The statue has a regal air, both artistically and ritually, which separates it from the very human quality of the folk *santos;* according to some, this air befits the capital (and once royal) city in contrast to rural villages. People do not turn her face to the wall or put her away until she grants a request, as they still do with some intercessors like Saint Anthony. Some devotees say they do not bother La Conquistadora with petty requests. She is a Marian advocation with whom devotees interact formally as with a queen rather than familiarly as with a friend. The formality does not make the devotion offered her any less genuine or passionate, but it does distinguish this Marian advocation from others.

La Conquistadora is a lady of few deeds of the kind which devotees can recite in mythic stories. She performs the tasks of "keeping our faith," "helping De Vargas," "hearing our prayers," and "reigning over us." Primarily, she is a providential presence rather than a doer of miracles. When devotees want a specific task done, they are much more likely to invoke Our Lady of Lourdes, for example, than Our Lady of the Conquest. When they want to invoke the sweep of southwestern history and culture, they are much more inclined to turn to La Conquistadora.

Devotees use perhaps more frequently the appellation Maria Santisima than La Conquistadora. Although "Most Holy Mary" is understood as a synonym for "La Conquistadora," it is a broader term. It allows for easier movement to other Marian titles which are less regal and less civic in connotation. Only during special occasions such as the rituals we have been considering do devotees begin to speak of Most Holy Mary more specifically as La Conquistadora.

The statue of La Conquistadora is a regal icon with a public, rather than a folk, following. She is venerated, not so much by village people, as the term "folk" usually connotes, or by the masses, as the term "popular" suggests, but by the *civitas*. She is a symbol of *ecclesia* offered as sufficiently public to warrant being considered patroness of the city and the region. She has a quasi-official air. Her devotional objects (such as medals and pictures) are sold only at the "crown church," the cathedral, not, for example, at San Miguel Chapel, where most of the devotional objects for other saints and advocations are sold. This is consistent with her quasi-official standing. La Conquistadora is queen of the city, not a familiar peasant girl.

The saints are "heroes of holiness," and some Marian advocations function as heroines. Being a heroine implies that one is admired for some act or quality and that admiration leads to imitation. It also implies a dramatic plot in which the heroine performs her paradigmatic deeds. No one speaks of La Conquistadora as a figure to imitate, as they might refer to Our Lady of Sorrows. One venerates and respects her but does not presume to imitate her. Whenever devotees imitate Mary as a model, they usually refer to her under some other title. Of course, for devotees Mary is always Mary under whatever title, in whatever form. Our Lady of the Conquest, Our Lady of Sorrows, and Our Lady of Guadalupe are different connotations of the same denotation, the Virgin Mary, so I am speaking only of different emphases, not different virgins. In trying to isolate what is unique about La Conquistadora as a Marian advocation, I do not mean to imply that devotees do not accept the church's prescribed theological unity of the various titles and forms. I am suggesting that each advocation has relatively consistent contexts which lead devotees to feel that one rather than another advocation is the one to invoke on such-and-such an occasion.

The statue's most elaborate title, only parts of which are used in popular references to her, is "Nuestra Señora del Rosario, La Conquistadora, Reina y Patrona del Antiguo Reino de la Nuevo Mexico y de su Villa Real de Santa Fe" (Our Lady of the Rosary, the Conqueress, Queen, and Patroness of the Ancient Kingdom of New Mexico and the Royal City of Santa Fe). Both De Vargas and La Conquistadora, along with the city of Santa Fe, have elaborate names which are employed on particularly solemn occasions. The title, "America's Oldest Madonna," is usually reserved for publicity purposes and is more characteristically employed by the confraternity or in tourist publications than by the people in general. In addition to her long title and the shortened versions of it, all of the usual attributes of Mary are also applied to her and sometimes used as titles, for example, virgin, lady, mother. Other titles have also been associated with her—some of them at earlier times and some of them by mistake. She is closely associated with Our Lady of Remedies, for example, and she has been mistakenly identified with Our Lady of Victory. In addition to these, La Conquistadora's relations to Our Lady of Guadalupe, the Assumption, and the Immaculate Conception are particularly valuable for our study. Therefore, we turn our attention now to some of the attributes and associated titles.

The Conqueress

The studies of Chávez (1948) and Espinosa (1936) have shown that the role played by La Conquistadora has roots in Mexico. Cortés had his *conquista*, his sacred battle image. The association of the Virgin with military conflict is not unique to New Mexico. "La Conquistadora," as Chávez has shown, is not an ecclesiastical title but a popular one (1948:16, 23). De Vargas preferred the less familiar, more refined title, "Nuestra Señora de la Conquista." Chávez argues that the statue called La Conquistadora was so named because she came with the first *conquistadores*, not "because of any conquests, bloody or unbloody" (*Viva*, July 1, 1963, p. 6). I would contend that whatever the origin of her name, popular devotion always links it, not generally to *conquistadores*, but specifically to her inspiration of the bloodless reconquest. Hence, our positions are not really antithetical, since Chávez is making a historical judgment about origins, while I am making a judgment about contemporary usage.

Because of her association with the reconquest, one might assume that La Conquistadora is interpreted primarily in military terms by her devotees. But despite the military interpretation offered in the Entrada drama, indigenous exegesis is surprisingly void of military references. Almost without exception devotees react with either puzzled consternation or surprise when asked if they think La Conquistadora can help men win wars. Both terms, "win" and "war," bother them, but they eagerly accept "victory" and "reconquest." Clearly, her association with military enterprises is restricted to a particular kind of military engagement, namely, conquest, and to a particular time, namely, the past.

I often posed this question to devotees: "How would you have reacted if in World War II Santa Feans like those in the Bataan Death March had carried a banner of La Conquistadora into battle?" Without exception the immediate response was, "I never thought of such a thing." As conversations proceeded, the almost unanimous conclusion was, "Well, I think that would be fine, provided our boys were doing it out of faith, but I don't think we have that strong a faith any more." After one such conversation I received a letter from a cloistered Carmelite nun who had thought further on the subject. She wrote:

Frankly, the question never came up before. So after you left, I asked myself, "What do I really believe in this matter?" Actually, in my own family we've had someone in nearly every war—"as a duty that must be fulfilled in spite of personal preferences." However, it would seem that the solution of man's problems is not in war, even though I also do not approve using violent measures to proclaim the fact. Here, Dr. Grimes, the whole aspect of Our Lady of Conquest would be the spiritual conquest of hearts. [September 2, 1973]

The Carmelite's response is typical only in one sense: she reinterprets the notion of conquest so it refers no longer to military but to spiritual matters. La Conquistadora becomes a symbol of civic *ecclesia* as her civil, militaristic, and ethnic connotations subside. The De Vargas symbol now carries the military-ethnic load, and La Conquistadora is left "pure." Devotees do not hesitate to say that she helped conquer Indians in the past, but when asked what she does in the present, they reply that she conquers human hearts, not Indian bodies. By virtue of the bloodless reconquest, La Conquistadora can be interpreted as a symbol either of conquest or of peace. She is both peacemaker and victor: she conquers violence with peace. While the Entrada emphasizes conquest, fiesta rhetoric and discussion emphasize peace. La Conquistadora's official prayer is instructive in illustrating what are the contemporary objects of her conquest:

O Lady Conqueror, promised in Eden as the Woman whose Seed would crush the Serpent's head, help us to conquer evil in our midst and in our hearts with the grace of your Son, Jesus Christ, Our God and Our Savior.

O Lady Conqueror, through your Motherhood of Our Savior, Who is True God and True Man, help us overcome all error regarding His Person and the Church that He founded for His Glory and our salvation.

O Lady Conqueror, through Jesus Who is the Prince of Peace and our Universal King, convert by His Divine Power which is above all human might the infidels and all the enemies of His Peace.

O Lady Conqueror, do conquer our hearts with your Immaculate loveliness, so that drawn from sinful ways to the precepts of your Son, we may glorify Him in this life and victoriously come to know Him, with you and all the Saints, forever in the next. Amen.

This prayer suggests that La Conquistadora conquers the serpent, evil, doctrinal error, infidels, enemies of Jesus' peace, men's hearts, sin, and death. Many devotees condense the matter by saying simply that she conquers evil. Conquering is spiritual-cultural; one does not use a sword on an error or a non-Christian ritual. No problem of interpretation exists as long as the object of conquest is a demonic spiritual power, but when evil is viewed as a bodily or cultural form, the issue of violence becomes important. The phrase "enemies of His peace" is crucial. No specific person or group is named, but almost all the devotees with whom I talked acknowledged that "enemies" and "peace" could in given circumstances apply to specific persons or groups. "Peace" could have political, as well as personal, dimensions. So even though one finds virtually no interpretation of the idea of conquest in terms of a contemporary, literal, military victory, because of her history, La Conquistadora is potentially a symbol for such, given sufficient faith and a righteous cause. Just as the latent power of Our Lady was actuated in De Vargas, and "enemies" was once concretized as a group of "rebellious Indians," so the principles, "conqueress" and "enemy" could once again become quite specific. Concretely, in 1973, the Santa Fe Police became personifications of La Conquistadora's power, while the thieves became "enemies of His Peace."

Devotees talk readily of peace, but the related questions of violence, pacifism, and war are left almost exclusively to clergy and a few select lay leaders. Twice during the fiesta the question of violent uses of power came to the fore. On both occasions the clergy were interpreters of La Conquistadora.

The first instance was the Solemn Pontifical Fiesta Mass, for which the Anglo archbishop delivered the sermon. He pointed out that the title "La Conquistadora" reflected the theology of the time in which it originated. Some are aware, he said, of the "utter lack of logic" of trying to spread the gospel by an assault on the person, which is what "conquest" means. Whole peoples will resist those who use coercion in trying to convert them, hence the incongruity of sword and cross. The archbishop went on to point out that Jesus never had an army; he needed none. "God needs no man's power." Conquest, the speaker insisted, is taking other people's riches and making those people into tiny images of ourselves. This, like the combination of baptism and murder, is a prostitution of religion. The archbishop preached this sermon with Franciscans, De Vargas, the queen, the staff, and the court seated in front of him. He pointed out that a few Franciscans had understood the contradiction between conquest and the gospel. He assured those before him that they "need not be ashamed of wearing Spanish military uniforms," for the fiesta is a morality play, and those wearing military uniforms remind us of our mistakes—of how impotent the reconquest really was. We cannot claim cultural superiority because of our heritage, he added, "we have some reforming to do." We must do as Jesus did, who raised his hand against no other man. Under La Conquistadora, then, he concluded, we must conquer ourselves, injustice, and oppression, not other men or other cultures.

Listeners asserted that the archbishop's sermon was quite typical, but by "typical" they meant, not "typical of the fiesta," but "typical of the archbishop." The sermon aroused considerable anger and resentment, especially among Hispanos close to the Santa Fe fiesta tradition. In fact, some were unwilling to discuss their reactions until weeks after the fiesta had concluded.

There are perhaps limited grounds for concluding that the

archbishop's interpretation was an ordinary one, as some informants said; he did, after all, demilitarize the notion of conquest. This is common. Nevertheless, he did so in the context of some atypical values and ideas. The usual mode of demilitarization leads to a view of conquest as a private, spiritual matter of the individual heart. The archbishop, on the other hand, interpreted conquest as a social matter. The usual interpretation shifts the idea of conquest from a context of war to one of Catholic devotion and dignity. The archbishop shifted conquest from a domain of war to one of justice.

The archbishop viewed De Vargas and his staff as reminders of the mistake of too closely allying church with state and army. Few who heard the sermon would have thought the fiesta soldiers were wearing their costumes in shame, or that an archbishop needed to remind them that they need not be ashamed of playing roles in a morality play. On the contrary, the military uniforms are worn with pride—not only in the role but in what the role signifies. The soldiers are viewed by most Santa Feans as the heroes of the Entrada and Hispanic Santa Fe, not as the villains of a morality play.

In essence what the archbishop did was to decompartmentalize what many devotees keep quite separate, namely, the spiritual conquest of the heart and the cultural-military conquest enacted in the Entrada. Even though fiesta-goers would never think of militarily reconquering contemporary Pueblos with a sword, they do so dramatically in the pageant. That is, they do so in one particular cultural form, the public drama. Perhaps I can make the matter of conquest clearer by listing its possible modes: (1) military conquest of the Indians in the past, 1692–1693; (2) symbolic-dramatic conquest of Indians in 1973; (3) conquest of individual hearts then and now; (4) corporate conquest of corporate injustice now.

The archbishop's sermon implies a rejection of the values latent in number one and number two. He said nothing about number three, and he affirmed the value of number four. In contrast, the ordinary Hispano participant affirms number one as an appropriate reaction to the revolt of 1680, affirms the values symbolized in number two, ignores number four, and places primary emphasis in discussion and public rhetoric on number three.

The ideological distance between Anglo archbishop and Hispano people is considerable. During the period of my field study, the people were still angered and humiliated by the archbishop's moving the chancery office of the Archdiocese of Santa Fe to Albuquerque. They viewed the move as both ideologically and economically motivated. During 1973 the name of the archbishop was frequently on the people's lips and in the newspapers. Four confrontations occurred, and in every case the issue was power and its mode of exercise. One situation involved a sit-in and occupation of vacant seminary buildings owned by the church. One involved a gun battle in a building which the archbishop had allowed a Chicano group to use. Another concerned the archbishop's participation in a protest march during a strike. And the last one had to do with the forcing of an experimental liturgy group from its buildings.

I do not mention these crises for the sake of locating blame, but because they illustrate how crucial the old ethos of conquest and the new ethos of power are to New Mexico. The conflict between devotees and the archbishop (who retired in 1974) was not essentially one of personalities but of basic ideological and hermeneutical principles. The archbishop was an Anglo liberal who interpreted La Conquistadora accordingly and in doing so found himself caught in a crossfire between Chicano radicalism and Spanish-American conservatism. The archdiocese now has its first Spanish-surnamed archbishop.

On one other fiesta occasion the question of conquest, violence, and power was central. After a candlelight procession from the cathedral along a path lit by *luminarias* (bonfires) to a hill overlooking the city, a sermon was delivered at the foot of the Cross of the Martyrs by a Hispano Franciscan. Like the archbishop's sermon, this one attempted to reinterpret what had occurred historically in order to discountenance violence and extol nonviolence. The sermon began with a reference to the burning of Zozobra, undoubtedly stirring in the minds of hearers an association with the burning *luminarias* which lined the procession path and the flames of martyrdom. But, said the Franciscan, unlike the Zozobra burning, this is a moment of absolute seriousness. The death of Zozobra is hardly comparable to the death of a martyr. As he began to recount the history of the revolt in which twenty-one Franciscans died, he admitted the existence of Spanish paternalism regarding the Indians. In fact, he put the matter even more strongly. The Spaniards, he insisted, had become "less than human." And "the Indians had cause." They had cause, because the Spanish invasion had become "an *indignity* to their humanity." But the friars, he recounted, "remained loyal to the dignity of the Indians." In the process of trying to regain this dignity, the Indians killed their benefactors, the Franciscan martyrs. Read your history books, he urged, and you will see that the friars "stayed behind with the people they loved," because they were committed to the theology of nonviolence. "Nothing good can be accomplished through coercion and violence," he concluded.

People said they were inspired by the sermon on the martyrs but viewed the Pontifical Mass as either "the same old thing" or were insulted by it. The differing reactions do not seem to depend merely upon occasion and personality but on the use of symbols. Of course, the use of symbols itself may have a direct connection with the fact that the archbishop was Anglo and the Franciscan, Hispano.

In many ways the second sermon is more directly critical of crusading ideologies than the first. The primary difference, though, lies in the relationship between symbol and countersymbol. In the archbishop's sermon, soldier (the man with the sword) and savior (the man who raised his hand against no one) are treated as symbolic opposites. The result is a forced choice on the part of Hispano listeners between their ethno-cultural symbol (the soldier) and their religious symbol (Jesus). The choice posed by the Franciscan is on a different level. The choice is between dehumanizing Spanish officials and humane Spanish Franciscans. The choice which is rhetorically forced on the audience is between dehumanization and nonviolence, but whichever choice the Hispano listener makes, he is not left without an Hispanic symbol. Furthermore, if he makes the rhetorically favored choice, he opts simultaneously for a symbol of *ethnos* and *ecclesia*.

I am sure that neither of the speakers nor most of their listeners consciously thought through the alternatives in precisely the way I have just outlined. The speakers did what they usually do, and if they are typical, they have already forgotten what they said on those occasions. The people did not know why they felt as they did about the two sermons. They simply knew that in one case they were bored or insulted and in the other they were inspired. But the difference lies in different modes of presenting and interpreting symbols which are part of the same system.

Whether La Conquistadora is a military conqueress, an ethno-cultural conqueress, a conqueress of injustice, or a conqueress of hearts depends on whether a given interpreter wants to emphasize *civitas*, *ecclesia*, or *ethnos*. This flexibility gives La Conquistadora more symbolic ambiguity than either De Vargas (a symbol of *ethnos*) or the fiesta queen (a symbol of *civitas*). She is primarily a bearer of *ecclesia*, but she also mediates the tensions between ethnicity and civicality.

Some interesting contrasts appear if we compare Our Lady

of the Conquest with the Irish Our Lady of Knock on the issue of violence. Victor and Edith Turner's study of this Marian queen of Ireland shows how a lady of peace becomes a goddess of war, a symbol of patriotic "Irish *'machismo'* " (n.d.:42–43). The picture of "a handful of lads with a gun and a rosary," which the Turners mention, is not to be found in the case of La Conquistadora except in history and pageantry. Her devotees have endeavored to reinterpret her as a symbol of tranquility and coexistence. La Conquistadora has not lost her crusading ethos, but the crusades she inspires are no longer military but civic and religious. La Conquistadora is still entwined in what the Turners call a "patriot game," but respectability, rather than bullets, is the ammunition. Whereas Our Lady of Knock and Our Lady of Guadalupe have both served as rallying images for insurrection, La Conquistadora has served the opposite purpose, to quell revolt and minimize conflict in the city.

One reporter summarizes the essence of the fiesta thus: "Peace on earth and good will to men . . . triumphed over war and dissension. (*New Mexican*, August 29, 1968, p. 2). He does not say "over injustice and oppression," a phrase appropriate to a more revolutionary ideology. The peace which La Conquistadora symbolizes presupposes, rather than challenges, the values of the political and military establishments. La Conquistadora inspires her devotees to fight for victory in determining the shape of a tranquil *civitas*. She challenges any claim to Anglo or Indian domination of the city, since her high civic status issues from a history and culture which are not dependent upon the westward movement of pioneers or the Pueblo world. She also challenges any claim that the legal separation of church and state must result in secularization, that is, in the separation of *ecclesia* and *civitas-civilitas*. La Conquistadora devotion is tactically defensive toward Protestant secularization and offensive toward

Pueblo religion. When conquest is defined primarily by the *civitas-ecclesia* nexus, its strategy passes from the arena of military incursion to that of mission and evangelism.

Devotees speak of "victory through her intercession." Theologically, she intervenes between men and God, but sociologically she intervenes between man and man. As a symbol, she interprets one religio-cultural tradition to another. She defines the religiosity of Hispanic Catholicism in Santa Fe, while the De Vargas symbol defines the ethnicity. A former archbishop referred to her as "the very soul of the Spanish Southwest." She is soul; De Vargas is body. Together they form a unit still capable of conquering forces which would sunder the soul and body of the city of Santa Fe.

One final association ought to be mentioned in connection with La Conquistadora's role as conqueress of evil, namely, that she is a symbolic conqueress of the atomic bomb and the mass destruction it has come to symbolize. That she should play such a role is appropriate, because some of her devotees work at the Los Alamos Scientific Laboratories. In 1954 Chávez had La Conquistadora "write" a paragraph which has since become a part of her public meaning:

Beneath my feet may also be seen a small gold-painted pedestal, which replaces the one sawn off and lost long ago. Though it is covered with antique rococo molding to go with my ancient self and the style of my garments, it is really a modern work of precision underneath; it is an eight-sided block of white pine that was cut and fitted together, and purposely, in the humming shops of the atomic city of Los Alamos, not long after the first bombs went off at Alamogordo, then at Hiroshima and Nagasaki. For as I myself am, allegorically speaking a prayer to her who crushed the infernal serpent's head, so this pedestal under my feet represents a continual prayer that Mary may hold vanquished underfoot whatever there may be of evil in atomic power.   [1954a:129; cf. 1950:306, n. 16]

Los Alamos is just a few miles from Santa Fe. The world was shocked by what happened there, and Santa Feans were even more shocked that such a thing could happen virtually under their noses without their knowing. The atomic bomb and occasionally Los Alamos are still potent symbols of evil. A prayer by Cardinal Spellman in 1954 which referred to La Conquistadora as "a power greater than all the energies wombed by atoms" has been reprinted by the confraternity in a small brochure. So even the link between La Conquistadora and established civil powers is not absolute. She will crush even these if they threaten to attain too much overt power, because in the end *ecclesia* defines the city as the Heavenly Jerusalem and refuses to allow the ideal city to be defined by power plays.

Queen, Patroness, First Lady

Our Lady is a conqueress, but she is also feminine, hence she does not go directly into battle. Only her champions actually engage in military, civil, civic, or ethnic conflict. She conquers, not from a horse, which would be too undignified for a lady, but from a throne. She does not sweat in the hot sun, raise swords, or sit in city council meetings— metaphorically or otherwise. Rather, she rides ritually on a throne, pedestal, or palanquin carried by her champions. At one time she was carried by women, but the Caballeros became her official escorts, because devotees considered it "more fitting that men should carry a lady."

The appropriateness follows, it seems, from the images of knight and queen which arise from the royal, courtly ethos of old Spain. During early fiestas De Vargas offered his sword and services at the feet of the fiesta queen. Courtly gestures of knight and lady still contribute to defining the roles of De Vargas, La Conquistadora, and fiesta queen, though this particular gesture is no longer used.

The symbol of Mary as queen has ritualistic importance to

the fiesta and novena-processions. A confraternity publication describes the cross on top of her crown as a "symbol of
her gentle rule." La Conquistadora must be served with
"knightly gallantry," to quote one informant. A queen might
seem to demand a king, as well as a knight, but given the
status of Mary in Catholic Christianity, the only way one
could carry out such a symbolic complement would be to
cast someone in the role of God and thus commit blasphemy.
The queen's ritual counterpart, then, must be symbolically
her inferior; thus there are only three possibilities. Mary as
queen can have knights, daughters, and sons. Symbolically,
Mary has only one son, Jesus, so the kinship metaphors of
knight and daughter are the ones which define most of the
relations between Mary and her devotees.

La Conquistadora is the queen in her tower, the regal figure on her throne, the one for whom the knight fights. She is
the queen of heaven and the American Southwest, and during fiestas of earlier days, strolling troubadours used to sere-
nade a replica of her before heading for the crowds on the
plaza. An unsigned, mimeographed article entitled "Tierra
de Maria Santisima: The Land of La Conquistadora" para-
phrases the words of Don Quixote to Sancho Panza and
applies them to La Conquistadora: "Without a Lady to love,
it would be like a tree without leaves and fruit, and more like
a body without a soul." A lady is complemented by a gentleman like De Vargas, a "gallant nobleman," a pious devotee
and a Knight of the Order of Santiago. Mary's queenship has
its complementary symbol in the knighthood of male devotees, while her motherhood has its symbolic complement in
the daughterhood of female devotees.

Not all queens are patronesses, only those who know how
to provide for the needs of the people. La Conquistadora is a
patroness; she hears the prayers of her people. Her queenship elevates her, but it does not stop up her ears. Because
she hears the prayers of the people, they in turn make La

Conquistadora their patroness. She is the official, unifying Marian symbol of the Southwest. (Perhaps for this reason she is seldom chosen as a personal patroness.) She is a spiritual and feminine version of the old Spanish *patrón*, under whose supervision labored the humble, and whose duty it was to look out for the well-being of the *partidario*. The connotation of the term "patroness" draws upon both the religious idea of a patron saint and the socioeconomic idea of a *patrón* (cf. Gonzalez 1969:45–70).

La Conquistadora reigns over the "Royal City of the Holy Faith." Santa Fe is now a royal city only in a metaphorical sense, but it is still the state capital and, according to some, the cultural capital, of New Mexico. La Conquistadora and the city of Santa Fe are thus complements to one another: queenly *ecclesia*, royal *civitas*. From Santa Fe she rules over the whole of her kingdom—sometimes identified as Santa Fe, sometimes as New Mexico, sometimes as the whole Southwest.

Symbolically, La Conquistadora is not only a queen of a royal Spanish city, she is also first lady in an American democracy. The appellation "First Lady of Santa Fe" is becoming increasingly common in popular usage. La Conquistadora is fully American, fully Catholic, and fully Hispano. She is the "First Lady" of the land in several senses, and her devotees refuse to allow Protestantism to define the civic-civil-religious nexus in the Southwest as it has done in federal, civil rituals. Hence, the *mayordomo* of her confraternity writes: "More than 150 years before Martha Washington became our nation's First Lady, a small, wood-carved statue of the Blessed Virgin Mary, a modest 31 or more inches tall, had already earned historic and spiritual right to the title "First Lady of the Land' " (*Official Program of the 1973 Fiesta de Santa Fe*, p. 4).

Virgin Mother

If La Conquistadora were the lady and queen elevated high on a pedestal, descending only occasionally to her people, she would hardly generate such intense devotion. As a Marian advocation, however, she not only has regionally specific connotations but also shares the more universally Catholic attributes of the Mother of God. But even the Mother of God would remain a vague spiritual abstraction unless she was also "our Mother." And the sense in which she is "our Mother" is unique to the Santa Fe area.

La Conquistadora is the symbolic mother of the lines of Hispanic descent from the *conquistadores*. Sometimes family genealogies are dedicated to La Conquistadora, whose picture is glued inside the front cover of the album containing the family tree. Most of my interviewees are extremely concerned with genealogy, and each new fiesta seems to occasion a wave of genealogical research among those who either play roles in the Entrada or serve on the queen's court. It is no accident that most of the research and writing done by Fray Angélico Chávez and Pedro Ribera-Ortega, each of whom is a devotee and historian, are genealogical. These two men have written the most about La Conquistadora and have most significantly influenced the shape of her devotion and its connections to Santa Fe's public ritual. Ribera-Ortega is a teacher of history at Santa Fe High School. His method of teaching New Mexico history is genealogical, and his genealogical studies are dedicated to La Conquistadora. One of Chávez' major publications, *Origins of New Mexico Families in the Spanish Colonial Period* (1954b), was serialized in the local newspaper because of the demand from ordinary people for a resource through which they could trace their ancestry to the original Spanish *conquistadores*. Chávez' enthusiasm for La Conquistadora is partly due to his discovery that his own genealogy is tied up with some of La Conquistadora's followers.

Le Conquistadora is the symbolic matrix of genealogical lines which lead to some of the most prominent families in Santa Fe and the Rio Grande valley. As symbolic mother, she is a source of cultural identity. In the face of this fact Chávez exclaims, "Religious piety mingled with ancestral pride raises my emotions to the point of tears" (1950). The prevalence of heraldic devices, coats of arms, and family trees among La Conquistadora's devotees and fiestaphiles is evidence that Chávez' emotion is widely shared. Particularly proud are those who can trace their genealogy either to a conquistador or to one of De Vargas' close associates.

Devotion to La Conquistadora is a way of sustaining loyalty to one's family lines. The Virgin Mother is the keystone of what George Mills calls "a familial cosmos" (n.d.:59). Those who have "filial devotion" to her are not only implicitly her knights and daughters but children of the *conquistadores*. Functionally, La Conquistadora is something of an ancient heirloom jointly possessed by a multitude of interlocking families. Hence, when they speak of "our" Mother, they are doing more than using a customary term. La Conquistadora is "ours" in two senses: she is our spiritual mother and our heirloom statue.

For her papal coronation La Conquistadora's devotees sent out a formally printed invitation that began *"Hijos mios"* (my children) and continued as if it were a personal note from the Lady herself. This intimate, first-person style probably has its origin in Chávez' *Autobiography*, written as if La Conquistadora herself had dictated it. As queen and lady she has champions and intermediaries, but as mother she speaks directly to her children. Significantly, the dedication page of Chávez' *Autobiography* reads, "To the memory of these and scores of other 'Conquistadora' progenitors and their consorts" (1954a).

La Conquistadora devotees say that she belongs to everyone in the Southwest, but, as far as I can tell, this concept applies only to her role as queen and patroness. As mother she belongs to Roman Catholics, particularly to Roman Catholics of Hispanic or conquistador descent. The summer novena-processions are times of family reunions and remembering the dead (through whom genealogies are traced). So even though an outer circle of inclusivism allows La Conquistadora rituals to be public, there is also an inner circle of ethnofamilial particularism. Publicly, no one is too concerned about the inner circle, but privately some devotees jealously guard La Conquistador as one would a revered, aged mother.

Public La Conquistadora rites are in part a ritualized "familizing" of the *civitas*. To be included in a family whether literally, temporarily, or symbolically is both a considerable compliment and a considerable obligation. Nancie González notes:

It seems safe to say that, although certain aspects of the former strongly knit family organization of the Hispano way of life have changed, the extended family unit remains important in ways unparalleled in the Anglo world. Indeed, several investigators have suggested that persons who cannot be fitted into a kinship category may be treated with suspicion, withdrawal, and perhaps even shown overt hostility. As Weaver has said recently, "Spanish-American society is kin-based society and the most lasting deepest ties are those between kin-based members." [1969:62]

The La Conquistadora cycle of rituals represents a symbolic effort to extend the Hispano family even beyond distant relatives, living and dead. This ritual "familization" of the city accounts for devotees' insistence that La Conquistadora belongs to all, not just Hispanos or Catholics. The familization of a city redefines the nature of the conflict so that interethnic violence becomes sibling rivalry. The change of focus enables "the fathers," whether city fathers or fathers in heaven, legitimately to adjudicate the squabbles between the siblings.

So far I have discussed Mary as mother of New Mexico's Hispano Catholics and of Santa Fe understood as a family-like brotherhood, but I have said little about her more traditional role as *theotokos* (God-bearer; mother of God). I shall not go into the very complicated business of Marian theology but will refer briefly to the Mother of God in the *Canticos de La Conquistadora*, a collection of popular songs used during the La Conquistadora rituals.

When Santa Fe devotees speak of the Virgin as Mother of God, they refer to a particular emotional quality rather than to a particular set of theological arguments about virginity, humanity, divinity, and original sin, though the language of piety is seldom completely divorced from the theological language of the church. One of the *canticos*, for example, "Pues Concebida," speaks of the Virgin Mother as "sweet refuge" (*refugio dulce*). Mary mitigates the harshness of the masculine, fatherly world.

The sexual aspects of Mary's virginity are almost never mentioned in the *canticos*. Her virginity is, rather, referred to as purity from sin, without specification of the nature of the sin involved. She comforts because she is free of what is so characteristic of the world. One informant refers to her with the formula, "tainted nature's solitary boast," and the taint is far more pervasive than sexuality. Sexuality is one way of "transmitting" sin; the "unnatural" but necessary institutions of ethnic group and city are others. The *canticos* do not locate pollution in sexuality so much as in the whole of culture, and to a lesser extent, history. Mary as virgin is removed from all this. Her sexual continence is but a symbol of her social continence whenever intercultural conflict is present. She is removed from the fray of *ethnos* and *civitas*. This does not make her any less powerful to her devotees, but it does mean that her power is accessible only insofar as the devotee leaves the fray momentarily and flees to her as a motherly refuge.

La Conquistadora is the refuge of the powerful, and she gives power. But she herself does not directly exercise it, thus her virgin purity. In the *cantico* "A La Conquistadora," she is asked to "free us from the other war." [1] She is petitioned for life and health so that the devotee can return in the coming year to celebrate another novena in order that life in the *agon* (contest) of the city will be possible. The Virgin Mother gives power; only men use it. And "to use" can mean "to prostitute" or "to employ."

In the *cantico* "Adios, Reina del Cielo," Mary is addressed by three major kinship terms: "daughter of the Father; mother of the Son; spouse of the Holy Spirit." The role of spouse is infrequently mentioned in the *canticos*, and that of daughter appears only in relation to God. In relation to God, Mary appears under every female kinship metaphor provided by the nuclear family except sister. In relation to man Mary appears only as metaphoric mother. For man she is basically origin and matrix—that from which man goes forth, as well as that to which he flees in time of trouble. La Conquistadora's special connection with the dead, as indicated by the location of Rosario Chapel in a cemetery, complements her close association with birth. Her symbolic strength, then, is at the beginning and end. Masculine symbols mark the impure, conflict-ridden middle.

The Rosary and Revolution

In addition to the popular title "La Conquistadora," the statue also bears the ecclesiastical title "Our Lady of the Rosary." Without knowing something of the history of the devotion to the rosary and the Marian advocations associated

[1] "Tu, que eres Virgen Santa, / En el cielo y en la tierra, / Te suplicamos, Senora, / Que nos libres de otra guerra."

with it, one would hardly suspect the underlying military and political overtones.

The feast day of Our Lady of the Rosary is the first Sunday in October. It was set at this time to commemorate the victory of the Christians over the Saracens (the "invincible Turkish Armada") in the naval battle of Lepanto (1571). Our Lady of the Rosary was the patroness of the Spanish fleets, and during this battle, Catholics said the rosary as they processed through the streets praying for victory. Chávez alludes to "the same old Spanish custom of turning specifically to Our Lady of the Rosary when the enemy was at the gates" (1954a:103).

Informants often mention Our Lady of the Rosary along with Our Lady of Fatima. According to the Marian apparition at Fatima (1917), recitation of the rosary was to have prevented the spread of communism and a second world war. Saying the rosary was a condition of the "peace plan from heaven" associated with the Fatima apparition. The repeated apparitions of Our Lady to the children of Fatima called for daily praying of the rosary in honor of Our Lady of the Rosary in order to obtain an end to war (Delaney 1961:193). The Fatima apparitions culminated in October, the month of the rosary. Devotion to Our Lady of Mount Carmel and to the Immaculate Heart of Mary were also encouraged in the appearances; thus several other Marian advocations, along with Our Lady of the Rosary, were promoted by Fatima.

It is obvious that the titles "Our Lady of the Conquest" and "Our Lady of the Rosary" are not connotative opposites but complement each other in their association with war and its cessation. The actual saying of the rosary is still prevalent in La Conquistadora activities despite post-Vatican II hesitancy about the rosary in other parts of the United States. Even though the saying of the rosary is regarded by some men as "a woman's devotion," men nevertheless consider the rosary an important symbol. The attendance at a rosary rally in 1973 at nearby Albuquerque drew over ten thousand people to the stadium. Though the rallies explicitly aim to encourage the various Fatima devotions, they have a certain political overtone which colors other rosary-related Marian advocations, including La Conquistadora. The following sign appeared on a bulletin board of a Catholic church in the Santa Fe area:

Rosary Rally, Albuquerque Sports Stadium
Remember OUR LADY TOLD US: SAY THE ROSARY + OFFER COMMUNION OF REPARATION + WEAR THE SCAPULAR + IF THIS BE DONE HER IMMACULATE HEART WILL TRIUMPH + RUSSIA WILL BE CONVERTED AND THERE WILL BE PEACE

—OR ELSE—

THERE WOULD BE—SOCIAL UNREST AND REVOLUTION—AND RUSSIAN COMMUNISM WILL SPREAD HER ERRORS—THE CHURCH WILL BE PERSECUTED— THE HOLY FATHER WILL HAVE MUCH TO SUFFER— FASHIONS WILL BE DESIGNED IN HELL—THERE'D BE MANY BAD MARRIAGES.

The sign goes on to call on the Legion of Mary, the Catholic Daughters, the Third Order of St. Francis, the Cursillistas, and the Knights of Columbus to pray to Mary to effect her promises.

In sum, the devotion to the rosary and to Our Lady of the Rosary traditionally connotes the conquest of pagan, godless, or non-Christian forces such as Saracens and Indians in the past and Russian Communists in the present.

De Vargas, as I noted earlier, placed many rosaries around the necks of Indians as a mark of their submission to Christianity and the church. The rosary employed, not only as an aid to devotion, but as a spiritual weapon, remains true to its origins. Saint Dominic, who is credited by tradition with the development of the rosary, used it to combat the Albigensian heresy. So the rosary still represents religiopolitical orthodoxy.

In addition to her ecclesiastical title, "Our Lady of the Rosary," La Conquistadora is also associated with Remedios, (Our Lady of Remedies), a title given the *conquista* which Cortés carried into Mexico City. Fray Angélico Chávez has shown that De Vargas actually employed a banner of Remedios, not a statue of La Conquistadora, in the reconquest of 1692. Because De Vargas returned in 1693 speaking frequently of La Conquistadora, the popular mind later associated Our Lady of Remedies and Our Lady of the Conquest.

Robert Ricard's excellent study, *The Spiritual Conquest of Mexico* (1966), describes Our Lady of Remedies as a distinctly Spanish cult which developed at the time of the conquest of Mexico. Remedios is said to have appeared to the fleeing Spanish army after the evacuation of Tenochtitlán. She gave them courage and dazzled the pursuing Indians, hence her role as patroness of the Spanish army during the War of Independence is not surprising. Remedios became the symbol of the royalist, peninsular Spaniards rather than the Mexican criollos (persons of Spanish descent born in the New World). Hence, she was the countersymbol of Our Lady of Guadalupe, who served as patroness of the revolting forces, and is now patroness of Mexico.

In "Hidalgo: History as Social Drama" (1974), Victor Turner offers an interpretation of the Mexican Revolution in social-dramatistic terms. He shows that Guadalupe, the "Brown Virgin," is a unifying symbol for Hidalgo, the revolutionary Mexican priest, and his Indian followers in their effort to "reconquer" Mexico, while Our Lady of Remedies symbolically leads the royalist forces.

The studies of both Turner and Ricard show that devotion to Guadalupe was initially propagated by secular priests but opposed by Franciscans. Hidalgo himself was a secular priest. Interestingly, New Mexicans sometimes pose a historical contrast between the faithfulness of Franciscans and the lack of dedication among secular clergy. The so-called Secular Period of New Mexico history (c. 1790–1850) is one in which Franciscan jurisdiction diminished as regular clergy were sent to replace men of the various religious orders. The secular clergy subsequently all but abandoned New Mexico, and when the first bishop was appointed in the mid-nineteenth century, only nine priests were in the territory (Armitage 1960:75). In modern Santa Fe some informants associate the secular priesthood, Mexico, and Our Lady of Guadalupe, on the one hand, and Franciscans, Spain, Our Lady of Remedies, and La Conquistadora, on the other. Turner's summary illustrates how different the Guadalupe ethos is from that of Our Lady of Remedies:

Our Lady of Guadalupe I would regard, therefore, not only as an Indian symbol but also as a joint criollo-Indian symbol, which incorporated into its system of significance not only ideas about the earth, motherhood, indigenous power, and so on, but also criollo notions of liberty, fraternity, and equality, some of which were borrowed from the atheistical French thinkers of the revolutionary period. [1974:153]

Eric Wolf shows that the pro-Mexican Guadalupe became a militantly anti-Spanish symbol:

And so on the eve of Mexican independence, Servando Teresa de Mier elaborates still further the Guadalupan myth by claiming that Mexico had been converted to Christianity long before the Spanish Conquest. The apostle Saint Thomas had brought the image of Guadalupe-Tonantzin to the New World as a symbol of his mission, just as St. James had coverted Spain with the image of the Virgin of the Pillar. The Spanish Conquest was therefore historically unnecessary, and should be erased from the annals of history. [1965:153].

Despite the symbolic opposition of Our Lady of Guadalupe and Our Lady of Remedies in Mexico, however, it would be erroneous to assume that Santa Feans view Our Lady of Guadalupe and La Conquistadora as countersymbols. According to John Meem, probably the oldest surviving shrine to Guadalupe in the United States is in Santa Fe (1972:21). Santa Fe's Guadalupe Parish is a strong supporter of La Conquistadora rituals. For Santa Feans, Our Lady of Guadalupe does not have the revolutionary ethos she has in Mexico, since Santa Fe was so far removed from the revolution. Informants know both the iconography and mythology of the Mexican Guadalupe, but their sociopolitical associations with her are largely royalist and Spanish, not Mexican and revolutionary. De Vargas thought nothing of conquering under the banner of Our Lady of Remedies and giving thanks for the victory before a statue of Our Lady of Guadalupe.

A prime factor which helped early Santa Fe devotees reconcile their simultaneous devotion to La Conquistadora and Our Lady of Guadalupe was the existence of two Guadalupes, one Spanish and one Mexican. The Mexican name "Guadalupe" is probably a Hispanisization of the Aztec word "Tecuatalope." This mis-hearing of the word seems to be the result of a Guadalupe devotion preceding the events which surrounded Juan Diego, to whom Guadalupe first appeared. The Spanish Guadalupe, whose name the Spaniards heard in "Tecuatalope," figured prominently in the conquest of the Moors at Santa Fe, Spain, in 1492. Santa Fe, New Mexico, of course, derives its name from this Spanish city. The Order of Santiago, of which De Vargas was a member, was quite powerful in the area of Santa Fe, Spain. And De Vargas was proud of having descended from the knights who had defeated the Moors. Hence, his view of Guadalupe, as well as that of many of the conquistadors and their descendants, was undoubtedly colored by the conquest ethos of the

Spanish Guadalupe more than the late, revolutionary ethos of the Mexican Guadalupe. For Santa Feans, Our Lady of Guadalupe does not have the qualities which would inspire a Chicano militant like César Chávez to carry her banner in protest to a state capital.

A certain fluidity exists between Marian titles, apparitions, and advocations in New Mexico. In addition to the theological assertion that Mary is one despite her plurality of forms, a factor adding to the confluence of differing Marian forms was New Mexico's relative isolation from competing nationalisms which employ Marian images. For example, La Conquistadora has even been confused with Our Lady of Victory, a title wrongly applied to her by the first bishop of Santa Fe. The confusion is ironic, because Our Lady of Victory was imbedded in French nationalism, and conflict between France and Spain in the New World was sometimes quite heated.

Not only is there a confluence of images in New Mexico, but there is also a confluence of titles for the same image. Santa Feans sing Guadalupe's story in La Conquistadora celebrations, associate her with Our Lady of Remedies, identify her with Our Lady of the Rosary, and occasionally mistake her for Our Lady of Victory; they have also given her several other titles in her long history. Iconographic study of the statue itself indicates that in all probability the present carving is an alteration of what originally was an image of Our Lady of the Assumption (Chávez 1954a:38–40; 1948:34–36). Subsequently, she served as an image of the Immaculate Conception as well. The iconographic attributes and the interpretation of the statue follow the pattern of conflation so typical of New Mexico *santos*. In *santero* art, for example, one can find representations of the Immaculate Conception in which the Virgin's heart is sword-pierced, an attribute normally linked to Our Lady of Sorrows. Veneration of the saints and the Virgin has always been intense in New Mexico, but never rigid in its iconography. New Mexico Catholic art is characterized by what we might call "intra-Catholic syncretism."

Other Marian advocations of importance to the Southwest are Our Lady of Lourdes, Our Lady of Fatima, Our Lady of Saint John of the Lakes, Our Lady of Light, Our Lady of the Blessed Sacrament, Our Lady of Sorrows, Our Lady of Solitude, Our Lady of Mount Carmel, and Our Lady Refuge of Sinners. José Espinosa's excellent study of Hispanic iconography, *Saints in the Valleys*, lists nineteen such titles which appear in New Mexican folk art (1967:91). All twenty of Mary's principle attributes and symbols also appear. The advocations, titles, and attributes are not distinguished on the basis of a common principle, but a rough classification is as follows: (1) those based on a biblical event (such as the Annunciation), (2) those evoked by an apparition or miracle (such as Our Lady of Lourdes), (3) those grounded in dogma (such as the Immaculate Conception), (4) those evolving from an historical or historico-mythical event (such as La Conquistadora), (5) those created expressly for artistic, iconographic, or liturgical purposes (such as Our Lady of Africa, Algiers). These categories are by no means complete or mutually exclusive. A Marian form may claim many reasons for being, and as we have seen, La Conquistadora, though belonging primarily to the fourth category, once belonged to the third. The bulk of Marian piety is rooted in the first three categories, so what we have said about La Conquistadora cannot be taken as typical of Marian devotion.

The Fiesta Queen

Of the three major fiesta symbols the fiesta queen is the most ambiguous. Devotees are quite ambivalent about her relation to both La Conquistadora and the De Vargas figure. Conceptually, the ambivalence concerns the relation of *ecclesia* and *ethnos* to *civitas*, of which the fiesta queen is the primary symbol. Indigenous discussions of the queen are marked with a curious combination of defensiveness and inarticulateness. There is no story to tell about her as there is about De Vargas and La Conquistadora. In 1972 the fiesta queen explicitly interpreted her queenship as symbolic of La Conquistadora's queenship, and in most years popular interpretations treat De Vargas and the queen as symbolic husband and wife. The defensiveness and inarticulateness arises because some church and fiesta officials have vigorously opposed both these interpretations, since they invert what is considered the proper hierarchy: Queen of Heaven, De Vargas, fiesta queen. Whereas the metaphor of kinship which describes Mary is mother, that of the fiesta queen is alternately sister or wife. The public discusses the relation between the De Vargas staff and the queen's court as if it were that of consorts, while the staff and court discuss it as if the relation were between siblings, particularly between older brother and younger sister. The femininity and purity of both the Virgin and the fiesta queen gives them much in common, but the motherhood of Mary and the sisterhood-wifeliness of the fiesta queen sets them somewhat at odds.

As ritualistic figureheads, queens are quite prevalent in New Mexico. One encounters many during a cycle of public rituals: fair queens, rodeo queens, parish queens, football queens, homecoming queens, and queens of various organizations. In addition, there is the usual array of "Miss" pageants: Miss New Mexico, Miss Junior Miss, Miss America, and Miss North American Indian. In almost every case when I inquired about the meaning of these queenly figures, the responses took two forms: "It's just the custom," or "She won the competition by her superior beauty, talent, personality, or ability." In Santa Fe one never hears a historical account of her presence and seldom even the claim that she has meaning. She does not "have meaning"; she simply "is." She "is what every girl wants to be," I was told. The question why the fiesta needs a queen at all instead of, say, a king, is one that consistently stops informants from talking. My impression is that, were it not for a controversy during recent years about the queen's role, informants would have been virtually silent about her.

The public discussion of the fiesta queenship surfaced on the heels of the controversy about the religious-commercial balance of the fiesta. What precipitated the discussion of her role was the realization of church and fiesta officials that the queen, rather than De Vargas, had become the primary symbol of the fiesta. Increasing commercialism and increasing emphasis on the queen seemed to co-vary in direct proportion. The present shift in emphasis from the queen to De Vargas represents in the minds of most informants a shift toward religion and away from secular, economic values in the fiesta. The queen seems to function as a symbol of what unifies the *civitas*, rather than of the religious ties that bind *ecclesia* or cultural-genealogical ties that bind Hispanic *ethnos*. The queen is "Miss Santa Fe" or "Miss Fiesta," while De Vargas is "Mr. Hispano" and La Conquistadora is "Mother Church."

Most informants say that the selection of the queen is just like the selection of De Vargas: each competitor makes a speech in both English and Spanish and then is voted upon by the Fiesta Council. As far as it goes, this opinion is correct, but additional restrictions on the queen make the roles significantly different. The following prerequisites should be compared with those for De Vargas listed above (p. 117). The queen must be: (1) interested in the role, (2) of good character, (3) of Spanish descent, (4) Spanish surnamed, (5) between ages nineteen and twenty-four, (6) unmarried before and during the fiesta, (7) born in Santa Fe County, (8) a resident of the county for the last five years, (9) bilingual, (10) able to present birth or baptismal certificate, (11) able to meet the public with responsibility, dignity, poise, and (12) able to secure an agreement for released time from her employer.

These are prerequisites for competition. After election each young woman on the court must sign a contract with three additional conditions. She aggrees (13) to attend all functions and rehearsals (two unexcused absences can be grounds for dismissal), (14) to cooperate fully with the Fiesta Council chairwoman of her supervisory committee, and (15) not to consume alcoholic beverages in either public or private appearances during her reign.

In effect the requirements for women are almost double the number for men, though some female informants say they do not feel these are "restrictions" but only "regulations." Regardless of their feelings, the structures for women are noticeably more demanding. The women are expected to be impeccable, while the men are only expected to be respectable. Some account for the double standard by saying that the "girls are younger and thus in need of more careful guidance." The queen's age is usually around nineteen and that of the De Vargas figure nearer the twenty-six to thirty range. But such a response is still no explanation. It does not explain why the queen is required to be younger or why she is required to be unmarried. One informant suggests that the age differential is "because De Vargas was historically older." This response only precipitates the question, "Older than who—his wife, his mistress, some Spanish queen?" Historically, De Vargas had no fiesta queen. Some informants say the queen is unmarried and De Vargas married "to prevent messing around." It is true that participants often describe their relations as brotherly-sisterly, but the public symbolically marries them despite this. And if one wanted to prevent "messing around," both figures could be married, perhaps even to each other, in ordinary life. So I suggest that the reason for the restrictions has to do with the logic of the queenly symbol. By prescription she is virginal (sexually not yet mature—a girl, not a woman) because the queen and her court are symbolically the plural cultures viewed as a city, a civic entity. And civic entities, unlike civil or legislative authorities, imply symbols relatively pure and free of the stain of maturity and power. Immaturity, powerlessness, and purity are marks of civic organizations and celebrations insofar as they are contrasted with the arena of civil and ethnic power.

The restrictive rules which bind all members of the court are paralleled by an equally protective mode of choosing the queen's court, which requires awarding the role of Spanish princess to the first four runners-up in the contest. The queen does not choose her court as De Vargas does his staff. Competition for both male and female roles occurs on the same night, a few days before the announcing of winners at the May Dance (Baile de Mayo). The full court consists of the queen, four Spanish princesses, two Indian princesses, and the so-called "little members" (two pages, two train-bearers, and one jester). These "little members" are young children, again emphasizing the symbolic purity associated with the court. The children are chosen by all members of the court except the two Indian princesses, who are usually Pueblos or Navahos, not Hispanos playing the roles of Indians as on the De Vargas staff. When I asked why only the Spanish royalty chose the "little members," two answers were offered—seven children would be too many to handle, and Indian children might have a hard time getting into town. Obviously, the responses do not explain why seven young women cannot choose five children nor why Indian children, like the Indian princesses, cannot come from Santa Fe as well as from distant pueblos.

The selection of the two Indian princesses follows a different procedure from that of the Spanish princesses. Only a few years ago they competed like the rest, but, informants

argue, competition is foreign to "the Indian way." Asking Indian women to make speeches would be as embarrassing to
them as asking the Spanish girls to take their clothes off, one
person noted. Consequently, Fiesta Council officials thought
it more appropriate to let the Pueblos choose their own representatives. Repeatedly, I was told by official sources that
the two Indian princesses had been selected by the governors
of the eight northern pueblos. In 1973 this became a matter
of considerable embarrassment for the two Indian girls, one
from Cochiti and the other of Picuris and Navaho lineage.
(See Figure 6.) Both princesses lived in Santa Fe, not on the
pueblos, and they quite candidly asserted that the governors
of their pueblos had nothing to do with their selection and
probably only knew about it by reading the erroneous accounts published in the newspaper. Their selection actually
came through informal friendship and kinship channels: a
relative on the Fiesta Council asked one of the girls who in
turn asked a friend, and so forth.

Figure 6. Indian princesses of the queen's court in procession to the Cross of the
Martyrs

The interpretations of their own roles offered by the queen, Spanish princesses, and Indian princesses did not differ significantly. All felt it an honor to occupy their roles; none offered any criticism of the fiesta. All were Catholics who felt they represented their people in an important religious celebration. All believed their interest in Santa Fe's civic and religious life was heightened by their participation. The Indian princesses initially worried that their people, especially males, might criticize them because of hostility to the Entrada, even though they had no connection with it. They were afraid a rumored AIM demonstration might precipitate a controversy. Instead they found their friends and relatives were proud of them. Both Hispano and Indian young women felt there was no discrimination among their group; they were all Santa Feans and all friends.

All the young women denied the existence of a courtly hierarchy paralleling the clearly defined military hierarchy of the De Vargas staff. But a subtle structural hierarchy of queen, Spanish princesses, and Indian princesses obviously determines most of their ritual gestures. Indian princesses do not choose "little members." Spanish princesses usually assist the queen with her robe. Seating arrangements follow a hierarchical pattern. These distinctions are reinforced by different modes of dress, kinds of crowns, and places in the marching order. Yet the court differs from the staff inasmuch as it aims at minimizing hierarchy. The fact that actual Indians participate in the court and that it tries to overcome its hierarchical elements is consistent with its civic ethos.

Some informants still speak of the queen and her court as "representatives of the Spanish culture," but others recognize this as an implicit assertion of cultural superiority and have consequently begun to speak of the queen and court as "representatives of the Fiesta Council," that is, of an organization which intends to represent the tricultural *civitas*. Although elements of *ethnos* are still present in the court, as soon as they are recognized as such, processes begin which move them toward *civitas*.

The actual duties of the court, as well as the structures for carrying out those duties, are considerably simpler than those for De Vargas and his staff. Organizationally, the group constituting the court disperses after the fiesta. Serving on the court is not an initiation into a continuing association like that provided by the Caballeros. Formally, the associative bonds formed between the young women dissolve. Older male informants say that the queens and princesses once tried to organize themselves into a Club Real (Royal Club), but, they claim, the club was dissolved because the queens tried to "rule over" the princesses. Other informants add that some wives of Caballeros have wanted to organize but were discouraged from doing so by some of the men.

The court's duties during the fiesta are limited to marching in processions, attending luncheons and teas, making short speeches of welcome, and being present on the various platforms as an *audiencia* for various performances. Informants sometimes describe fiesta entertainment using the language of command performances, as if the entertainment were "for" the queen. The 1973 queen said of her duties, "Mostly, I just make appearances." The women play no part in the pageant, nor do their positions as fiesta royalty have names or historical counterparts, as is the case for male roles. Whereas the meaning of the male roles can be explored both historically and organizationally, the meaning of the female roles has largely to be inferred from behavior. Participants and officials alike do little more than guess the meanings of the female roles.

To provide some idea of the self-interpretations offered by informants I have reproduced below most of the winning speech given by the 1973 queen:

For 261 years, honor, respect and religion have survived in the hearts and souls of the people of the city of the Holy Faith. What is the secret of this long-lived trust? Perhaps La Conquistadora focused her gleaming eyes on this land and was determined to obtain it for the Spanish people. Through her valiant servant, Reconquistador Don Diego de Vargas, this rich treasure was won without bloodshed.

The glorious return of María Santísima is another example of her enchanting past. Her spiritual presence will live in the people of Santa Fe until the end of time. La Fiesta de Santa Fe is a rare celebration that preserves our unique Spanish heritage. Preserving the past is a vital part of our American heritage.

To be selected Reina of this activity is a royal title which every young lady considers an honor and privilege. It is a role that should be carried out with dignity. With complete understanding of these responsibilities, if selected your Queen, I will try to live the role of La Reina de la Fiesta de Santa Fe with dignity, poise and humility. Mil gracias y que Viva La Fiesta! [*Official Program of the 1973 Fiesta de Santa Fe*, pp. 16–17]

As usual the speech refers to two major fiesta symbols, De Vargas and La Conquistadora, and then catalogues many of the value-virtues already discussed, such as honor, dignity, and humility. In discussions the queen for 1973 clearly shied away from identifying herself as a symbol of La Conquistadora as the 1972 queen had done, although she insisted that her role was a religious one. The 1973 queen remarked on several occasions, "I guess I am here to remind the people of La Conquistadora's presence." Her mode of reminding is verbal and didactic rather than symbolic. And reminding is quite different from symbolizing. The queen embodies La Conquistadora in neither her role nor her person. Instead she calls upon devotees to remember. This reluctance to identify the queen as a symbol of La Conquistadora is supported by the chairwoman of the Fiesta Council's Queen Committee who observed, "Some say she is a symbol of La Conquistadora, but I wouldn't dare say that. That would be stepping into somebody's shoes that couldn't be filled."

In contrast is the interpretation offered by the queen of the previous year, 1972. She saw herself as a "living symbol of La Conquistadora":

Although a queen is an American tradition, I feel that the Fiesta de Santa Fe queen should be and is symbolically representing La Conquistadora because to the Spanish people La Conquistadora is a queen. . . .

Calling the queen representative of La Conquistadora instead of just a "queen," would mean more to the Spanish people and would enhance the queen's position in the significance of Fiesta de Santa Fe. [*Official Program of the 1972 Fiesta de Santa Fe*, p. 16]

Most informants are quite aware of the differences between reminding and symbolizing. No one objects to reminding, though many are ambivalent about symbolizing. For several years religiously conscious participants in the fiesta have tried to make the celebration more overtly religious, and the queenship is, in their view, one of the most secularized of the fiesta symbols. Yet the inclusion of the queen in the *ecclesia* complex of symbols inevitably leads to an association of the queen and the Virgin Mary, which results in an implied ascendancy over De Vargas. Devotees do not balk at an iconic representation of the Virgin, but a "living symbol," a figurehead, is quite another matter. A minority of informants view the interpretation of the 1972 queen as illustrative of genuine, pious depth; others view it as presumptuous and overstated. Many feel that the fiesta queenship has no historical roots and no theological dimensions and thus should be clearly marked as secondary.

One way of emphasizing the secondary status of the queen is the use of spatial metaphors like "behind." To quote the 1972 De Vargas, "But these men [the reconquerers] were not alone. For *behind* [my emphasis] them stood a Lady; yes, a

Lady—our Lady of the Rosary, La Conquistadora, Our Patroness" (*Official Program of the 1972 Fiesta de Santa Fe*, p. 9).
Both the fiesta queen and La Conquistadora are spoken of as
"behind," though devotees also speak of the Virgin as
"above" (as on a pedestal). The "behindness" of the fiesta
queen implies that her status is inferior to that of De Vargas,
who is symbolically "out on the battle front," while the
"aboveness" of Our Lady suggests her superiority over all
human roles, regardless of their status or rank. It is perfectly
acceptable for the supernatural feminine (Mary) to be above
the human masculine (De Vargas). However, ranking the
human feminine (the fiesta queen) over the human masculine
is not.

The Mary who is queen of heaven has power. She is no
mere figurehead, even though her power is above the fray in
which men exercise power. She delegates the administration
of power to De Vargas, but it is her prerogative to do so,
hence the necessity for prayer to her. La Conquistadora's
power is markedly recessive in quality; it lacks the daring
aggressiveness of De Vargas, as an excerpt from a conversation with a devotee makes clear:

A: In the fiesta we relive the same faith that the Spaniards had 200
   years ago.
Q: Do you really believe in the same way that De Vargas did that
   La Conquistadora can help win battles?
A: Yes. If you believe hard enough, she will help. I am sure of it.
Q: Could you share some examples either from your own life or
   from the lives of others in which La Conquistadora helped?
A: I don't really know of her helping anyone specifically, but I am
   certain that it must have happened.

La Conquistadora has the power of maintaining men's faith
and unifying the Hispanic genealogy, rather than the power
of miracle and marvelous deed. Still, in comparison, the fiesta queen is a figurehead, not a source of power. She repre-

spatial, while those of masculine figures like Jesus and De Vargas are strongly historical-temporal. De Vargas as a symbol dominates New Mexico's history; the queen as a symbol dominates Santa Fe as a tricultural *civitas*.

During the Conquistadors' Ball people still speak of it as the Queen's Ball. Furthermore, the queen is enthroned— given a symbolic place—while De Vargas is not. People say, "This is the queen's fiesta," never, "This is De Vargas' fiesta." There is a Queen's review, but no De Vargas review. People speak of the *audiencia* with all the fiesta figures as "the audience with the queen." In sum, the De Vargas symbol is extended in time, while the queenly symbol is limited in time and concentrated in space. The "fiestafied" city is hers; the historical city is his. Her symbolic "kingdom" lasts for only four days. Power is no necessity; in fact, it is a hindrance. What is necessary, under the reign of the fiesta queen, is suspension of ethnic and religious jealousy.

The people, of course, recognize that *civitas* and *ethnos* cannot be neatly isolated from one another, hence their frequent reference to the queen and De Vargas as married. De Vargas, "Mr. Hispano," crystallizes the self-assertive power of Hispanic culture. He is its dynamic aspect, which resists assimilation. The queen, on the other hand, is its open, flexible aspect, which allows it to assimilate and blend with the other two cultures. "Miss Fiesta de Santa Fe," like the Statue of Liberty, is a feminine symbol who beckons men to gather without exercising their normal competitive, conflictive powers.

Power is symbolically linked to "our forefathers" and "the city fathers." Patrilineality, patriarchiality, and paternalism are powerful factors in Santa Fe. When power usage becomes conflictive, men are involved most of the time. Both cowboy and conquistador symbols emphasize the female's "place of honor," which is either behind or above direct culture contact. But culture contact need not be wholly identified with culture conflict. So when culture contact means intercultural cooperation, the feminine "behind" becomes the feminine "between." Feminine symbols mediate between competing masculine symbols. As William Blake observed, man is not joined to man except by woman.

One can assert that La Conquistadora is queen of the "kingdom of New Mexico" or that the fiesta queen is the symbol of Santa Fe without provoking any of the controversies that would arise if someone asserted that De Vargas were "king of Santa Fe." The queenship is uncontroversial and innocent, except when someone tries to make it an ally of some special interest. The specifically civic symbol is grounded in the noncontroversial. People fight about "religion and politics," but they "admire their queen." Symbols of civic cooperation, like fiesta rhetoric, maximize unity by minimizing content. The fiesta queen is a symbol largely empty of specific content—at least, as empty as a symbol can be and still function to bear meaning. Some individuals try quite hard to fill the symbol with more content, but their efforts are not supported by community consensus. What many do not recognize is that the functioning of the role depends on its very emptiness. One has only to assent to the symbolic form of the figurehead to have filled four days with rituals of unification.

That this feminine symbol is created by the civic imagination, and is not the product of religious revelation, as in the case of La Conquistadora, or of Hispanic history, as in the case of De Vargas, is sometimes an embarrassment to fiesta participants. They feel that the queens and princesses have little or no meaning. My interviews provoked discussions among the princesses about the meaning of their roles, because they themselves were not sure what they represented. Some informants say they think the roles came out of an era when queenships were being devised all across America, but beyond this they could see little more than civic concoction.

Incidentally, the role of Pueblo princess has as little historical rootage as the role of Spanish princess or fiesta queen. But there is no reason to denigrate these roles simply because they are the creations of the civic imagination or because they seem to be forms without content. The roles are symbolic grounds for intercultural cooperation, and even friendship, as the presence of Pueblo girls in the court amply illustrates.

One anomaly, which is an exception to my thesis about the civic nature of the queen and court, is the absence of Anglo participants. Informants account for this in two ways. On the one hand, they say that the Anglos who were instrumental in reviving the fiesta in the early part of the century wanted Hispanos and Indians to have the primary roles. On the other hand, informants suggest that the historical events being commemorated involved Hispanos and Indians but not Anglos, since they occurred between 1680 and 1692.

One might expect a truly tricultural celebration to include Anglo symbols as well as Hispano and Indian ones. And if Anglo symbols were to be included, the queen's court would be the logical place. By design the queen is Hispano; there can be no Indian queen. And so far there are no Anglo princesses; these factors militate against my contention that the feminine symbols represent the unity of tricultural Santa Fe. I can only account for them by suggesting that the unity and equality of the ethnic groups is as fragmented as the symbols are, and by saying again that the fiesta is not a neutrally civic celebration but rather a civic-religious celebration employing Hispanically defined symbols.

The enthronement is to the queen what the Entrada is to De Vargas. These are their respective "moments." Both of them consider their coronation and knighting as important. The coronation-knighting ceremony is their moment, but the Entrada is De Vargas', while the enthronement is the queen's (see Figure 7).

Figure 7. The 1973 fiesta queen making her enthronement speech

The enthronement of the queen is a prelude to the burning of Zozobra, thus making it, along with the burning, the best-attended event of the fiesta. The non-Catholic populace tends to regard the enthronement-burning as the fiesta's beginning. Only on this occasion is the "Star Spangled Banner" played, as if it were announcing that *civitas* were at the core of the event. And significantly, *civitas* is accompanied by a "pagan" celebration, that is, a non-Catholic, non-Protestant, non-Pueblo celebration. The national anthem is played by a mariachi band and followed by the Mexican national anthem. Only on this occasion, the governor of the state and the mayor of the city make welcoming addresses—again empha-

sizing civic over ethnic concerns. Ethnically, the fiesta has
begun early in the morning with the De Vargas Mass. Everything about the queen's enthronement declares its civicality—the size of the crowd, the presence of governor and
mayor, the national anthems, the singing of the official fiesta
song, speeches by new and retiring fiesta queens, and the
"pagan" celebration which follows immediately. So even
though La Conquistadora, De Vargas, and the fiesta queen
share in all the rites of Santa Fe's public celebrations, each
seems to dominate one of the rites as peculiarly his or her
own. La Conquistadora is most at home in processions and
masses; De Vargas in the Entrada; and the fiesta queen in the
enthronement and entertainment events.

Perhaps we are now at the point where I can summarize
the dominant meanings of each of the three major symbols.
Informants indicate the systemic unity of the symbols by
speaking of De Vargas and the queen as if they were married
and by speaking of De Vargas as La Conquistadora's knight.
A few, as I have noted, also speak of the fiesta queen as a

Chart 1. The major symbols in Santa Fe's public ritual system

	La Conquistadora	De Vargas	Fiesta queen
Ethos	*Ecclesia*	*Ethnos*	*Civitas*
Symbolic form	Icon	Dramatic role	Figurehead
Level of reality	Supernatural, eternal	Historical, temporal	Natural, spatial
Gender	Feminine	Masculine	Feminine
Marital image	Virgin Mother	Married father	Single
Corporate image	Soul	Body	Clothing
Rite	Mass, procession	Entrada	Enthronement
Music	*Canticos*	"El Cid"	National anthem
Organization	Church, Confraternity	Caballeros	Fiesta Council
Metaphor of motion	Receptive	Dynamic	Static
Metaphor of location	Above	In front	Behind
Mode of legitimation	Spiritual hierarchy	Military hierarchy	Public mandate
Mode of power	Inspiration	Pressure	Representation
Mode of intercultural relations	Conversion	Conquest	Cooperation

symbolic embodiment of La Conquistadora. But along with the unity of the symbols in this public ritual system, there is a division of labor among the symbols, which is recognized by informants, at least fragmentarily. Chart 1 outlines the symbolic work, the meaning, of each symbol. Each shares certain secondary qualities with the other symbols, but I have eliminated these for the sake of clarifying their differences. The chart is an oversimplification, but, I think, a useful one provided it is not used too rigidly.

This chart, a summary of conclusions and observations from preceding chapters, indicates the positional links between symbols. It outlines the heart of a system which is for Hispanos a world view and for Anglos and Indians both a spectacle of local color and a competing ideology. By appealing to any one of these symbols on a given occasion Hispano Santa Feans can emphasize alternately the ecclesiastical, ethnic, or civic aspects of the city. And because they do not inquire into the consistency of the symbols as a system but treat them as a varied collection, the contradictions of public ritual seldom become an issue. Participants may argue vehemently about the accuracy of symbols, that is, their referential meanings, but seldom about their positional consistency. Furthermore, they do not typically interpret the symbols as having distinguishable contextual meanings, hence the frequent response, "They say pretty much the same thing." I hope I have made evident that they do not merely repeat one another's messages nor are they merely a neutral, representative sampling of Santa Fe's ethnic and religious constituencies. Considerable power is expended to enable these symbols to continue defining the character of public ritual.

Santa Fe
Chronology, 1100–1973

1100– Drought forces evacuation of cliff dwellings; beginning of Rio
1300 Grande Pueblo cultures
1400 Navahos arrive in New Mexico; raid Pueblos
1521 Cortés conquers Aztec empire
1531 Our Lady of Guadalupe appears to Juan Diego
1536 Cabeza de Vaca crosses the Southwest
1539 Fray Marco de Ninza's report on Seven Cities of Cibola
1540 Coronado begins to explore Southwest
1598 Oñate colonizes New Mexico; sets up first capital at San Juan de los
       Caballeros
1610 New capital established at Santa Fe by Pedro de Peralta; approxi-
       mate date of "oldest church," San Miguel Chapel
1625 Fray Alonso Benavides brings La Conquistadora to Santa Fe
1680 Pueblos revolt, kill 21 missionaries, drive Spanish to El Paso
1692 Diego de Vargas' bloodless reconquest of Santa Fe
1693 De Vargas' second, bloody reconquest; recolonization of Santa Fe
1712 First Santa Fe Fiesta decreed by City Council
1717 Le Conquistadora Chapel built
1726– Deterioration of Confraternity of La Conquistadora
1770
1770 Revival of Confraternity of La Conquistadora
1787 Secular clergy introduced to New Mexico
1790– "The Secular Period"; "Golden Age of Santo-Making"
1850
1803 Louisiana Purchase brings United States into Southwest
1807 Rosario Chapel built; first procession to Rosario
1821 Mexican rule in New Mexico; opening of Santa Fe Trail
1823 City Council makes Saint Francis patron of Santa Fe
1833 Gold discovered in New Mexico
1846 Mary of Immaculate Conception declared patroness of United
       States; United States at war with Mexico

1848   Treaty of Guadalupe Hidalgo; General Stephen Kearny raises U.S. flag in Santa Fe

1849   Stagecoaches begin using Santa Fe Trail; first Baptist missionary arrives in New Mexico

1850   John Baptist Lamy becomes vicar-apostolic of Santa Fe; French clergy begin to replace Mexican clergy; first Methodist missionary arrives

1851   First Presbyterian missionary arrives

1853   Gadsden Treaty sets final U.S.–Mexico boundary; Santa Fe becomes a diocese

1854   Immaculate Conception of Mary declared dogma by Pius IX

1862   Texas Confederacy invades New Mexico during Civil War

1863   First Episcopal missionary arrives

1866–   Erection of Santa Fe plaza monument
1868

1867   "Long Walk" of Navahos to Fort Sumner

1870–   Building of the present St. Francis Cathedral
1889

1875   Santa Fe becomes archdiocese

1885   Death of Archbishop Jean Baptiste Lamy

1889   Archbishop Salpointe issues criticisms of Penitentes

1912   New Mexico becomes a state

1914   New section of Rosario Chapel built

1919   Beginning of revival of Santa Fe Fiesta; "Franciscan revival" ends line of French clergy

1920   Erection of the Cross of the Martyrs

1925   Founding of Spanish Colonial Arts Society

1926   Zozobra introduced into Santa Fe Fiesta; Old Santa Fe Foundation begins

1927   Incorporation of the fiesta; first of the fiesta queens

1935   Founding of La Sociedad Folklorica

1936   Archbishop Rudolf A. Gerken receives Penitentes back into church

1940   Coronado Cuarto-Centennial Celebration

1945   Atomic bomb test at Trinity site

1948   Publication of Chávez' *Our Lady of the Conquest*

1950   Bodily Assumption of Mary declared dogma by Pius XII

1954   Marian Year; centennial of Immaculate Conception dogma; Episcopal coronation of La Conquistadora; La Conquistadora's "pilgrimage"; publication of Chávez' *La Conquistadora: The Autobiography of an Ancient Statue*

1956   Re-establishment of Confraternity of La Conquistadora

1957 Founding of Caballeros de Vargas
1958 Scenario written for Entrada pageant by Edmundo Delgado
1960 Siglos de Santa Fe Celebration (Santa Fe's 350th anniversary); papal coronation of La Conquistadora
1962–1965 Second Vatican Council
1964 Archdiocese of Santa Fe withdraws from fiesta
1966 Caballeros de Vargas gain control over Entrada; church rejoins fiesta; Fiesta Council comes under jurisdiction of City Council
1967 Fiesta's Entrada script revised by Pedro Ribera-Ortega; Reies Lopez Tijerina's confrontation at Tierra Amarilla
1969 Tijerina convicted and sentenced to prison; Episcopal and Presbyterian responses to Tijerina's demands
1970 Tear gas employed to contain troubles during Santa Fe Fiesta
1971 Tijerina released from prison
1972 Brotherhood Awareness Conferences initiated by Tijerina
1973 March 19   La Conquistadora stolen
      April 15   La Conquistadora recovered
      April 29   Celebration of La Conquistadora's return
      May 6   The *New Mexican* introduces Chávez' column on New Mexico families
      May 12   Announcement of fiesta royalty at Baile de Mayo
      June 24 (Sunday)   Corpus Christi procession
      June 28–June 30   Special triduum of masses
      July 1 (Sunday)   La Conquistadora Procession to Rosario; vespers; enthronement
      July 2–July 7   Masses at Rosario celebrate novena
      July 8 (Sunday)   La Conquistadora procession back to St. Francis; coronation; consecration of New Mexico; Mass
      July 9   Last Mass of novena
      July 12   Santa Fe Rodeo Parade
      July 26   Controversy over plaza monument begins
      July 29   Special pre-fiesta music begins
      Aug. 26   Pre-fiesta events begin
      Aug. 31–September 3   Fiesta de Santa Fe
      Dec. 8   Initiation of Caballeros de Vargas (Usually on October 4, Feast of St. Francis)

Fiesta Schedule, 1973

August 27 (Pre-fiesta)
    8:00 P.M.   Exhibicion de Modas (style show)

August 28
    7:30 P.M.   Variety show (sponsored by local merchant)
    8:30 P.M.   Fiesta melodrama, "The Burgeoning Blight of Biggy's Brown Bags" (performed nightly)

August 29
    8:00 P.M.   Quisicosas ("Anything Goes," a variety show)

August 30
    8:00 P.M.   Desafio de Mariachis (mariachi concert)

August 31 (Fiesta)
    6:30 A.M.   Pregon de la Fiesta (fiesta proclamation) by the mayor of the City of Santa Fe
    6:35 A.M   De Vargas Mass, Rosario Chapel
    10:00 A.M.   Grand opening of fiesta arts and crafts market (market open daily)
    12:00 P.M.   Carnival rides and booths open (continues daily)
    5:00 P.M.   Music on plaza platform
    6:30 P.M.   Pre-enthronement entertainment
    6:30 P.M.   Vespers; knighting of De Vargas; crowning of fiesta queen (St. Francis Cathedral)
    7:30 P.M.   Plaza entertainment (continuous)
    8:00 P.M.   Enthronement of fiesta queen and court; queen's show
    9:00 P.M.   Burning of Zozobra (Old Man Gloom) and fire dance
    10:00 P.M.   Baile de la Gente (People's Dance) on plaza nightly

September 1 (Fiesta's American Indian Day)
    9:00 A.M.   Plaza entertainment
    10:00 A.M.   Desfile de los Niños (children's costume and pet parade)
    1:00 P.M.   American Indian Day program (proclamation by governor followed by Pueblo dances)
    3:00 P.M.   Mariachi and other entertainment
    4:00 P.M.   Audiencia con General Don Diego de Vargas y la Reina

de la Fiesta (audience with fiesta royalty; opportunity for picture taking)

9:00 P.M.   Gran Baile de los Conquistadores (Conquistadors' Ball)

September 2 (Sunday)

9:30 A.M.   Solemn procession

10:00 A.M.   Solemn Pontifical Fiesta Mass ("Misa Panamericana")

12:30 P.M.   Mariachi and other entertainment

1:30 P.M.   Entrada pageant

2:00 P.M.   Spanish dances on plaza

2:00 P.M.   Indian dances at the Governor's Palace

2:45 P.M.   Plaza entertainment

3:30 P.M.   Dancers on plaza

3:30 P.M.   La Merienda de la Fiesta (old-fashioned style show)

4:00 P.M.   Judging and prizes for fiesta costumes

4:00 P.M.   Indian dances

7:00 P.M.   Mass of the Martyrs at St. Francis Cathedral

7:45 P.M.   Candelight procession to Cross of the Martyrs; sermon beneath the cross

8:30 P.M.   Plaza entertainment, fiesta melodrama, etc.

9:00 P.M.   De Vargas Ball

September 3

10:00 A.M.   Arts, crafts, carnival rides, dancers, etc.

10:30 A.M.   Dancers on plaza

11:00 A.M.   Mariachi music; presentation of food booth awards

12:30 P.M.   La Sociedad Colonial Española and other entertainment

1:30 P.M.   Band music

2:00 P.M.   Desfile de Fiesta (general fiesta parade)

4:00 P.M.   Military Order of the Purple Heart steer raffle

4:30 P.M.   Queen's review of 1973 fiesta

6:00 P.M.   Official closing, thanksgiving, blessing

8:30 P.M.   Final performance of fiesta melodrama

Map of Santa Fe with Fiesta Events (from program)

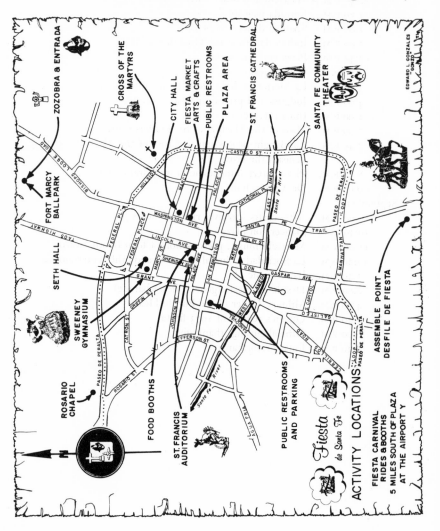

References

Aradi, Zsolt. 1954. *Shrines to Our Lady around the World.* New York: Farrar, Straus & Young.

Armitage, Merle. 1960. *Pagans, Conquistadores, Heroes and Martyrs: The Spiritual Conquest of America.* Assisted by Peter Ribera-Ortega. N.p.: Manzanita.

Arnold, Oren. 1953. *New Mexico Brags.* Phoenix: Bob Petley Studios.

Bacigalupa, Andrea. 1972. *Santos and Saints' Days.* Santa Fe: Sunstone.

Bellah, Robert N. 1968. "Civil Religion in America," in *The Religious Situation, 1968.* Ed. Donald R. Cutler. Boston: Beacon.

———. 1973. "Liturgy and Experience," in *The Roots of Ritual.* Ed. James D. Shaughnessy. Grand Rapids: Eerdmans.

Berkhofer, Robert F., Jr. 1965. *Salvation and the Savage: An Analysis of Protestant Missions and American Indian Response, 1787–1862.* New York: Atheneum.

Bodine, John J. 1968. "A Tri-Ethnic Trap: The Spanish Americans in Taos," in *Spanish-Speaking People in the United States.* Proceedings of the 1968 Annual Spring Meeting of the American Ethnological Society. Ed. June Helm. Seattle: University of Washington Press.

Breese, Frances, and E. Boyd. 1966. *New Mexico Santos: How To Name Them.* Santa Fe: Museum of New Mexico.

Bullock, Alice. 1972. *Living Legends of the Santa Fe Country.* Rev. ed. Santa Fe: Sunstone.

Burke, Kenneth. 1968. *Language as Symbolic Action: Essays on Life, Literature Method.* Berkeley: University of California Press.

———. 1969. *A Grammar of Motives.* Berkeley: University of California Press.

Burridge, Kenelm. 1969. *New Heaven, New Earth: A Study of Millenarian Activities.* New York: Schocken.

Castaneda, C. E. 1936. "The First American Play," *Preliminary Studies of the Texas Catholic Historical Society,* 3:5–39.

Chávez, Fray Angélico. 1948. *Our Lady of the Conquest.* Albuquerque: University of New Mexico Press.

———. 1950. "La Conquistadora Is a Paisana," *El Palacio*, 57:299–307.

———. 1954a. *La Conquistadora: The Autobiography of an Ancient Statue.* Paterson, N.J.: St. Anthony Guild.

———. 1954b. *Origins of New Mexico Families in the Spanish Colonial Period.* Santa Fe: Historical Society of New Mexico.

———. 1965. "The Penitentes of New Mexico," *New Mexico Historical Review*, 40:97–123.

———. 1967. "Pohe-Yemo's Representative and the Pueblo Revolt of 1680," *New Mexico Historical Review*, 42:85–126.

Christian, William, Jr. 1972. *Person and God in a Spanish Valley.* New York: Seminar.

Cirlot, J. E. 1962. *A Dictionary of Symbols.* Trans. Jack Sage. New York: Philosophical Library.

De Borhegyi, Stephen F. 1956. "The Miraculous Shrines of Our Lord of Esquipulas in Guatemala and Chimayo, New Mexico," *El Santuario de Chimayo.* Santa Fe: Colonial Arts Society.

Delaney, John J., ed. 1961. *A Woman Clothed with the Sun: Eight Great Appearances of Our Lady in Modern Times.* Garden City: Doubleday.

Deloria, Vine, Jr. 1969. *Custer Died for Your Sins: An Indian Manifesto.* New York: Avon.

Douglas, Mary. 1973. *Natural Symbols: Explorations in Cosmology.* New York: Vintage.

Dozier, Edward P. 1970. *The Pueblo Indians of North America.* New York: Holt, Rinehart & Winston.

Eliade, Mircea. 1963. *Myth and Reality.* Trans. Willard R. Trask. New York: Harper & Row.

Ellis, Richard N. 1971. *New Mexico Past and Present: A Historical Reader.* Albuquerque: University of New Mexico Press.

Englekirk, John E. 1940. "Notes on the Repertoire of the New Mexican Spanish Folktheater," *Southern Folklore Quarterly*, 4:227–237.

Espinosa, J. Manuel. 1936. "The Virgin of the Reconquest of New Mexico," *Mid-America*, 7:79–87.

———. 1942. *Crusaders of the Rio Grande: The Story of Don Diego De Vargas and the Reconquest and Refounding of New Mexico.* Chicago: Institute of Jesuit History.

———, trans. and ed. 1940. "Vargas' Campaign Journal and Correspondence, August 21 to October 16, 1692," in *First Expedition of Vargas into New Mexico.* Albuquerque: University of New Mexico Press.

Espinosa, José. 1967. *Saints in the Valleys: Christian Sacred Images in the History, Life and Folk Art of Spanish New Mexico.* Albuquerque: University of New Mexico Press.

Fergusson, Erna. 1951. *New Mexico: A Pageant of Three Peoples.* New York: Knopf.

Fiorina, Betty, ed. 1971. *New Mexico Blue Book.* Santa Fe: Media Services.

Firth, Raymond. 1973. *Symbols, Public and Private.* Ithaca, N.Y.: Cornell University Press.

Foster, George M. 1953. "Cofradía and Compadrazgo in Spain and Spanish America," *Southwestern Journal of Anthropology,* 9:1–28.

Foy, Felican A., ed. 1972. *1973 Catholic Almanac.* Huntington, Ind.: Our Sunday Visitor.

Gardner, Richard. 1970. *Grito: Reies Tijerina and the New Mexico Land Grant War of 1967.* New York: Harper & Row.

Geertz, Clifford. 1966. "Religion as a Cultural System," in *Anthropological Approaches to the Study of Religion.* Ed. Michael Banton. A.S.A. Monographs, no. 3. London: Tavistock.

Gerth, Hans, and C. Wright Mills. 1953. *Character and Social Structure: The Psychology of Social Institutions.* New York: Harcourt, Brace & World.

Gillmor, Frances. 1943. "The Dance Dramas of Mexican Villages," *University of Arizona Humanities Bulletin,* 14:5–28.

González, Nancie. 1969. *The Spanish Americans of New Mexico: A Heritage of Pride.* Albuquerque: University of New Mexico Press.

Hahn, Robert A. 1973. "Understanding Beliefs: An Essay on the Methodology of the Statement and Analysis of Belief Systems," *Current Anthropology,* 14:207–229.

Hammond, George P., and Agapito Rey. 1953. *Don Juan de Oñate: Colonizer of New Mexico, 1595–1628.* Cuarto Centennial Publications, vol. 5. Albuquerque: University of New Mexico Press.

Harvey, Byron, III. 1972. "An Overview of Pueblo Religion," in *New Perspectives on the Pueblos.* Ed. Alfonso Ortiz. Albuquerque: University of New Mexico Press.

Hewett, Edgar L. 1926. *The Fiesta Book, 1926.* Papers of the School of American Research. Santa Fe: Archaeological Institute of America.

Hollis, Martin. 1970. "Reason and Ritual," in *Rationality.* Ed. Bryan R. Wilson. New York: Harper & Row.

Hollon, W. Eugene. 1968. *The Southwest: Old and New.* Lincoln: University of Nebraska.

Horgan, Paul. 1954. *Great River: The Rio Grande in North American History.* New York: Minerva.

———. 1965. *The Centuries of Santa Fe.* New York: Dutton.

Jackson, Anthony. 1968. "Sound and Ritual," *Man,* N.S. 3:293–299.

Jung, C. G. 1958. "Transformation Symbolism in the Mass," in *Psyche and Symbol: A Selection from the Writings of C. G. Jung.* Ed. Violet De Laszlo. Garden City: Doubleday.

Klapp, Orin E. 1962. *Heroes, Villains and Fools: The Changing American Character.* Englewood Cliffs: Prentice-Hall.

Kurath, Gertrude Prokosch, and Antonio Garcia. 1970. *Music and Dance of the Tewa Pueblos.* Museum of New Mexico Research Records, no. 8. Santa Fe: Museum of New Mexico.

LaFarge, Oliver, and Arthur N. Morgan. 1959. *Santa Fe: The Autobiography of a Southwestern Town.* Norman: University of Oklahoma.

Lea, Aurora Lucero-White. 1953. *Literary Folklore of the Hispanic Southwest.* San Antonio: Naylor.

Lewis, Brother B. 1957. *Oldest Church in U.S.: The San Miguel Chapel.* Santa Fe: n.p.

Macleod, Xavier Donald. 1866. *History of the Devotion to the Blessed Virgin Mary in North America.* New York: Virtue & Yorston.

Madsen, William. 1964. *Mexican-Americans of South Texas.* New York: Holt, Rinehart & Winston.

Major, Mabel, and T. M. Pearce. 1972. *Southwest Heritage: A Literary History with Bibliographies.* 3d ed. Albuquerque: University of New Mexico Press.

Marie, Sister Joseph. 1948. *The Role of the Church and the Folk in the Development of the Early Drama in New Mexico.* Philadelphia: University of Pennsylvania Press.

Meem, John G. 1972. *Old Santa Fe Today.* Albuquerque: University of New Mexico Press.

Meyer, Theodosius. 1926. *St. Francis and Franciscans in New Mexico.* Santa Fe: El Palacio.

Mills, George. n.d. *The People of the Saints.* Colorado Springs: Taylor Museum.

Mills, George, and Richard Grove. 1956. *Lucifer and the Crucifer: The Enigma of the Penitentes.* Colorado Springs: Taylor Museum.

Morris, Charles. 1938. *Foundations of the Theory of Signs.* Chicago: University of Chicago.

Mullahy, B. I. 1967. "Processions, Religious," *New Catholic Encyclopedia,* 11:819–821.

Myers, Lewis A. 1965. *A History of New Mexico Baptists.* N.p.: Baptist Convention of New Mexico.

Nabokov, Peter. 1970. *Tijerina and the Courthouse Raid.* 2d ed. Berkeley: Ramparts.

Ortiz, Alfonso. 1969. *The Tewa World: Space, Time, Being and Becoming in a Pueblo Society.* Chicago: University of Chicago Press.

———. 1972. "Ritual Drama and the Pueblo World View," in *New Perspectives on the Pueblos.* Ed. Alfonso Oritz. Albuquerque: University of New Mexico Press.

Pandey, Triloki Nath. 1972. "Anthropologists at Zuñi," *Proceedings of the American Philosophical Society*, 116:321–337.

Paul VI, Pope. 1965. *Mysterium Fidei: Encyclical on Eucharistic Doctrine and Worship*. Commentary by Anthony T. Padovano. Glen Rock, N.J.: Paulist Press.

Pearce, T. M. 1956. "The New Mexican 'Shepherds' Play,'" *Western Folklore*, 15:77–88.

———. 1965. *New Mexico Place Names: A Geographical Dictionary*. Albuquerque: University of New Mexico Press.

Phares, Ross. 1971. *Bible in Pocket, Gun in Hand: The Story of Frontier Religion*. Lincoln: University of Nebraska Press.

Philibert, Sister Mary. n.d. "Did Vargas Win His Battle with a Banner?" N.P.: Howard N. Rose.

Pollock, Duncan. 1973. "New Mexico: An Earthbound Iconography," *Art in America*, 61:98–101.

Ribera-Ortega, Peter. 1961. *Christmas in Old Santa Fe*. Santa Fe: Ancient City.

Ricard, Robert. 1966. *The Spiritual Conquest of Mexico*. Trans. Lesley B. Simpson. Berkeley: University of California Press.

Ricoeur, Paul. 1967 *The Symbolism of Evil*. Trans. Emerson Buchanan. New York: Harper & Row.

Rosaldo, Renato. 1968. "Metaphors of Hierarchy in a Mayan Ritual," *American Anthropologist*, 70:524–536.

Ross, Calvin. 1934. *Sky Determines: An Interpretation of the Southwest*. New York: Macmillan.

Santa Fe Cathedral, The n.d. Rev. ed. Santa Fe: Schifani Bros.

Schwartz, Gary, and Don Merten. 1968. "Social Identity and Expressive Symbols: The Meaning of an Initiation Ritual," *American Anthropologist*, 70:1117–1131.

Shalkop, Robert L. 1967. *Wooden Saints: The Santos of New Mexico*. Colorado Springs: Taylor Museum.

Smith, Henry Nash. 1950. *Virgin Land: The American West as Symbol and Myth*. New York: Vintage.

Stevens, Thomas Wood. 1940. *The Entrada of Coronado: A Spectacular Historic Drama*. Albuquerque: University of New Mexico Press.

Theil, A. Paul. 1955. "The Ancient City's Fiesta," *El Palacio*, 62:259–267.

Turner, Victor. 1967. *The Forest of Symbols: Aspects of Ndembu Ritual*. Ithaca, N.Y.: Cornell University Press.

———. 1969. *The Ritual Process*. Chicago: Aldine.

——— 1973a. "The Center Out There: Pilgrim's Goal," *History of Religions*, 12:191–230.

———. 1973b. "Symbols in African Rituals," *Science*, 179:1100–1105.

———. 1974. *Dramas, Fields, and Metaphors: Symbolic Action in Human Society*. Ithaca, N.Y.: Cornell University Press.

Turner, Victor and Edith. N.d. "The Queen of Ireland:Knock Shrine Pilgrimage." Unpublished ms.

Twitchell, Ralph Emerson. 1925. *Old Santa Fe: The Story of New Mexico's Ancient Capital*. Santa Fe: Santa Fe New Mexican.

———. 1967. *The Conquest of Santa Fe, 1846*. Truchas, N.M.: Tate Gallery.

United Presbyterian Church, U.S.A., General Assembly. 1969. *Minutes of the General Assembly*. Philadelphia: Office of the General Assembly.

Van Gennep, Arnold. 1960. *The Rites of Passage*. Trans. Monika B. Vizedom and Gabrielle L. Caffee. Chicago: University of Chicago Press.

Vatican Council, Second. 1964. *The Constitution on the Sacred Liturgy*. Commentary by Gerard S. Sloyan. Glen Rock, N.J.: Paulist Press.

Vatican Council, Second, and Pope Paul VI. 1970. *The Roman Missal: General Instruction and the Order of the Mass*. Collegeville, Minn.: Liturgical Press.

Wallace, Anthony. 1966. *Religion: An Anthropological View*. New York: Random House.

———. 1970. *Culture and Personality*. 2d ed. New York: Random House.

Weigle, Marta. 1970. *The Penitentes of the Southwest*. Santa Fe: Ancient City.

Wellman, Paul I. 1954. *Glory, God and Gold: A Narrative History*. Garden City: Doubleday.

Wolf, Eric. 1956. "Aspects of Group Relations in a Complex Society," *American Anthropologist*, 58:1065–1078.

———. 1965. "The Virgin of Guadalupe: A Mexican National Symbol," in *Reader in Comparative Religion: An Anthropological Approach*. Ed. William A. Lessa and Evon Z. Vogt. New York: Harper & Row.

Index

SYMBOL AND CONQUEST

Designed by R. E. Rosenbaum.
Composed by Vail-Ballou Press, Inc.,
in 11 point VIP Janson, 2 points leaded,
with display lines in Helvetica.
Printed offset by Vail-Ballou Press
Warren's No. 66 text, 50 pound basis.
Bound by Vail-Ballou Press
in Columbia book cloth
and stamped in All Purpose foil.

Library of Congress Cataloging in Publication Data
(For library cataloging purposes only)

Grimes, Ronald L
  Symbol and conquest.

  (Symbol, myth, and ritual series)
  Bibliography: p.
  1. Santa Fe, N. M.—Festivals, etc. 2. Santa Fe, N. M. Cathedral of San
Francisco de Asis. La Conquistadora (Statue) 3. Mary, Virgin—Cultus—Santa Fe,
N. M. 4. Symbolism. I. Title.
GT4811.S26G74   394.2   76-13657
ISBN 0-8014-1037-1